PEOPLE'S BIBLE COMMENTARY

ROMANS

ARMIN J. PANNING

PBC

CONCORDIA PUBLISHING HOUSE · SAINT LOUIS

Revised edition first printed in 2004.
Copyright © 2000 Concordia Publishing House
3558 S. Jefferson Ave., St. Louis, MO 63118-3968
1-800-325-3040 · www.cph.org

Commentary and pictures are reprinted from ROMANS (The People's Bible Series), copyright © 1999 by Northwestern Publishing House. Used by permission.

Interior illustrations by Glenn Myers.

Manufactured in the United States of America
ISBN 0-7586-0444-0

1 2 3 4 5 6 7 8 9 10   13 12 11 10 09 08 07 06 05 04

CONTENTS

EDITOR'S PREFACE

The *People's Bible Commentary* is just what the name implies—a Bible and commentary for the people. It includes the complete text of the Holy Scriptures in the popular New International Version. The commentary following the Scripture sections contains personal applications as well as historical background and explanations of the text.

The authors of the *People's Bible Commentary* are men of scholarship and practical insight gained from years of experience in the teaching and preaching ministries. They have tried to avoid the technical jargon which limits so many commentary series to professional Bible scholars.

The most important feature of these books is that they are Christ-centered. Speaking of the Old Testament Scriptures, Jesus himself declared, "These are the Scriptures that testify about me" (John 5:39). Each volume of the *People's Bible Commentary* directs our attention to Jesus Christ. He is the center of the entire Bible. He is our only Savior.

We dedicate these volumes to the glory of God and to the good of his people.

The Publishers

Resinol

INTRODUCTION TO ROMANS

The opening verse of Romans—in fact, the opening *word*—informs us that Paul is the author of this profound epistle. Statements within the letter also support that conclusion, for the author calls himself "the apostle to the Gentiles" (11:13). Furthermore, the scope of the author's missionary work, "from Jerusalem all the way around to Illyricum" (15:19), accords with what Acts tells us about the apostle Paul's remarkable ministry.

Date and place

The date of Paul's writing to the Romans can be determined with relative accuracy by piecing together bits of internal evidence. At the time of his writing of Romans, Paul was about to return to Jerusalem with the collection that gentile Christians had gathered for needy Jewish believers in Jerusalem (15:25,26). From Acts and the Corinthian correspondence, we learn that this gathering of funds took place during Paul's third missionary journey. That journey is usually dated about A.D. 53–57.

Paul spent a large part of that missionary tour at Ephesus, in Asia Minor. At the end of his three-year stay in Ephesus, Paul set out overland through Macedonia and Greece, intending en route to pick up the funds that had been collected by the various congregations. The last stop on his swing through Macedonia and Greece would have been Corinth. Hence when Paul writes to the Romans, "Now . . . I am on my way to Jerusalem" (15:25), he most likely is writing from Corinth.

In his correspondence to the Corinthians, Paul had promised to spend some time in Corinth—perhaps even spend the winter with them (1 Corinthians 16:6). This intention on the apostle's part seems to have been realized (Acts 20:2,3). Hence Paul is likely to have written his letter to the Romans from Corinth during the winter or early spring of A.D. 57.

Occasion

No doubt Paul would have liked to go directly from Corinth to visit the Romans. For many years he had been wanting to visit them (1:13), but until now he was prevented from doing so. A complicating factor up until now had been Paul's God-given assignment to plant the gospel in the major urban centers of Asia Minor and southeastern Europe—cities like Ephesus in Asia Minor, Philippi and Thessalonica in Macedonia, and Corinth in Greece. Now, however, that work had been completed (15:19,22-24), and Paul could think of turning his attention to other areas. His immediate interest was to go to the West, to Rome and the regions beyond, including Spain.

Only one other task needed the apostle's attention before heading west, and that was the delivery of the collection to the poverty-stricken Christians in Jerusalem (15:25). Because of that delay and in preparation for his eagerly awaited visit to Rome, Paul sent ahead the letter we have come to call Romans.

Another lesser but still important detail contributed to Paul's sending a letter to the Christians in Rome at this time. Paul had the service of a trusted letter carrier. Recall that in Paul's day there was no such thing as an international postal system. If you wanted to send a letter to your distant friend, you had to find a traveler willing to carry your letter who was traveling to the place where your friend lived. In the closing chapter of his letter, Paul urged the Romans, "I commend to you our sister Phoebe, a servant of the church in Cenchrea. I ask you to receive her in the Lord in a way worthy of the saints and to give her any help she may need from you, for she has been a great help to many people, including me" (16:1,2). Phoebe was obviously a highly regarded Christian woman who was traveling to Rome for some reason. It seems entirely probable that she served as the carrier of Romans. Incidentally, Phoebe's hometown of Cenchrea is one of the two seaports serving Corinth, which further reinforces the conclusion that Paul wrote Romans from Corinth.

Purpose

From the fact that Paul had not previously been to Rome, we may safely conclude that he was not the founder of the congregation there. In fact, there is no record of any apostolic activity in connection with the founding of this group. The tradition that Peter served as the bishop of Rome for 25 years is unfounded and highly improbable. Given the somewhat unusual beginning of the group in Rome, it is plausible that Paul sent his letter, at least in part, to give them the benefit of his apostolic teaching.

But the intended edification was by no means to proceed in only one direction, with Paul providing all the good things for the Romans. Rather, Paul envisioned a two-way exchange when he came to them. He not only says, "I long to see you so that I may impart to you some spiritual gift to make you strong," but also immediately adds, "that is, that you and I may be *mutually encouraged by each other's faith"* (1:11,12).

Obviously, Paul's joy over the faith of the Romans was a major factor in penning a letter to them, but the letter also had a very practical purpose. Paul was looking to the Romans for help and support in connection with the mission work he was contemplating for Spain and the West. Paul is very open in asking for their aid. He writes, "But now that there is no more place for me to work in these regions, and since I have been longing for many years to see you, I plan to do so when I go to Spain. I hope to visit you while passing through *and to have you assist me on my journey there,* after I have enjoyed your company for a while" (15:23,24).

We need to realize that in Paul's day there was no world mission board to mobilize the resources of the entire church body in order to support those going to "foreign" fields. Recall that at times Paul provided his own support by tent-making (Acts 18:2,3; 1 Thessalonians 2:9) or received help from private sources and individual congregations (1 Corinthians 16:6,10,11; 2 Corinthians 1:16; Titus 3:13; 3 John 5-8). In the current situation, Paul is very candidly asking for help from the Romans. His hope may well have been that Rome would become his base of operation to the West as Syrian Antioch had been in the East.

Recipients

We have already indicated that Paul, who had not yet been to Rome, could not be the founder of the Roman church. We have also discounted a 25-year Roman ministry for Peter. There is insufficient evidence to support the idea that he founded the congregation in Rome, although he later may have sealed his ministry with a martyr's death there.

How, then, did the Roman congregation get its start? Perhaps the best answer is that we do not know. Some possibilities may be suggested, however. One theory gives credit for that accomplishment to the "visitors from Rome (both Jews and converts to Judaism)" who were in Jerusalem at the time of Pentecost (Acts 2:10,11). The assumption is that they returned home to plant the Christian faith in the capital city of the empire. That is entirely possible, and even if they were not the prime movers in actually starting the church, they might have been among the earliest representatives and spokespeople for the Christian faith there.

An unusual feature of the epistle to the Romans is the large number of people whom Paul greets in the final chapter. Paul mentions some two dozen people by name. How could he know that many people in a place he had not yet visited? An answer to that question may also bring with it a possible solution to the mystery of who founded the Roman church. In the ancient world, there was a proverbial saying to the effect of "All roads lead to Rome." Rome, the capital of a sprawling empire, was the center of a bustling and thriving world community. Traveling considerable distances was common, even if not easy or comfortable. Many people moved around a great deal. Think of the movement of Aquila and Priscilla: from Pontus (near the Black Sea) to Rome, to Corinth (Acts 18:1,2), to Ephesus (Acts 18:18,19), and back to Rome (Romans 16:3).

It is possible that the people named in Romans chapter 16 were people whom Paul had met in the East and had brought into the church with his gospel message. When these people in the course of business or public life subsequently found their way to Rome, they took their Christianity with them and became prominent members of the Christian community in Rome.

Incidentally, speaking of a Roman Christian *community* may be a more appropriate use of terminology than speaking of a Roman Christian *church,* for there does not seem to have been a central organized congregation there. Rather, the readership of Paul's letter seems to have consisted of a series of smaller groups meeting in private homes. Call them house churches, if you will. A number of such groups seem to be discernible in Paul's section of greetings (16:5,10,11,14,15).

Another item that has raised some discussion is the ethnic makeup of Paul's readership in Rome. Were they of gentile or Jewish extraction? The view reflected in this commentary is that the numerical majority of the Christians in Rome at this time was of gentile background.

For support of such a view, note that at the outset of his letter Paul describes himself as an apostle who had received "grace and apostleship to call people from among *all the Gentiles* to the obedience that comes from faith," and then immediately adds, "You also are among those who are called to belong to Jesus Christ" (1:5,6). Later in the same chapter, he gives a reason for his eagerness to visit them by saying it was "in order that I might have a harvest *among you, just as I have had among the other Gentiles*" (1:13). Even in chapters 9 to 11, which deal so directly with the spiritual status of the Jewish nation, Paul says regarding the imagery of wild olive branches being grafted into a domesticated olive tree, "I am talking to you Gentiles" (11:13).

However, even though Gentiles likely were the majority in number, there still remained a very influential Jewish minority. Strong influence from the Jewish community perhaps should not surprise us. After all, Jesus said to the Samaritan woman, "Salvation is from the Jews" (John 4:22). Add to that what we also know from Acts regarding the usual pattern in the founding of fledgling Christian congregations. Paul's first approach regularly was to go to the Jewish synagogue in urban centers and preach there as long as he was tolerated. When the synagogue leaders objected to Paul's message, as they regularly did, Paul and his little group of Christian followers would find other quarters—often in private homes.

The time available to Paul for giving guidance and training to these young congregations was decidedly limited. Therefore, the grounding in the Old Testament Scriptures that the ex-synagogue people brought was excellent preparation for their taking leadership roles in the new Christian congregation when Paul moved on to the next mission site. In this way, even though the number of Jews may have been relatively small, Jewish leadership was a significant factor in the young Christian congregations whose converts were gained largely from the local gentile population.

Paul does not overlook this Jewish element in the Roman congregation. His incisive preaching of the law, charging all people with lacking the righteousness that avails before God, is directed also at those who call themselves Jews (2:17-24). At another place he identifies himself with his Jewish readers when he speaks of Abraham as "our forefather" (4:1). And he introduces the extended three-chapter discourse on Israel with the poignant, Moses-like petition, "I could wish that I myself were cursed and cut off from Christ for the sake of my brothers, those of my own race" (9:3; see also Exodus 32:31,32). In conclusion, both Jews and Gentiles are the object of Paul's loving concern in his letter to the Romans.

Content

Unlike most of the correspondence we have from the apostle Paul's pen, his letter to the Romans does not seem to have been written to solve any particular problem in the congregation or to settle a theological debate. The letter is calm and dispassionate. In some respects it resembles an essay, setting forth a broad, systematic treatment of God's plan of salvation. Dominant throughout is the concept of *righteousness.*

Natural man's lack of righteousness (1:18–3:20) is offset by the righteousness that comes from God, the righteousness earned by Christ and received by the sinner through faith (3:21–5:21). Having received Christ's righteousness through faith, the justified sinner is now moved to live a life of righteousness that conforms in ever greater degree to God's will (6:1–8:39).

After a three-chapter interlude in which he speaks of God's righteousness in dealing with Israel (9:1–11:36), the apostle addresses specific situations in the faith-lives of the Romans. Included among these is a request for their support in sharing the good news of God's righteousness with those in the West who still need to hear that saving message.

Outline

    I. Introduction of the letter (1:1-15)
       A. Greetings and personal introduction (1:1-7)
       B. Paul's thankfulness for the faith of his readers (1:8-10)
       C. Paul's motive for wanting to visit the Roman Christians (1:11-15)
   II. Theme: righteousness from God (1:16,17)
  III. The unrighteousness of all people (1:18–3:20)
       A. Gentiles (1:18-32)
       B. Moralists (2:1-16)
       C. Jews (2:17–3:9)
       D. Summary: all people (3:10-20)
  IV. Righteousness credited: justification (3:21–5:21)
       A. Righteousness through Christ by faith (3:21–4:25)
         1. God's justice demonstrated (3:21-26)
         2. Faith established (3:27-31)
         3. Faith illustrated (4:1-25)
       B. The effects of justification (5:1-11)
       C. Summary: Man's unrighteousness contrasted with God's gift of righteousness (5:12-21)
    V. Righteousness in Christian living: sanctification (6:1–8:39)
       A. Freedom from the clutches of sin (6:1-23)
       B. Freedom from domination by the law (7:1-25)
       C. Freedom from the fear of death (8:1-39)

Continuing significance

If a person were to settle on one specific reason for Paul's writing this letter, it might seem that preparing the Romans to be the base of support for future mission work ranked high in Paul's thinking. To be sure, if the Romans were to anchor the new wave of gospel outreach to the West, then they themselves would need to be firmly grounded in the basic truths of justification and sanctification.

But with the passage of time and the benefit of hindsight, we can safely say that God saw fit to serve a larger readership with this letter than just its original recipients in Rome. In his wisdom God has provided and preserved a letter that has edified its readers for nearly two thousand years now. And it will continue to serve as long as there are sinners in need of its message of law and gospel. All of Scripture is useful and profitable to the Last Day, of course, but it is perhaps not an overstatement to say that nothing is more so than Romans. Luther expressed that same evaluation in the preface to his translation of Romans:

> This epistle is really the chief part of the New Testament, and is truly the purest gospel. It is worthy not only that every Christian should know it word for word, by heart, but also that he should occupy himself with it every day, as the daily bread of the soul. We can never read it or ponder over it too much; for the more we deal with it, the more precious it becomes and the better it tastes. (*Luther's Works,* American Edition, Volume 35, page 365)

With the prayer that the letter may become ever more precious to the reader, we offer the following commentary on Paul's masterful epistle.

PART ONE

Introduction of the Letter
(1:1-15)

Greetings and personal introduction

1 **Paul, a servant of Christ Jesus, called to be an apostle and set apart for the gospel of God—²the gospel he promised beforehand through his prophets in the Holy Scriptures ³regarding his Son, who as to his human nature was a descendant of David, ⁴and who through the Spirit of holiness was declared with power to be the Son of God by his resurrection from the dead: Jesus Christ our Lord. ⁵Through him and for his name's sake, we received grace and apostleship to call people from among all the Gentiles to the obedience that comes from faith. ⁶And you also are among those who are called to belong to Jesus Christ.**

⁷To all in Rome who are loved by God and called to be saints:

Grace and peace to you from God our Father and from the Lord Jesus Christ.

In ancient times the standard form used for beginning a letter differed somewhat from what we're accustomed to. We place the author's signature at the end of the letter; the ancients put it up front. The letter to the Romans opens with the first word of the first verse identifying Paul as the author.

A second item always stated up front in ancient letters was an indication of whom the letter was intended for. That comes in verse 7 of Paul's letter, where the recipients are identified as "all in Rome who are loved by God and called to be saints."

The third standard item in every ancient letter was a greeting. Here in Romans the greeting, "Grace and peace to you

11

from God our Father and from the Lord Jesus Christ," is very similar to the phrase that opens virtually all of Paul's New Testament letters.

What is unusual about the letter to the Romans is the extensive treatment given the first item, namely, the author describing himself and his message. That description occupies verses 1 to 5. In it Paul calls himself "a servant of Christ Jesus." Literally, he says he is a slave, a person who doesn't follow his own will but who takes orders. Paul was in the service of Christ Jesus. His particular task had been shaped by his having been "called to be an apostle." An apostle, by definition, is one who has been sent out. Paul was *called* to be an apostle." On his own he never would have chosen to be one. Recall that formerly he was Saul, the great persecutor of Christians. This Saul was so opposed to Christians that he not only persecuted Christians in Jerusalem, but he even went out looking for them in the outlying areas. In the course of Saul's trip to Damascus to arrest Christians there, Jesus met Saul on the road, struck him blind, and brusquely confronted him with the stern rebuke, "Saul, Saul, why do you persecute me?" (Acts 9:4).

Paul did not choose to become a Christian. Rather, God called him and "set [him] apart for the gospel" (1:1). When Ananias, the pious Christian whom the Lord sent to minister to Paul in his blindness, objected to going near this flagrant persecutor, God told him, "Go! This man is my chosen instrument to carry my name before the Gentiles and their kings and before the people of Israel" (Acts 9:15). Paul truly was chosen by God and set apart for the gospel.

Mention of the gospel sets Paul off in a different direction, moving from the description of himself to an extended description of the gospel of which he is a privileged servant and apostle.

He describes this message as "the gospel he [God] promised beforehand through his prophets in the Holy Scriptures regarding his Son, who as to his human nature was a descendant of David, and who through the Spirit of holiness was declared with power to be the Son of God by his resurrection from the dead: Jesus Christ our Lord" (1:2-4).

When Paul calls himself God's "servant," he is using a term that was a standard description for Old Testament prophets (Ezra 9:10,11; Jeremiah 7:25; Daniel 9:6; Amos 3:7). And it is with good reason that Paul identifies himself with God's Old Testament servants, the prophets. The gospel he is preaching is really the same message they already had proclaimed. They had pointed to the Messiah, the promised Christ, who was to come into the world as Savior and Redeemer. Paul's gospel message proclaims and extols that same Christ, who now has come. Paul can claim that his gospel is one that God proclaimed "beforehand through his prophets in the Holy Scriptures regarding his Son" (1:2,3). Paul tells the Romans at the outset of his letter that he really is saying nothing new. His message is in line with what God's servants, the prophets, had foretold.

And what was that message? At its core it is the claim that true God and true man are united in one and the same person in Christ. Paul expresses that truth in a set of parallel expressions (verses 3,4). That parallel, however, is better reflected in the rendering the NIV translators have put into their footnote than in what they have chosen for the text. The footnote reads "who as to his spirit" of holiness rather than their first choice, "who through the Spirit of holiness."

Note the difference. In the footnote *spirit* is lowercased and refers to Christ's "spirit of holiness," in distinction to the uppercase *Spirit,* which would refer to the Holy Spirit. Literally, Paul says that his gospel is a message about God's Son:

who, in relation to his flesh, was born of the
seed of David
> and
who, in relation to his spirit of holiness, was
declared to be the Son of God.

He *became* true man, the seed of David, when he was
born of Mary, but from eternity he always was true God.
He didn't become the Son of God; rather, he was *declared,*
he was powerfully shown as such by his resurrection.

Of the many miracles the God-man did while here on
earth, the crowning miracle was his resurrection after he had
died as our substitute. His perfect life earned righteousness
for us. His innocent death paid for our many sins and misdeeds. The Father's raising him from the dead proves that he
is indeed the Savior, totally acceptable to his heavenly Father.

Paul calls this God-man "Jesus Christ our Lord." We
have come to understand that combination as a simple
title, which is all well and good, but in a greater sense,
every word of that four-word expression is individually significant. The name *Jesus* means "Savior" and was given to
the Son of Mary born in Bethlehem. *Christ* means "the
Anointed One," the Messiah, God's Son, who deigned to
take on human flesh so that he could die as the sinner's
substitute. In so doing he redeemed sinners—he bought
them back—at the price of his lifeblood so that they are
now his. He is their owner, their lord and master. But the
key word that personalizes the whole expression is the
possessive adjective *our.* By faith we receive all the benefits he came to bring. By faith he is *our* Lord, as he was
Paul's Lord. Under the guidance of the Holy Spirit, Paul
had come to accept Jesus Christ as his Lord, and he now
proclaims Christ as the heart of the gospel message that he
is about to share with his Roman readers.

The recipients of Paul's letter are "all in Rome who are loved by God and called to be saints" (verse 7). Although Paul has not been to Rome, as he will be informing us shortly (1:13), he does know a considerable number of people in Rome. In the closing chapter of this letter, he will be sending personal greetings to some two dozen people. The real bond between them, however, is that, like Paul, they are loved by God, who has called them to be saints. As Paul uses the term, *saints* are people who are holy by faith in Christ Jesus. Call them believers, if you will.

On the basis of their common faith in Christ, Paul can extend the following greeting: "Grace and peace to you from God our Father and from the Lord Jesus Christ" (verse 7). "Grace" was the common greeting in the Greek-speaking world. "Peace" *(Shalom)* was, and is, the standard greeting in the Jewish world. Since this letter was written to an ethnically mixed audience of Jews and Gentiles, both of these greetings are appropriate. Coming from Paul's pen, however, these two terms are far more than just a commonplace secular greeting. In Paul's Christian vocabulary, *grace* is the quality that makes God willing, even eager, to give good gifts to believers. And God's gifts—such as forgiveness of sins, a good conscience, and the certainty of heaven—bring peace to those who are the objects of God's grace. Thus grace and peace go together as cause and effect.

Paul's thankfulness for the faith of his readers

[8]First, I thank my God through Jesus Christ for all of you, because your faith is being reported all over the world. [9]God, whom I serve with my whole heart in preaching the gospel of his Son, is my witness how constantly I remember you [10]in my prayers at all times; and I pray that now at last by God's will the way may be opened for me to come to you.

15

We have noted the standard form Paul uses to open his letters. Another feature that is standard with Paul's letters is the "laudatory" sentence he includes as the second paragraph of virtually every letter. In that sentence Paul regularly commends the faith and spiritual growth of his readers. (For examples of laudatory sentences in other letters of Paul, see 1 Corinthians 1:4; Ephesians 1:3; Philippians 1:3; 1 Thessalonians 1:2; 2 Thessalonians 1:3.)

Here Paul thanks God for the growth and maturity in faith that have become evident in the lives of the Roman Christians. In fact, so prominent is their faith that Paul can say it is "being reported all over the world." With this hyperbole, or intentional overstatement, Paul calls attention to the significant growth in the Romans' faith-life, and thanks God for them, as he does regularly. Paul asserts that he "constantly" remembers them in his prayer "at all times."

What catches our attention, however, is the strength of Paul's assertion. He calls on God as a witness to the fact that he has thought of the Romans regularly. Also of note is the careful wording he uses when he says, "and I pray that now at last by God's will the way may be opened for me to come to you."

Recall that this letter is being written from Corinth. As Paul indicates in his second epistle to the Corinthians, written shortly before this letter to the Romans, it had been necessary for him to clear up a major misunderstanding with the Corinthians. A change in Paul's travel plans had resulted in his not coming to them as early or as often as they were expecting—and the Corinthians took offense at this! Paul doesn't want to let a similar misunderstanding arise in his dealings with the Romans. That he has not yet come to visit them is not because of a lack of interest on his part. Under oath Paul assures them that he remembers them constantly and prays that "now at last by God's will the way may be opened" for him to come to them. Paul will return to this thought shortly (1:13), but first he explains his reasons for wanting to come to them.

Paul's motive for wanting to visit the Roman Christians

[11]I long to see you so that I may impart to you some spiritual gift to make you strong—[12]that is, that you and I may be mutually encouraged by each other's faith. [13]I do not want you to be unaware, brothers, that I planned many times to come to you (but have been prevented from doing so until now) in order that I might have a harvest among you, just as I have had among the other Gentiles.

[14]I am obligated both to Greeks and non-Greeks, both to the wise and the foolish. [15]That is why I am so eager to preach the gospel also to you who are at Rome.

Paul has absolutely the noblest of motives for wanting to come to Rome and visit the Roman Christians. He wants to come so that he may impart "some spiritual gift" to them for the strengthening of their faith. Faith grows through the use of the means of grace, and it is these means that Paul intends to share with them. But at this point there's an intriguing break in Paul's sentence. After telling them that he longs to see them so that he might strengthen them, he adjusts his line of thought to head off a misunderstanding that might arise in the minds of his readers, namely that the upcoming visit will be a one-way street with Paul dispensing all the good things. Actually, Paul envisions the visit as a two-way street. He will be strengthened too. He's coming so that the Roman Christians and he himself "may be mutually encouraged by each other's faith." Their faith will strengthen him! Paul's laudatory sentences in verses 8 to 10 weren't just a formality. He really does treasure the faith of his fellow believers. A moment's reflection will reveal an engaging picture here: Paul, the great missionary, being strengthened and encouraged by the faith of

17

the people to whom he's ministering. But there's a lesson here too. We all might learn to treasure more fully the fellowship of the believers the Lord lets us associate with.

In line with his previously expressed concern for the Romans, Paul now returns once more to the matter of his not having visited them previously. The double negative he uses actually becomes a strong positive: "I do not want you to be unaware [meaning: I want you to be very sure] . . . that I planned many times to come to you (but have been prevented from doing so until now)."

No doubt many things might have kept Paul from going to Rome earlier. He himself identifies the major cause later in the letter (15:19-22) when he tells us that unfinished mission work in the Eastern Mediterranean region ("from Jerusalem . . . to Illyricum") was the main reason for his not being able to go earlier. Now, however, that work is finished, and he can go to Rome "in order that I might have a harvest among you, just as I have had among the *other* Gentiles" (verse 13).

We noted in the introduction to Romans that the Christian church (or churches) in Rome was a mixed group of Jews and Gentiles. Although a small number of Jews, well versed in the Old Testament Scriptures, might have provided much of the leadership, the majority of the Roman Christians was most likely of gentile background. Hence Paul can say that he is looking forward to having a gospel "harvest" among them just as he had among the other Gentiles.

Paul, however, did not feel restricted in the scope of his ministry. Although primarily a missionary to the Gentiles, Paul never hesitated to go first to the Jewish synagogue when he came to a new mission field. Paul alludes to the broad scope of ministry when he says, "I am obligated both to Greeks and non-Greeks, both to the wise and the foolish. That is why I am so eager to preach the gospel also to you who are at Rome."

PART TWO

Theme of the Letter: Righteousness from God
(1:16,17)

¹⁶I am not ashamed of the gospel, because it is the power of God for the salvation of everyone who believes: first for the Jew, then for the Gentile. ¹⁷For in the gospel a righteousness from God is revealed, a righteousness that is by faith from first to last, just as it is written: "The righteous will live by faith."

Although the text of Romans is inspired by God, the chapter and verse divisions are not. Division into chapters seems to date back to the 12th century, while numbered verses did not appear until the 16th century, when printed editions of the Bible became common. The point is that Paul did not intend for a division between what we have come to designate as verses 15 and 16. In fact, in the Greek text, verses 15 to 21 are all connected with causal conjunctions such as our *because, since,* and *for.* These causal conjunctions regularly connect a key concept from the preceding statement with a following reason or rationale.

Therefore, verse 16 provides the rationale for what was said in verse 15. There Paul said, "I am so eager to preach the gospel also to you who are at Rome." Verse 16 adds the reason: *because* "I am not ashamed of the gospel."

Being ashamed of the gospel would imply that Paul was hesitant about proclaiming it, that he was afraid of making claims and promises from it that might go unfulfilled. If such unreliability was the case, when all is said and done, Paul would end up embarrassed and discredited for making false claims and promises that he couldn't keep.

19

But Paul isn't hesitant at all about proclaiming the gospel, because "it is the power of God for the salvation of everyone who believes." When Paul calls the gospel a power, he uses the Greek word dynamis, a basis for the English word *dynamite.* The gospel has that kind of power not because it originated with Paul—remember, he's just a "servant" (1:1)—but because it is the power of God. It brings the greatest possible blessing, eternal salvation. Even more amazing, that salvation is for everyone.

When Paul says the gospel is "the power of God for the salvation of everyone *who believes"* (verse 16), he is not limiting the power of the gospel, as though salvation were intended only for some and not for others. When he speaks of the salvation "of everyone who believes," he's talking about the *how* of salvation, not the *who.* Paul will be saying more about this shortly.

In verse 14 Paul had indicated that as a gospel preacher, he was obligated "both to Greeks and non-Greeks," in other words, to everyone. Here in verse 16 he uses a slightly different designation in speaking of the universal scope of the gospel. The gospel is the power of God for everyone, "first for the Jew, then for the Gentile."

Historically and chronologically, one could make a case for the priority of the Jewish nation in God's plan of salvation. God chose Abraham from all the families of the earth and made of him a special nation from whom the Savior was born. Jesus' earthly ministry was largely limited to his Jewish compatriots, as he explained to the Canaanite woman (Matthew 15:24). To the Samaritan woman at Jacob's well, Jesus said, "Salvation is from the Jews" (John 4:22). One could therefore say that God's plan of salvation was "first for the Jew."

But salvation was never intended only for the Jewish nation. Inclusion of Gentiles was always in God's plan (Isaiah 60:1-9;

Acts 15:13-18). Wholesale conversion of Gentiles, however, did not happen until the arrival of the New Testament Christian church and the apostles' carrying out Christ's commission to preach the gospel to all nations (Mark 16:15). The gospel was "first for the Jew," but then also "for the Gentile." The same gospel works for all.

Why can it work for all? Because "in the gospel a righteousness from God is revealed, a righteousness that is by faith from first to last, just as it is written: 'The righteous will live by faith'" (1:17).

In the original Greek, the expression translated "a righteousness from God" has simply the possessive form of *God*. It might therefore be translated "God's righteousness." But that translation is ambiguous. It could allow for two meanings: the righteousness God has whereby he himself is holy, or the righteousness he demands from every person. It was this second understanding of God's righteousness that caused Luther so much trouble early in his life. He became angry with God for demanding a righteousness that even the best human effort could not provide.

Only when Luther learned another meaning of "God's righteousness" did his troubled soul find peace. That other meaning is the righteousness that God gives. The NIV is interpretive but correct when it translates the phrase as "a righteousness *from* God."

The gospel can bring salvation for everybody who believes because God is the one providing the righteousness everybody needs. Sinful human beings produce nothing useful. God in Christ has done it all! By his perfect life as the sinner's substitute, Christ earned the righteousness that all people owe to a just and holy God. By his innocent death on the cross, Christ paid for the many things we and a world of sinners have done wrong.

In the gospel God now invites the sinner to accept Christ's righteousness as his own. And when sinners in faith accept Christ's merit, God looks at them as though they were just and holy. God declares the sinner innocent of all wrongdoing. It's like a judge in a courtroom pardoning a convicted offender. This marvelous exchange whereby Christ takes our sin on himself and gives us his righteousness is called *justification*. As Paul tells us, this way of receiving righteousness from God is "by faith from first to last." It's purely by grace, without any merit on the sinner's part. The prophet Habakkuk indicated this already centuries earlier when he said, "The righteous will live by his faith" (2:4).

PART THREE

The Unrighteousness of All People
(1:18–3:20)

The focal point of Paul's letter to the Romans is the teaching that the only righteousness that avails before God is the righteousness that comes from God—through faith in Christ. The need for righteousness from God is universal because, ever since Adam and Eve's fall into sin, no one is righteous. No one can stand before God's bar of justice and claim on the basis of personal performance to have the merit necessary to qualify for heaven. All people, by their very nature, fall short of God's just and holy requirements. All are unrighteous.

In the next section (1:18–3:20), Paul documents this lack of righteousness, dividing all people into three major categories. The first group he depicts are the open and coarse sinners (1:18-32), whom Paul's readers would identify as gentile unbelievers living lifestyles of blatant sinfulness.

The second group Paul describes are those of somewhat higher and more noble standards. We might call them moralists, namely, people who feel that living a moral life gives them the grounds for expecting a more favorable verdict from God. They agree that the coarse sins Paul identified and denounced in the first group are intolerable to God. However, because they themselves aren't caught up in these coarse sins, they think themselves to be better off before God. On the basis of their supposedly more acceptable conduct, they feel they're not under God's wrath. Paul deals with their misunderstanding in 2:1-16.

Paul's third category of people who lack righteousness assume that they always have possessed it. They are the Jews.

Because they are descendants of Abraham and members of God's chosen people, blessed with God's revealed Word, many of them suppose they must already be on the road to heaven. Paul clearly points out that a mere outward, external connection will not do (2:17–3:9).

In a summary statement (3:10-20), Paul concludes that no one, neither Jew nor Gentile, has the righteousness a just and holy God rightly demands. Righteousness is not to be found in the fallen human family. If there is to be any hope of a solution, the remedy has to come from the outside—from God himself. How that remedy is provided will be the emphasis of Paul's next section.

The unrighteousness of the Gentiles

¹⁸The wrath of God is being revealed from heaven against all the godlessness and wickedness of men who suppress the truth by their wickedness, ¹⁹since what may be known about God is plain to them, because God has made it plain to them. ²⁰For since the creation of the world God's invisible qualities— his eternal power and divine nature—have been clearly seen, being understood from what has been made, so that men are without excuse.

It is useful to note the parallelism between verses 17 and 18. In the former verse, Paul asserted that the righteousness of God is revealed in the gospel. In the next verse, he now says, "The wrath of God is being revealed from heaven against all the godlessness and wickedness of men." The connection between these two verses becomes even more apparent when we recall that all the major thoughts from verses 16 to 21 are connected with causal conjunctions. Although the NIV translation doesn't indicate it, there is a causal conjunction at the start of verse 16. The progression of Paul's thought is this: If there is to be any righteousness for fallen mankind, it has to come from God *because* "the wrath of God . . . revealed from heaven" is the only thing unrighteous people can reasonably expect on the basis of what they have done and continue to do.

Why is God angry with sinners? Because they "suppress[ed] the truth by their wickedness." Our human minds often find difficulty in accepting God's being angry with all sinners. We're inclined to pose the questions, Don't some people have many advantages over others? Don't some have the opportunity to gain a much fuller understanding of God's will, while others seem to be shortchanged? Is it fair for God to be equally angry with all people?

It's helpful to follow Paul's logic here. He points out that the heart of the matter is not the quantity of knowledge people have. God is not angry with people for having too little knowledge but rather for going against what knowledge they do have. It's not ignorance or a lack of information that leads them to do bad things; it's perversity on the sinner's part. Against better knowledge the sinner rebels against God and defies him with conscious and deliberate disobedience. Hence Paul brands such conduct as "wickedness."

But is it too strong to call this "wickedness"? Again, Paul's causal conjunction is helpful. Paul maintains that sinners can fairly be charged with rebellion against better knowledge because they have "truth" that they suppress. How can Paul say that they have truth to wickedly suppress? *Because* "what may be known about God is plain to them." Why can Paul say it is plain to them? *Because* "God has made it plain to them." How can Paul know that it's plain to them? *Because* "since the creation of the world God's invisible qualities—his eternal power and divine nature—have been clearly seen, being understood from what has been made, so that men are without excuse."

People have a natural knowledge of God written in their hearts, and this knowledge is supplemented and reinforced by what Paul now adds, namely, proof gained by looking around at the created world. Anyone can see that the world was brought into being by something far greater than mere chance, by someone with "eternal power and divine nature." Only the fool says, "There is no God" (Psalm 14:1). All people have information about God, "so that men are without excuse."

In the context of our letter, it is clear that Paul is directing this verdict primarily against the Gentiles. He now goes on to show that suppressing the truth and following wrong thinking leads to wrong actions—with disastrous results for gentile sinners.

²¹**For although they knew God, they neither glorified him as God nor gave thanks to him, but their thinking became futile and their foolish hearts were darkened. ²²Although they claimed to be wise, they became fools ²³and exchanged the glory of the immortal God for images made to look like mortal man and birds and animals and reptiles.**

In verse 20 Paul made the sobering observation that the Gentiles in open rebellion to God were "without excuse." Why can he say they are without excuse? *Because* "although they knew God, they neither glorified him as God nor gave thanks to him." Again, Paul's point is not how much the Gentiles knew or how clearly they knew God. His point is that they went against what they did know. For in God's creation they could see his invisible qualities of eternal power and divine nature, but they refused to glorify him or to acknowledge that they owed him thanks for the many temporal blessings that came their way day after day. Consequently "their thinking became futile and their foolish hearts were darkened."

Paul uses passive verbs here when he speaks of the Gentiles becoming futile and being darkened; their thinking and hearts are being acted upon. The question is, Who made them futile? Who darkened their hearts? The answer is that they did it to themselves. Two observations would seem to support that conclusion. First of all, note that the passive verbs stand among a cluster of active verbs: they (the Gentiles) did not glorify God; they did not give him thanks; they claimed to be wise; they exchanged the glory of God for mortal images. Furthermore, the stress in this section is entirely on what the Gentiles do in their natural, unregenerate state. The point is that the people Paul describes here are not some unfortunates who were doomed in advance by God's decree and thus never had a chance. These are people who are sinning by choice and against better knowledge. They're doing what they want to do. For a fuller statement on their willing commitment to evil, look ahead to verse 32. God did not "program" them for an evil lifestyle, but he does indeed respond to their wickedness. That response will be treated in verses 24, 26, and 28.

The kind of fools the Gentiles made of themselves when they suppressed their knowledge of God is illustrated in one example that Paul cites: "Although they claimed to be wise, they became fools and exchanged the glory of the immortal God for images made to look like mortal man and birds and animals and reptiles." Keep in mind that Paul is talking here of people who knew God but suppressed that knowledge. The result of such bad thinking is bad actions and bad choices. In their supposed wisdom, they acted so foolishly that they traded the reality of the immortal God for likenesses, images—and images of frail, mortal things like people, birds, animals, and reptiles at that. Not a wise trade at all!

²⁴Therefore God gave them over in the sinful desires of their hearts to sexual impurity for the degrading of their bodies with one another. ²⁵They exchanged the truth of God for a lie, and worshiped and served created things rather than the Creator— who is forever praised. Amen.

One of the sobering truths about our holy God is that, although he is unalterably opposed to sin and evil, he does not forcibly keep people from sinning. Fallen humanity retains the awful ability to defy God. And when people insist on doing wrong and opposing God, he does not prevent them. We see an example of this in the Gentiles' being able to fashion images and idols to replace the true God. Paul says of their reckless folly, "They exchanged the truth of God for a lie, and worshiped and served created things rather than the Creator."

That God did not prevent such folly does not mean that it went unnoticed or unpunished. It's occasionally said, Virtue is its own reward. The opposite is also true: Vice is its own punishment. When people defy God and thumb their noses at him as they flagrantly disobey his holy will, he does not prevent them or punish them immediately. Rather, he lets them wallow in their sin. So it went here with the Gentiles. Paul says, "Therefore God gave them over in the sinful desires of their hearts to sexual impurity for the degrading of their bodies with one another."

Paul becomes more explicit regarding their "sexual impurity" when he continues:

²⁶Because of this [exchanging the truth of God for a lie], God gave them over to shameful lusts. Even their women exchanged natural relations for unnatural ones. ²⁷In the same way the men also abandoned natural relations with women and were inflamed with lust for one another. Men committed indecent acts with other men, and received in themselves the due penalty for their perversion.

Homosexuality truly is a grievous and disgusting sin, but it is by no means the only sin God allows blatant sinners to become entangled in. A dreadful catalog of vices and evils now follows in regard to God's dealing with crass sinners.

[28]Furthermore, since they did not think it worthwhile to retain the knowledge of God, he gave them over to a depraved mind, to do what ought not to be done. [29]They have become filled with every kind of wickedness, evil, greed and depravity. They are full of envy, murder, strife, deceit and malice. They are gossips, [30]slanderers, God-haters, insolent, arrogant and boastful; they invent ways of doing evil; they disobey their parents; [31]they are senseless, faithless, heartless, ruthless. [32]Although they know God's righteous decree that those who do such things deserve death, they not only continue to do these very things but also approve of those who practice them.

Note the sequence: The Gentiles had a knowledge of God that they didn't consider worthwhile to retain, so they refused God's guidance and struck out on their own evil course of action. In response God "gave them over to a depraved mind." What their depraved minds thereupon proceeded to do is then outlined in the devastating list that follows.

But it wasn't bad enough for these people to do these things themselves. They compounded their wickedness by propagandizing for their sin and recruiting others to join them. "Although they know God's righteous decree that those who do such things deserve death, they not only continue to do these very things but also approve of those who practice them."

The practice of homosexuality served as Exhibit A for Paul in his case against the Gentiles (1:26,27). Certainly, homosexuality is not the only sin, nor before an impartial God necessarily the worst sin, but it still today serves as a graphic example of the wicked and perverse mind-set that Paul is describing in writing to the Romans. We live in an age when many people are no longer content to live an "alternative" lifestyle quietly. Rather, they openly advocate and promote it. We see organized marches and campaigns for "gay *rights*" as though that were something they are entitled to. In all of this, it's perfectly clear that those clamoring for change are not merely seeking acceptance for themselves but are trying to gain advocates for their perversion. They "not only continue to do these very things but also approve of those who practice them."

Whether the focus is on ancient gentile libertines or their modern counterparts, Paul's point stands: Don't look for any righteousness before God from this group!

The unrighteousness of moralists

Paul has just finished a graphic section indicting the Gentiles for their grievous sins and obvious lack of righteousness. Because they turned their backs on him, God gave them over to all sorts of disgusting sins and degrading vices.

In the present section, Paul envisions a person who agrees with Paul's denunciation of these evildoers. In effect the person says, "You're right, Paul. People who do things like that are definitely out of God's good graces. They deserve the dreadful fate that's in store for them."

The moralist's approach rests on the principle that people have to lead better lives if their status before God is to improve. His assumption is that he himself knows what is better and that he is doing so. He fancies himself as having more righteousness than others. That's why he can criticize others and presume to give them advice on how to improve. Paul's response is, Wait a minute! Watch out—lest by the approach you're using, you actually condemn yourself.

2 You, therefore, have no excuse, you who pass judgment on someone else, for at whatever point you judge the other, you are condemning yourself, because you who pass judgment do the same things. ²Now we know that God's judgment against those who do such things is based on truth. ³So when you, a mere man, pass judgment on them and yet do the same things, do you think you will escape God's judgment? ⁴Or do you show contempt for the riches of his kindness, tolerance and patience, not realizing that God's kindness leads you toward repentance?

With supposed superiority, the moralist passes judgment on someone else. In this instance he is condemning the evil actions Paul has identified as characteristic among the Gentiles. Paul does not dispute the correctness of the moralist's assessment of the situation. Paul agrees, "Now we know that God's judgment against those who do such things is based on truth." The Gentiles' sins deserve punishment. The problem, however, is that the moralist, in his arrogance and presumption, doesn't see that he himself is committing the same kind of sins. In doing so, he falls under the same condemnation—in fact, under his own condemnation.

Paul exposes both the moralist's arrogance and faulty logic when he asks, "So when you, a mere man, pass judgment on them and yet do the same things, do you think you will escape God's judgment?" In Paul's mind there is absolutely no doubt that the moralist, with his present mind-set, will not escape God's just judgment. But the moralist doesn't know that and doesn't agree. He's going to protest, But I'm *not* doing the same things as those Gentiles!

Hence, good teacher that he is, Paul asks a follow-up question to get at the heart of the matter. Paul continues, "Or do you show contempt for the riches of his kindness, tolerance and patience, not realizing that God's kindness leads you toward repentance?"

The main problem is that the moralist has an unrepentant heart—and understandably so. He has been comparing his life and conduct to the depraved conduct of the Gentiles. He's not doing the gross things they do; therefore, he feels self-righteously superior. Trusting in his relatively more moral life, he thinks he's fine with God just as he is.

But he's been comparing himself to the wrong standard. Instead of looking at Gentile misbehavior, he should have been looking to the kindness, tolerance, and patience of a loving God, who takes care of him day in and day out. He should have been recognizing his obligation to love the Lord with his whole heart, soul, and mind. He has not done this. Instead, by ignoring this kind, tolerant, and patient God, he has actually been doing just the opposite of loving God. He's been "show[ing] contempt" for the richness of God's grace. As such, he's no better than the Gentiles who "suppress[ed] the truth by their wickedness" (1:18), who "neither glorified him as God nor gave thanks to him" (1:21), and who "did not think it worthwhile to retain the knowledge of God" (1:28).

Paul goes on to point out what the inescapable consequences of such conduct, if not repented, must necessarily be.

⁵But because of your stubbornness and your unrepentant heart, you are storing up wrath against yourself for the day of God's wrath, when his righteous judgment will be revealed. ⁶God "will give to each person according to what he has done." ⁷To those who by persistence in doing good seek glory, honor and immortality, he will give eternal life. ⁸But for those who are self-seeking and who reject the truth and follow evil, there will be wrath and anger. ⁹There will be trouble and distress for every human being who does evil: first for the Jew, then for the Gentile; ¹⁰but glory, honor and peace for everyone who does good: first for the Jew, then for the Gentile. ¹¹For God does not show favoritism.

The self-righteous moralist compares his life and conduct to that of wayward Gentiles and concludes that he's significantly better than they are. He's comfortable with his life and actions, and therefore he sees no reason to repent. But his complacency, Paul points out, is a delusion.

"Because of your stubbornness and your unrepentant heart," Paul tells him, "you are storing up wrath against yourself for the day of God's wrath, when his righteous judgment will be revealed."

Taking note of the root of the verb that is here translated as "storing up" yields an interesting insight. Literally, the verb means "*treasuring* up." People usually try to accumulate good and useful things, things of value. But in stubborn impenitence, the moralist is treasuring up wrath for himself. The actions he thinks are so good and acceptable are really reprehensible acts of self-righteousness, not things pleasing to God. They're what the church father Augustine called "glittering vices."

Why are they vices? Not because the moralist's actions in themselves are necessarily bad, but because his motive for doing them is wrong. The difference between good works flowing from faith and bad works motivated by self-righteousness and a self-seeking spirit may not be readily apparent to human eyes at the present time. The difference, however, is very real and will become obvious to all on "the day of God's wrath, when his righteous judgment will be revealed." "For those who are self-seeking and who reject the truth and follow evil, there will be wrath and anger."

From what Paul has already said in this letter, "the righteous will live by faith" (1:17), and from what he says in his other letters, it is perfectly clear that salvation is a gift of God's grace. The Scriptures consistently teach that salvation comes to the believer by faith, without requiring any merit or any fulfillment of the law. Good works do not earn salvation, but they are nonetheless important. They are the manifestation of faith, the physical evidence that faith, which is invisible, is in fact present and resides in the heart of the believer. Good works are the proof that faith is living and active. Recall James' evaluation of the situation when he says, "Faith by itself, if it is not accompanied by action, is dead" (James 2:17).

Note also the place our Savior gives works in his description of judgment day (Matthew 25:31-46). The division between "sheep" and "goats" is made purely on the basis of faith or lack of faith in the heart. Faith, although invisible to us, is clearly visible to the omniscient God. Vindication of God's just verdict, however, is made on the basis of the fruits of faith that are clearly visible to all.

In the case of the righteous, God defends his placing them among the sheep by saying, "For I was hungry and you gave me something to eat, I was thirsty and you gave me something to drink, . . ." (verse 35).

When the unrighteous complain about the negative verdict against them, the same measuring stick is used. The standard of works as the fruit of faith is applied to them also. Only in this case, their lack of good works verifies the damning lack of living faith that has justly condemned them to a place with the other goats.

Good works are not necessary for salvation, but they are an important indicator as to the presence or absence of saving faith. Works are the standard evidence of living faith that an impartial God applies to every individual, regardless of status or nationality. Hence Paul can say, "There will be trouble and distress for every human being who does evil: first for the Jew, then for the Gentile; but glory, honor and peace for everyone who does good: first for the Jew, then for the Gentile. For God does not show favoritism."

Throughout the Old Testament, God dealt with the Israelites in a unique way, beginning with his choice of Abraham as the father of the special nation from which the Savior was to be born. Jesus was born a Jew, and in his ministry, which was carried out almost entirely on Jewish soil, he declared, "Salvation is from the Jews" (John 4:22). The Jewish nation obviously had significant advantages, leading Paul, when he earlier spoke of the power of the gospel for salvation, to say, "first for the Jew, then for the Gentile" (Romans 1:16). That same pattern, first for the Jew and then for the Gentile, however, also holds true in God's final verdict. The Jews had great advantages, but greater advantages means greater obligations. Of his unbelieving compatriots, Jesus said, "If I had not come and spoken to them, they would not be guilty of sin. Now, however, they have no excuse for their sin" (John 15:22). Jesus states the principle clearly when he declares, "From everyone who has been given much, much will be demanded; and from the one who has been entrusted with much, much more will be asked" (Luke 12:48).

Although God's dealing with people is not identical in each case, that is, in the quantity of blessings he bestows on one person as compared to another, yet God's dealing with all people is absolutely just and evenhanded. In the final accounting, he judges all people on the basis of their response to his grace. That is just another way of saying that he looks for and rewards the actions that flow from a heart filled with faith and trust in what God's Son has done. Conversely, God rejects and punishes everyone who has spurned his grace in Christ and who tries to stand before him on the basis of personal merit. Judgment on the basis of faith showing itself in action is God's fixed pattern of dealing with everyone, Jew or Gentile. That is the case, "for God does not show favoritism."

While that principle holds true for both reward and punishment, Paul here expands upon only the latter, the negative

35

verdict spoken by God upon the unbeliever whose life does not reflect the obedience of faith in Christ.

¹²All who sin apart from the law will also perish apart from the law, and all who sin under the law will be judged by the law. ¹³For it is not those who hear the law who are righteous in God's sight, but it is those who obey the law who will be declared righteous. ¹⁴(Indeed, when Gentiles, who do not have the law, do by nature things required by the law, they are a law for themselves, even though they do not have the law, ¹⁵since they show that the requirements of the law are written on their hearts, their consciences also bearing witness, and their thoughts now accusing, now even defending them.) ¹⁶This will take place on the day when God will judge men's secrets through Jesus Christ, as my gospel declares.

It may be helpful to take a look at the structure of the five verses quoted above. The NIV translators have done us a service by putting verses 14 and 15 into parentheses. They are thereby indicating that these two verses form a separate thought, an aside Paul adds to answer an objection he anticipates may arise.

If for the moment we leave verses 14 and 15 aside, it will be evident that the thought expressed in verse 16 hooks up directly with verses 12 and 13. Those two verses told us about God's negative verdict against sinners, a verdict that "will take place on the day when God will judge men's secrets through Jesus Christ, as my [Paul's] gospel declares."

What God will be judging on judgment day are "men's secrets." That is just another way of saying that God's verdict will be determined by what people's motives were, by what moved them to do the actions and activities that marked their lives. We can't see people's motives. To us they're secret, unless by chance people make them evident to us by what they say or do. There is, of course, a close connection between what people feel in their hearts and what they do with their hands, as Paul points out when he says, "All who sin apart from the law will also perish apart from the law, and all who sin under the law will be judged by the law. For it is not those who hear the law who are righteous in God's sight, but it is those who obey the law who will be declared righteous."

There's a great difference between hearing the law and obeying it. Perhaps an illustration can help to clarify this. You may be totally convinced of the value of limiting highway speeds to 55 miles per hour. It reduces wear and tear on your vehicle; it saves gasoline and lives. You agree with the law; you "hear" what it says. But if you've been driving 70 miles per hour in a 55 zone, and a highway patrol officer pulls you over to the side of the road, all your agreeing with the law isn't going to prevent you from receiving a ticket. The officer has seen your performance, your lack of obedience to the law.

So too before God. It's not "those who *hear* the law" but "those who *obey* the law" who will be declared righteous. And the same principle, the same standard of judgment, applies also to declaring people unrighteous. "All who sin apart from the law will also perish apart from the law, and all who sin under the law will be judged by the law."

Note that in both cases, Paul is talking about people who have sinned and as such are now subject to punishment. The difference (or rather, *apparent* difference) is that one group sinned "apart from the law" while the others sinned "under the law."

Paul is dividing them into two groups because of the different circumstances surrounding the two groups—one of them Jewish; the other, gentile. The Jews had the benefit of God's revealed law, notably in the Mosaic Law given to them through Moses on Mount Sinai. The Gentiles were "apart from the law" in the sense that they didn't have that specific set of God-given regulations.

But the Gentiles still sinned and therefore are subject to God's wrath and punishment. Paul is expecting an objection at this point: How can it be fair for God to punish the Gentiles if they didn't have the benefit of the law's guidance?

Paul now addresses this complaint in the two-verse aside (verses 14,15) we called attention to earlier. Paul points out that although the Gentiles didn't have the Mosaic regulations, they were not without "law," information about God's holy and unchangeable will.

"By nature" pagans do things required by God's law. Guided by the natural knowledge of God written in their hearts, they know and decide that it is wrong to kill, to steal, to dishonor authority, and the like. This does not mean that they know the whole will of God; to the extent that they have a natural impulse to do things in a moral way, "they are a law for themselves."

A related way in which Gentiles show that they have "the requirements of the law . . . written on their hearts" is the activity of conscience. Conscience operates on the innate feeling that there are certain natural rules of conduct to be followed, certain things that should be done and others that should not be done. When a person's conscience judges that his actions are in conformity with the rules, then he is inclined to defend himself. On the other hand, there are times when the person knows he's going against the law written in his heart. He's doing what he knows he shouldn't be doing. Then there comes a voice from within him that rightly accuses him and convicts him of sin. Such a person may have sinned "apart from [God's written, revealed] law," but he is still guilty before God, because he has consciously and intentionally defied God and rebelled against the natural knowledge of God's law, as reinforced by conscience. As he has sinned "apart from the law," so he will "perish apart from the law."

God is serious about having his will done and having his law kept. Relative goodness will not do. Recall that this section has been addressed to the moralist, the person who feels that because he isn't as bad as the coarse gentile sinners, he is acceptable to God. Paul makes it unmistakably clear that such a moralist, either Jew or Gentile, has been disobedient to God and deserves eternal punishment. The moralist has no righteousness upon which he can stand before God and therefore is just as bad off as the gross gentile sinners he looks down on.

The unrighteousness of the Jews

[17]**Now you, if you call yourself a Jew; if you rely on the law and brag about your relationship to God;** [18]**if you know his will and approve of what is superior because you are instructed by the law;** [19]**if you are convinced that you are a guide for the blind, a light for those who are in the dark,** [20]**an instructor of the foolish, a teacher of infants, because you have in the law the embodiment of knowledge and truth—**[21]**you, then, who teach others, do you not teach yourself? You who preach against stealing, do you steal?** [22]**You who say that people should not commit adultery, do you commit adultery? You who abhor idols, do you rob temples?** [23]**You who brag about the law, do you dishonor God by breaking the law?** [24]**As it is written: "God's name is blasphemed among the Gentiles because of you."**

These eight verses, forming a rather complex paragraph, divide themselves into three major thoughts. First there are four "if" clauses. They outline the advantages many Jews supposed themselves to possess by virtue of their Jewish heritage. The next two verses (21,22) pose four searching questions to those Jews, the answers to which will be extremely incriminating. The last two verses (23,24) seem best understood as Paul's negative evaluation of the Jews' status before God, a verdict supported by a quotation from the Old Testament Scriptures.

Supposed Jewish advantages

Paul lines up a series of bold claims that Jews were inclined to make of themselves. The sentence could be diagrammed out like this:

> If you call yourself a Jew;
> if you rely on the law and brag about your relationship to God;
> if you know his will and approve of what is superior because you are instructed by the law;
> if you are convinced that you are a guide for the blind,
>> a light for those who are in the dark,
>> an instructor of the foolish,
>> a teacher of infants,
>> because you have in the law the embodiment of knowledge and truth—

Note that, in one way or another, almost all of the perceived advantages center on knowing God's revealed law. Armed with that knowledge, the Jews feel themselves superior to those less fortunate. They assume that they are the embodiment of knowledge and truth and are in a position to correct others.

Searching questions

Interestingly, Paul's "if" clauses don't have the usual conclusion we expect with a conditional sentence (If this is the case, then . . .). Because of this lack of conclusion, the NIV translators have put a dash at the end of verse 20, indicating that the sentence doesn't end in the ordinary way. Instead of finishing out the conditional sentence with a concluding clause, Paul rather asks four questions that are intended to have the proud Jew reassess himself and his supposed superior status.

Equipped with God's law, the Jew feels he's in a position to instruct others and show them the error of their ways. Paul now asks, "You, then, who teach others, do you not teach yourself?" Paul's point is, You who claim to be able to teach others the right way, shouldn't you be taking your own advice? Shouldn't you be doing what you're urging others to do? The answer—implied here and directly stated a few verses later—is, You *should* do so, but you're not. Essentially, Paul is accusing them of hypocrisy, the sin that Jesus also charged his Jewish compatriots with, time and time again.

Paul goes on with more searching questions: "You who preach against stealing, do you steal?" Again, the proper assessment: You shouldn't, but you do—if not by actually taking your neighbor's property, then by *wanting* to take it, by coveting.

"You who say that people should not commit adultery, do you commit adultery?" You shouldn't, but you do commit adultery—if not by the outward act, then by lusting in your heart.

"You who abhor idols, do you rob temples?" In ancient times there were no banks as we think of them today. For this reason sacred places like temples often became the storage place for valuables like precious metals and jewels. It is not likely, however, that Paul is accusing the Jews of literally raiding these temples for their treasures. What seems a more likely interpretation here is that while the Jews as a nation claimed to abhor idols and false gods, they were all too willing to take up the false teaching and disgusting religious practices of their heathen neighbors. In this way they would be robbing ideas and customs from temples. Whichever of the two interpretations one settles upon, in either case Paul's question implies that while the Jews claim to abhor idols, they haven't remained unaffected by them.

The NIV translators have rendered verse 23 as a question, in line with the previous four questions—and grammatically, that is a very possible construction. There is an alternative, however, that seems more likely within the context. That alternative is to take this verse as a statement rather than a question.

The ancient Greek language in which Paul wrote his epistles had some practices that seem very strange and terribly clumsy to us today. For example, there were no word divisions in written Greek, simply an unbroken line of letters. In the earlier centuries, those letters were all capitals, and eventually they came to be all lowercase letters. Furthermore, for centuries there was little or no punctuation—no commas, periods, or question marks. There were some interrogative words that signaled a question to the reader, but if the sentence lacked such a word, the reader had to decide from context whether the writer intended a declarative sentence or a question.

We're faced with such a contextual decision in verse 23. From the fact that the next verse is an Old Testament quotation that seems to serve as a proof passage supporting the apostle's previous statement, it seems better to take verse 23 as a declarative statement rather than as a question. Taken as a question, the verse would read, "You who brag about the law, do you dishonor God by breaking the law?" In its context, however, the verse rather seems to be Paul's evaluation of the situation, a declarative statement giving the proper answer to the previous four questions. Paul would then be saying, "You who brag about the law, you dishonor God by breaking the law."

As support for this rather harsh judgment, Paul cites an Old Testament reference: "As it is written: 'God's name is blasphemed among the Gentiles because of you.'" The passage Paul is using seems to be an adaptation of Isaiah 52:5.

Paul's point is that even with all their supposed advantages in having the law, the Jewish people do not have the righteousness that a just and holy God requires. Instead of honoring God by cheerfully obeying the law they claim to value so highly, through their disobedience they are actually causing his name to be blasphemed among the Gentiles.

It is evident from Paul's argument that there is no inherent righteousness that comes from having the law, and, as Paul now adds, external observance of the rite of circumcision isn't of any help either.

²⁵Circumcision has value if you observe the law, but if you break the law, you have become as though you had not been circumcised. ²⁶If those who are not circumcised keep the law's requirements, will they not be regarded as though they were circumcised? ²⁷The one who is not circumcised physically and yet obeys the law will condemn you who, even though you have the written code and circumcision, are a lawbreaker.

Circumcision was the sign and seal of God's covenant with Abraham and Abraham's descendants, the Jewish nation. For a Jewish male, to accept circumcision was to enter into a covenantal relationship with God. That covenant relationship entailed two things: God's promise to be Israel's God, and Israel's promise to be God's devoted people, committed to doing his will and obeying his commands.

For a Jew to claim the promises of God through the covenant sealed with circumcision but then to ignore the will of God in his life and conduct was a contradiction in terms. This inconsistency leads Paul to make the observation, "Circumcision has value if you observe the law, but if you break the law, you have become as though you had not been circumcised."

It will be evident, therefore, that circumcision in itself was not the essential feature of a proper relationship with God. The essential feature rather was the attitude of the heart reflecting itself in a life of love and trust in the Lord. Where the heart is right (and that, of course, can come about only through faith in the promised Savior), there circumcision really becomes a nonfactor. Paul alludes to this when he poses the hypothetical question, "If those who are not circumcised keep the law's requirements, will they not be regarded as though they were circumcised?"

The answer to Paul's question is that such people will indeed be regarded as true children of God. In fact, because of their faith-born obedience to God, they will become the judges of circumcised but disobedient Jews. Paul declares, "The one who is not circumcised physically and yet obeys the law will condemn you who, even though you have the written code and circumcision, are a lawbreaker."

The Jews were inclined to put their confidence in having the law and being circumcised. But these things were merely outward and formal; they did not provide the righteousness God looks for. They did not succeed in bringing about a right relationship between the sinner and God. Such a relationship can't come through "the written code." It has to come by faith in the heart, worked by the Holy Spirit. That is something totally different from simply accepting physical circumcision. Therefore, Paul can summarize his case against these self-satisfied and boastful Jews with the following generalization:

[28]A man is not a Jew if he is only one outwardly, nor is circumcision merely outward and physical. [29]No, a man is a Jew if he is one inwardly; and circumcision is circumcision of the

heart, by the Spirit, not by the written code. Such a man's praise is not from men, but from God.

The last sentence, with its reference to "praise . . . from God," is perfectly understandable as it stands. It may be of interest, however, to note that Paul has built a pun, a play on words, into this sentence. In Hebrew the word for "praise" has a sound close to that of the name *Judah*, from which the designation *Jew* is derived. For similar plays on the *praise/Judah* combination, see Genesis 29:35; 49:8.

Three Jewish objections and Paul's responses

Paul has clearly and forcefully made his point that having the Mosaic Law and observing circumcision do not, in and of themselves, assure the Jews of a place in heaven. These external things are not what makes a person truly Jewish, in the sense of being someone whose "praise is . . . from God." No, that commendation rests on something else. What's necessary is the internal state of a believing heart, marked by the true circumcision, which is spiritual, not literal.

In effect, Paul's answer to the Jews is a call to repentance, a call for them to let go of their prideful claim to superiority by virtue of having the law and circumcision. Their pride, however, prevents that, and instead of repentance we hear three resentful and challenging questions theoretically given by Jewish objectors. Paul deals with each objection in turn as they are raised in verses 1, 5, and 9.

3 **What advantage, then, is there in being a Jew, or what value is there in circumcision? ²Much in every way! First of all, they have been entrusted with the very words of God.**

³What if some did not have faith? Will their lack of faith nullify God's faithfulness? ⁴Not at all! Let God be true, and every man a liar. As it is written:

**"So that you may be proved right when you speak
and prevail when you judge."**

First Jewish objection

Paul has indicated that being a descendant of Abraham is
not a ticket to heaven by itself. In fact, Gentiles obedient to
God's will are going to condemn these Jews who have the
written law and circumcision and yet are lawbreakers (2:27).

This induces the Jewish objection "What advantage,
then, is there in being a Jew?" Paul takes the question seriously, and his answer concentrates on just one advantage
the Jews have (there are more, as Paul will be pointing out
in 9:4,5). What advantages? Paul responds, "Much in every
way! First of all, they [the Jews] have been entrusted with
the very words of God."

All people have a measure of knowledge about God
through the natural knowledge written in their hearts. God,
however, honored the Jewish nation by revealing and
recording his will in a written record. For them he "put it in
writing," as we might say today. On Mount Sinai, God had
Moses inscribe his holy Commandments on stone tablets—
Commandments that showed Israel their sins and their need
for a Savior. Through both the verbal and written messages
of his many prophets, God repeated his promise to send the
Savior that sinners needed. And when the time finally came,
God sent his Son, whom the evangelist John calls "the
Word" (John 1:1), to reveal his saving message especially to
the Jews. Regarding "the Word," John expressly declares,
"No one has ever seen God, but God the One and Only,
who is at the Father's side, has made him known" (verse
18). Because of this the writer of Hebrews can say, "In these
last days he [God] has spoken to us by his Son (1:2). Paul's
point stands: The Jewish nation had a significant advantage

over all other people in that they were given the inspired Scriptures, the very Word of God.

At this point Paul is expecting his antagonists to raise a difficulty. "If having the Word of God is so great a blessing," they might object, "why is it that so many of the Jews are going to be condemned in the judgment, as you, Paul, stated previously?"

Paul's answer is, The problem lies with those who are lost. They failed to trust the Word. Their not believing God's Word doesn't make the Word false or ineffective. The unbeliever's faithlessness doesn't cancel out God's *faithfulness,* does it?

God's Word is sure and reliable, and possessing it must be considered a great advantage. If ever there seems to be a conflict between what God's Word says and what human logic suggests, then the wise person—that is, the believer—will side with God and say with the apostle, "Let God be true, and every man a liar." Such reliance on God's Word and submission to its message also mirrors a psalmist's approach, as shown in Psalm 51. Paul quotes only a small portion of the psalm, assuming that the readers will know the context. The 51st psalm is one where King David, the murderer and adulterer, has to acknowledge that he is in the wrong and that God is right. In contrite humility he acknowledges his guilt and says:

I know my transgressions,
    and my sin is always before me.
Against you, you only, have I sinned
    and done what is evil in your sight,

[continuing with the words Paul quotes in his rebuttal to the Jewish objection]

so that you are proved right when you speak
    and justified when you judge. (Psalm 51:3,4)

Second Jewish objection

⚡️ ⁵**But if our unrighteousness brings out God's righteousness more clearly, what shall we say? That God is unjust in bringing his wrath on us? (I am using a human argument.) ⁶Certainly not! If that were so, how could God judge the world? ⁷Someone might argue, "If my falsehood enhances God's truthfulness and so increases his glory, why am I still condemned as a sinner?" ⁸Why not say—as we are being slanderously reported as saying and as some claim that we say—"Let us do evil that good may result"? Their condemnation is deserved.**

If, as the psalmist says, God is always "proved right" when he speaks and "justified" when he judges, doesn't it follow that each conviction of a sinner serves to demonstrate God's justice? The sinner's being proved wrong shows the rightness of God, thus resulting in glory and honor to God. Isn't that doing God a favor? And if so, why should the sinner be punished for glorifying God?

Both verse 5 and 7 reflect the "human argument" that underlies this grossly false, even blasphemous, line of reasoning. The logic of verse 5 suggests that if God always prevails over evil, then our unrighteousness brings out God's righteousness all the more clearly. It's like a jeweler displaying a fine pearl. To make its milky whiteness stand out all the more, the pearl is displayed on a foil of black velvet to highlight the contrast. Likewise, the argument goes, our sins serve as a foil for God's holiness. He looks better in comparison to us.

Verse 7 expresses a parallel idea, but in addition it raises the question of whether guilt is still involved. "Someone might argue, 'If my falsehood enhances God's truthfulness and so increases his glory, why am I still condemned as a sinner?'" Isn't the sinner really doing God a service when he creates a situation wherein God can gain glory by showing his justice? And doesn't that take away the guilt from him who has brought glory to God?

Paul's answer is, If that were so, how could God judge the world? Note the basic assumption on Paul's part that God is going to judge the world. That's a given for both Jew and Gentile. If God can't punish the evildoer, as he must do in judging the world, then any kind of evil is permissible. Then one might as well say, "Let us do evil that good may result."

There apparently were people who not only said that but who also attributed this blasphemous teaching to Paul. Perhaps this erroneous idea stemmed from a misunderstanding (deliberate or innocent) of Paul's teaching that salvation is a gift of God's grace without the requirement of any personally earned merit or worthiness. This apparently was interpreted as allowing the sinner to do whatever he pleased. Regarding those who misunderstood grace and distorted the teaching of Christian liberty into sinful license, and then as a crowning insult laid that false teaching at Paul's doorstep, the apostle simply says, "Their condemnation is deserved." God is indeed going to judge the world. Then such people will get what is rightly coming to them.

Third Jewish objection

⁹**What shall we conclude then? Are we any better? Not at all! We have already made the charge that Jews and Gentiles alike are all under sin.**

Paul has leveled a stinging rebuke against those in the Jewish camp who would distort his teaching about God's grace and turn Christian liberty into sinful license. This response from Paul draws a third objection from his Jewish antagonists. They ask, "What shall we conclude then? Are we any better?"

Translators are divided on the handling of the second of those two questions. The NIV translators opted for the rendering "Are we any *better?*" In the footnote they suggest the alternative "Are we any *worse?*" Those sound like contradictory and conflicting statements, don't they? How can two such different understandings be legitimate contenders for what Paul intended to say? For an explanation you will have to bear with a few grammatical technicalities.

Our English verbs have two voices: the *active* voice, where the subject does the action of the verb (the boy hit a home run), and the *passive* voice, where the subject receives the action of the verb (a home run was hit by the boy). The Greek language had a voice that fits between these two. It has come to be called—not very imaginatively—the *middle* voice. It conveys the sense of the subject doing the action of the verb for the subject's own benefit or interest (the boy hit himself a home run).

A further complication is that the verb forms for the middle and passive voices sometimes look alike, so context has to decide which one of the voices the author intended. That's the situation here. The Greek verb in question could be either middle (do we have ourselves an advantage?) or passive (are we being taken advantage of?). The translation "Are we any better?" would be taking the verb as middle. "Are we any worse?" would reflect the passive sense.

The NIV translators decided in favor of the former. Other translators have chosen the second alternative. A moment's reflection will show that the answer to either of the questions would be the same: a resounding negative. Are Jews any better than other people? Not at all! Are Jews any worse than other people? Not at all!

Why is that? Paul's answer is, "We have already made the charge that Jews and Gentiles alike are all under sin." Both groups are lacking the righteousness that God looks for. The whole previous section, from 1:18 on, has been a devastating description of the spiritual bankruptcy of both the Jews and the Gentiles.

Both groups are "under sin." That means they are dominated by sin. It's not just a chance or accidental thing that occasionally happens to them. Sin permeates them; it brands them. It's the dominant force in natural human life, for both Jews and Gentiles. Paul substantiates this double indictment with Scripture, which asserts that *total* domination by sin marks the life of *every* man, woman, and child.

Summary: the unrighteousness of all people

Support from Scripture

[10]**As it is written:**

> **"There is no one righteous, not even one;**
> [11]   **there is no one who understands,**
>   **no one who seeks God.**
> [12]**All have turned away,**
>   **they have together become worthless;**
>   **there is no one who does good,**
>   **not even one."**
> [13]**"Their throats are open graves;**
>   **their tongues practice deceit."**
>   **"The poison of vipers is on their lips."**
> [14]   **"Their mouths are full of cursing and bitterness."**
> [15]**"Their feet are swift to shed blood;**
> [16]   **ruin and misery mark their ways,**
> [17]**and the way of peace they do not know."**
> [18]   **"There is no fear of God before their eyes."**

A casual reading of these verses could leave the impression that this section is a single block of quotation taken from a single book of the Bible. A closer look will show, however, that this is not the case. It is, rather, an artfully woven-together collection of numerous Old Testament passages. They have all been neatly assembled to make one point, namely, that there is a universal lack of righteousness that besets the whole human family. The reader is invited to check out the sources of the individual quotations Paul has put together with this collage, but that need not detain us just now.*

Paul's point will be served if we simply keep in mind his basic emphasis: Absolutely no one has any righteousness at all before God. Some subpoints that could be noted under that major heading would be a threefold division into sins of *thought* (10-12a), *word* (13,14), and *deed* (12b-17). Verse 18 identifies the root cause for all of the above, namely, "no fear of God."

Paul's collection of quotations starts out with the assertion that the heart of the human problem lies in an abysmal lack of understanding and a woeful lack of appreciation for who God is and what he has done for sinners. Quoting the psalmist, he says:

> "There is no one who understands,
>   no one who seeks God.
> All have turned away, . . .
>   there is no one who does good,
>   not even one."

A lack of understanding, or a profound misunderstanding, reflects itself in what people say, and the tongue betrays the evil that lurks in the sinner's mind and heart:

> "Their throats are open graves;
>   their tongues practice deceit."

---

* Compare verses 10 to 12 with Psalm 14:1-3; 53:1-3; and Ecclesiastes 7:20. Compare verse 13a with Psalm 5:9; verse 13b with Psalm 140:3; verse 14 with Psalm 10:7; verses 15 to 17 with Isaiah 59:7,8 and Proverbs 1:16; verse 18 with Psalm 36:1.

"The poison of vipers is on their lips."
"Their mouths are full of cursing and bitterness."

Wrong thoughts and deceitful words lead to wicked and often violent actions:

"Their feet are swift to shed blood;
ruin and misery mark their ways,
and the way of peace they do not know."

All these deplorable situations are traceable to a common root cause:

"There is no fear of God before their eyes."

[19]Now we know that whatever the law says, it says to those who are under the law, so that every mouth may be silenced and the whole world held accountable to God. [20]Therefore no one will be declared righteous in his sight by observing the law; rather, through the law we become conscious of sin.

A word Paul uses very frequently in Romans is the Greek word *nomos*. Basically it translates as "law," but it allows for considerable variation in how it is used and what it means. An important consideration often is, Does it have a definite article, "*the* law," or is it without the definite article, "*a* law," in the sense of a general legal requirement? This difference in construction, coupled with its placement into different contexts, results in some significant variation in meaning from one instance to the next.

As noted, the term "*a* law," without a definite article, can refer to any system or pattern of laws. With the definite article, "*the* law" very often refers to the Mosaic Law given to God's chosen people on Mount Sinai. "*The* law" may, however, also refer to the five books of Moses—the Pentateuch, Genesis to Deuteronomy. And "*the* Law" is also used to refer to other books of the Old Testament as well. This latter

53

use is less common than the others, but there are some clear examples of it.*

The significance of this becomes apparent when we realize that there are three different meanings for the four instances in verses 19 and 20 where Paul uses the term *nomos.* Let's treat the first two uses separately before attempting to follow the logic of Paul's summarizing statement.

Paul states, "Now we know that whatever the law says, it says to those who are under the law." In the first use of *nomos* (which has the definite article in Greek), Paul uses "the law" to refer to the cluster of passages previously quoted (3:10-18). These passages, drawn largely from the psalms, thus give *nomos* a meaning equivalent to the Old Testament. These Old Testament passages, given specifically to God's chosen people, were addressed primarily to those "under *the* law," that is, under the covenantal arrangement regulated by the Mosaic Law. We might therefore paraphrase this verse, with its two *nomos* meanings, by saying, "Now we know that what the Old Testament says, it says specifically and directly to Jews under the Mosaic regulations."

The apostle now proceeds to his logical conclusion by what we might call an argument "from the greater to the lesser." If God's recorded Word convicts even the greater, his own chosen people, of not having any righteousness, then what hope is there for the lesser, the Gentiles, whom Paul has on another occasion described as "without hope and without God in the world" (Ephesians 2:12)? It's similar to the logic Peter uses when he writes, "It is time for judgment to begin with the family of God; and if it begins with us, what will the outcome be for those who do not obey the gospel of God?" (1 Peter 4:17).

---

* In John 10:34 "the Law" that is quoted is not from the Pentateuch but from Psalm 82:6; in John 15:25 it's Psalm 69:4; in 1 Corinthians 14:21 it's Isaiah 28:11,12.

Paul reasons, If even God's chosen people, with all their advantages, have no inherent or earned righteousness, then certainly no one else can have any either. Then every mouth must remain silent. Then the whole world, Jew and Gentile, is accountable before God.

Paul moves on to a very important point regarding the law when he continues, "Therefore no one will be declared righteous in his [God's] sight by observing the law." With the word *therefore,* Paul is drawing a conclusion. It is a conclusion, however, that hinges on a proper understanding of the term *nomos,* which will be used twice in this verse. Both times it is without the definite article. As such, it has the general meaning of "a law" or "any law." The NIV, with its translation "by observing *the* law," would be improved by removing the English article *the.* Paul is saying that no one will be declared righteous in God's sight by doing law-works of any kind. It makes no difference which legal pattern people may choose to be under, whether it be Gentiles following the natural knowledge written in their hearts or Jews observing the Mosaic code. In their sinful perversity, the Gentiles "suppress the truth" as they know it (1:18); the Jews, while paying lip service to the revealed law, hypocritically live contrary to it, so that God's name is blasphemed among the Gentiles (2:17-24). The result is the same in both cases: through obedience to the law (which they both fall short of), neither group has any righteousness to offer at God's bar of justice.

In fact, Paul goes even further when he declares that providing righteousness for people is not the law's real function. It serves quite another purpose. He writes, "Through the law we become conscious of sin." A set of legal regulations (again *nomos* is without the definite article here, therefore "any law") has the twofold effect of perversely bringing out disobedience in rebellious sinners and also of serving as a standard by which to measure such sinful disobedience. As such, its most notable function is to lead to an awareness of sin.

In subsequent chapters Paul will be saying much more about this dual function of the law, but for the moment his emphasis is this: Jews and Gentiles alike are all under sin. No one has any righteousness of his own. Consequently, humanity's case is desperate. We are helpless and hopeless. If there is to be any hope for us, it can't come from ourselves. It has to come from outside of us. Thank God such "outside help" is available, as Paul will explain shortly!

PART FOUR

Righteousness Credited: Justification
(3:21–5:21)

Sinners cannot provide the righteousness a holy God justly requires. Acquiring such righteousness is possible only by the grace of a loving God, who gives righteousness freely as a gift through faith in Jesus Christ. This exchange whereby God takes away the guilt of our sins and credits us with the righteousness of Christ is called *justification.*

Righteousness by faith in Christ

²¹But now a righteousness from God, apart from law, has been made known, to which the Law and the Prophets testify. ²²This righteousness from God comes through faith in Jesus Christ to all who believe.

The problem Paul has described so fully (1:18–3:20) is that there can be no righteousness from trying to observe the law. Nobody can earn any credit with God by imperfectly following a set of rules, whatever those rules may be. Sinners can do nothing that would please God and thus serve as a basis for God to reward them. Sinners don't have the righteousness that avails before God.

But now, marvel of marvels, a righteousness has been made known. It's exactly what sinners need but can't produce on their own. It's a righteousness *(a)* from God and *(b)* apart from law.

Let's look at the second item first. It's a righteousness "apart from law." We've already commented on the significant difference in meaning that occurs when the word for "law" *(nomos)* appears with or without a definite article. Here it is without. The NIV translators have accurately reflected that. This righteousness comes "apart from law." It has no connection to obeying any law. It follows then that there is nothing sinners can do to add anything to this righteousness.

But even more important, there is nothing a person *has* to do. God has done it all! A righteousness "from God" has been made known. It bears repeating that this is all God's doing. Hence this righteousness can stand by itself; it has a separate existence without any input from humanity. That's why it must be "made known" to us.*

And how has this righteousness been made known? It is a truth to which "the Law and the Prophets testify." Here *nomos* has the definite article and refers to a specific "law," namely, that body of revealed information which was set forth in the Pentateuch, the five books of Moses. Thus the Law, together with the Prophets, forms Paul's term for the Old Testament.** The righteousness that comes from God is made known and testified to by the Scriptures.

So far, the apostle has established that there is a righteousness of precisely the type that sinners need, but how do they get it? Paul answers, "This righteousness from God comes through faith in Jesus Christ to all who believe."

It is a righteousness that God gives "through faith in Jesus Christ." Faith, in the sense of trust and confidence in God's promise, is the avenue, the channel, through which righteousness comes to the believer. Or, to use a slightly different picture, faith is the hand that receives this righteousness from God.

---

* For a parallel idea expressed with a different verb, see 1:17, where Paul speaks of this righteousness as being "revealed."

** See Luke 16:29 for a similar designation. In the parable of the rich man and Lazarus, Abraham states that the rich man's brothers should listen to "Moses and the Prophets," that is, the Old Testament Scripture.

Righteousness comes in only *one* way, and it comes in the *same* way to all: by faith, by believing. When Paul says "to all who believe," he is not limiting the scope of God's righteousness, as though it is intended only for some and not for others. Paul here is addressing the *how* of God's saving plan (by faith), not the *for whom*. This latter point, regarding the scope of God's gracious plan, is addressed next.

There is no difference, ²³for all have sinned and fall short of the glory of God, ²⁴and are justified freely by his grace through the redemption that came by Christ Jesus.

Paul stated earlier (2:11) that God shows no favoritism in dealing with sinners. Those who are disobedient (which is everyone, Jew and Gentile alike) are under his wrath. But that same impartiality also shows itself when God deals with people in grace and mercy. In that aspect of God's dealing "there is no difference" as well, Paul tells us.

How can he say that? On what does he base his statement? By inspiration the apostle supplies the rationale for his bold assertion: "for all have sinned and fall short of the glory of God, and are justified freely by his grace." All have sinned, and consequently all "fall short of the glory of God." One explanation offered for the second half of that line is that by its fall into sin, the human race lost the glory God gave it at creation, which he fully intended for people to have. That is a plausible explanation that does no violence to the verb paired with it, namely, that all sinned.

But the Greek word here translated as "glory" has another meaning in some contexts. It can also be translated as "praise," in the sense of approval. A clear example of this occurs in John 5:43,44, where Jesus takes his unbelieving compatriots to task with the rebuke, "I have come in my Father's name, and you do not accept me; but if someone else comes in his own name, you will accept him. How can you believe if you accept praise [or approval] from one another, yet make no effort to obtain the praise [approval] that comes from the only God?"*

According to the latter interpretation, Paul would be saying, "All have sinned and lack God's approval." Lacking God's approval is surely a serious indictment, and yet Paul can go on to say an absolutely amazing thing. He continues, "All have sinned . . . and are justified." The grammar of the original Greek here makes it perfectly clear that the ones justified are the same "all" who sinned. That's why Paul can say that with God "there is no difference." All sinned; all are justified.**

How can that be? The answer: because God justifies (declares people just) "freely by his grace." These two terms are virtually synonymous. *Freely* means "free of charge, without price or cost." *By his grace* means "as a gift." Because no person has any merit to bring, justification has to come as a gift. Being declared just is something that is done to or for the sinner. It's not something he does for himself. Therefore, receiving justification as a gift is the *only* way justification works—and that's also the way it *always* works.

When Paul says that all are justified, we need to be careful, however, not to misunderstand him, as though he were saying that all will be saved. That would be the false teaching of universalism. Natural man, wicked and perverse sinner that

---

* Other examples of this word having the meaning of approval can be found in John 12:42,43 and 1 Thessalonians 2:6.

** Other passages asserting the worldwide scope of God's justifying love are Ezekiel 33:11; 1 Timothy 2:3,4; and especially John 1:29 and 2 Corinthians 5:19. Taking away "the sin of the world" and "not counting men's sins against them" are the equivalent of declaring all people to be righteous, or justifying all people. The counterpart to this teaching, namely, the need for repentance and faith on the part of the individual to receive God's blessing, is also well documented, both in Paul's letters (Romans 3:28; Galatians 2:15,16; Ephesians 2:8) and in the rest of Scripture (Genesis 15:6; Habakkuk 2:4; Mark 1:15).

he is, retains the awesome power to resist God's grace. In their stubborn unbelief, many people unfortunately refuse to accept Christ's merit, and they will be lost forever for their unbelief. Our Savior's sobering verdict, "Whoever does not believe will be condemned" (Mark 16:16), is still true. In the case of those who are lost, unbelief has rejected the right-eousness from God that truly was there for them.

Paul's teaching of *general justification,* or *objective justification* as it is sometimes called, has far-reaching implications. It is really the heart of the gospel. Think of what it implies for you personally. If all sinners are justified, then surely you are too—despite all the sins and shortcomings that Satan argues should disqualify you. Because "there is no difference," God assures you that his grace is for all, including you. Righteous-ness from God is there—to be accepted by faith.

General justification has great significance also for our outreach and evangelism efforts. If all have been justified, then there is no one to whom you cannot go with the gospel's good news. You can tell anyone and everyone, "Your sins have all been forgiven by Christ's substitutionary death. He has earned a robe of righteousness for you. It's there for you. Accept it; believe it." (See Acts 16:29-31).

Paul has stressed the absolute necessity of faith if sinners are to receive righteousness from God. But to be true faith, in the sense of trust and confidence, it has to have some-thing to hang on to. It has to have a proper object of trust. Paul now addresses this point.

25God presented him [Christ Jesus] as a sacrifice of atonement, through faith in his blood.

God's motive for justifying sinners is mercy; his method is redemption. The term *redemption* is intended to bring to mind for his readers the idea of a slave, or a prisoner of war, or perhaps even a kidnapped person—anyone who needs to be ransomed, to be "bought back." The purchase price is greater than anything the captive can raise on his own. Somebody on the outside has to step in and help if there is to be a rescue. And that is exactly what God did! He provided "the redemption that came by Christ Jesus" (3:24).

God is a holy God who can't just wink at sins and dismiss the sinner's many infractions as if they didn't matter. God, in his Word, is clear and direct on that matter: "The wages of sin is death" (Romans 6:23). The sinner's life was forfeit. Sin had to be paid for with a life. Again Scripture is clear: "Without the shedding of blood there is no forgiveness" (Hebrews 9:22). Sin carried a heavy price that had to be paid—and it was! God sent his very own Son to be the substitute to die in our place. Christ became true man so that he might shed his blood as a sacrifice and die the sinner's death, or as Paul puts it, "God presented him as a sacrifice of atonement."

The apostle's terminology here reflects the activity God had directed Israel to observe annually on the great Day of Atonement. God commanded this festival as a graphic reminder of Israel's need to confess its sins and then symbolically transfer those sins to a scapegoat that was driven out into the wilderness, bearing away the sins of the people (Leviticus 16:1-34, particularly 20-22).

God's intent was to remind Israel of its need for a Savior and to strengthen in them a longing for the promised Messiah, the Redeemer, who would do for them literally what was being enacted symbolically.

In writing to the Romans, Paul is, of course, speaking from the New Testament perspective in which Christ already has come and offered himself as the sacrifice, thereby putting us at one with God. Hence Paul can say that all have been justified by God's grace "through faith in his [Christ's] blood."

God's justice demonstrated

God's *motive* for justifying sinners is grace; his *method* is redemption. His *objective,* or goal, for doing so is now described by Paul. It's a twofold objective on God's part: to demonstrate that he is just, and to demonstrate that he is a God who justifies those who have faith in Jesus.

He did this [presenting Christ as a sacrifice of atonement] to demonstrate his justice, because in his forbearance he had left the sins committed beforehand unpunished—²⁶he did it to demonstrate his justice at the present time, so as to be just and the one who justifies those who have faith in Jesus.

God is just. His integrity requires a negative reaction to sin and disobedience. However, in his great patience and "forbearance," he moves slowly in dealing with sinners. Often he moves so slowly, in fact, that sinners may get the idea that sin isn't so serious; that God doesn't really care all that much; and that, in the final analysis, he may not do anything about it at all. Past experience with God's seeming inactivity could be misunderstood. Sins "committed beforehand" could appear to be left unpunished, because there has not been any open and obvious day of judgment.

Paul, however, leads us to understand that such a casual view of sin is dead wrong. If you doubt this, Paul says, then look at what God did to Christ because of sin. He required the lifeblood of his Son to pay the price for human sin. Sin is serious! It needs to be repented.

Paul preached the same message in Athens to people whom he called to repentance because of their worship of idols and false gods. He warns them, "In the past God overlooked such ignorance, but now he commands all people everywhere to repent. For he has set a day when he will judge the world with justice by the man he has appointed. He has given proof of this to all men by raising him from the dead" (Acts 17:30,31; for a similar statement, see Acts 14:15,16).

The same warning also fits us, who are all too prone to underestimate the seriousness of our sin and guilt. We would do well to heed the reminder from Thomas Kelly's Lenten hymn:

> If you think of sin but lightly
> Nor suppose the evil great,
> Here you see its nature rightly,
> Here its guilt may estimate.
> Mark the sacrifice appointed;
> See who bears the awful load—
> 'Tis the Word, the Lord's Anointed,
> Son of Man and Son of God.
> (*Christian Worship: A Lutheran Hymnal* [CW] 127:3)

Look at what God did to Christ, the sinner's substitute, and know that God is a just God who punishes sin.

But God had another objective in mind when he made Christ a "sacrifice of atonement" (3:25). It was not only to "demonstrate his justice" but also to demonstrate that he is "the one who justifies those who have faith in Jesus."

Later in this epistle, Paul will write, "Consider therefore the kindness and sternness of God" (11:22). Both of those qualities are clearly evident here. God's sternness toward sin is shown by the severe treatment meted out on the Son for the sins that were laid on his innocent shoulders. But the payment for sin that Christ's death achieved satisfied God's justice. That was proven by the Father raising his Son from the grave on Easter morning.

In Christ, justice has been served. Now, without compromising his integrity as a just and holy God, the Father can show kindness to redeemed sinners, whose guilt has been pardoned and whose debt has been paid. In Christ, God can see the sinner as just and holy.

In this way Christ's sacrifice of atonement does double duty. It demonstrates that God is just, but it also demonstrates that God is the God "who justifies those who have faith in Jesus."

The principle of faith established

²⁷Where, then, is boasting? It is excluded. On what principle? On that of observing the law? No, but on that of faith. ²⁸For we maintain that a man is justified by faith apart from observing the law.

In Christ, God has demonstrated that he is a God who justifies those who have faith. Objectively, God has declared the whole world righteous (Romans 5:18,19; 2 Corinthians 5:19). The benefit of this general justification, however, comes to the individual by faith, by believing and trusting in Christ, by accepting the merit Christ has earned. This personal, individual justification is often called *subjective justification,* to distinguish it from the former *general justification.*

Speaking of this justification of the individual believer, Paul now reasons as follows: If, by definition, faith is trust and confidence in what someone else has done, then it can't be of any credit to the person who trusts and believes. There is no ground for boasting about benefits received.

That is Paul's point here. If the sinner had kept God's law and thereby had earned something, then he'd have grounds for boasting. But that's not the case. Justification doesn't come on the principle of obeying the law but on accepting righteousness from God by faith as a free gift. Paul repeats and emphasizes that principle when he says, "We maintain that a man is justified by faith apart from observing the law."

This, incidentally, is the verse where Luther in his German Bible inserted the word *alone*. While that word is not in the Greek text, the context overwhelmingly supports the sense that justification is by faith *alone,* apart from law-works of any kind.*

²⁹Is God the God of Jews only? Is he not the God of Gentiles too? Yes, of Gentiles too, ³⁰since there is only one God, who will justify the circumcised by faith and the uncircumcised through that same faith.

Recall that earlier Paul had spent considerable time on the subject of the Jews having an advantage by virtue of their covenant relationship with God regulated by the Mosaic Law. The Jewish advantage had been ruled out when Paul declared that God shows no favoritism (2:11). Here the apostle returns briefly to that subject. He agrees that if having and doing the law were the essence of a right relationship with God, then the Jews would have an advantage. But a right relationship with God does not rest on obedience to the law, but on having faith. Since such a right relationship comes by faith, it's there for all believers, Jew and Gentile alike. Hence God is the God of Gentiles as well as Jews, because he will "justify the circumcised [Jews] *by faith* and the uncircumcised [Gentiles] *through that same faith.*"

³¹Do we, then, nullify the law by this faith? Not at all! Rather, we uphold the law.

Paul has left no doubt that the law is not the basis upon which sinners are reconciled to God. That's accomplished

---

* Luther's defense for the addition of *alone* can be found in the American Edition of *Luther's Works,* Volume 35, pages 185-189,195-202. For scriptural support of the concept of faith alone, see Ephesians 2:8,9.

by faith alone. But does this mean that by extolling faith Paul is thereby nullifying, or rejecting, the law as though it were bad or useless? Paul responds, "Not at all! Rather, we uphold the law." In subsequent chapters, particularly 6 and 7, Paul will have much more to say about the proper function of the law. But for the moment he continues his emphasis on the priority of faith. He points us first to the case of Abraham.

The principle of faith illustrated: Abraham

We have noted that the recipients of Paul's letter to the Romans were a mixed group of Jews and Gentiles. When Paul now speaks of Abraham as "our forefather," he is including himself among the Jewish readers. In doing so he is picking up on a point critical to the discussion on righteousness, namely, Abraham's salvation. Note first of all that Abraham's salvation and life in heaven was a given. This was the assumption in popular opinion, and it is also substantiated by Scripture (for example, John 8:56 and Luke 16:22). He is in heaven. The question simply is, How did he get there?

The question is important because many Jews looked to Abraham as the classic example of a man who pleased God with works. After all, he left his homeland and followed God's leadership to the Promised Land. He obeyed God and would have sacrificed his son Isaac if God had not stopped him. This "friend of God," as he came to be called (2 Chronicles 20:7), looked to them like a prime candidate for salvation on the basis of works and personal performance.

4 What then shall we say that Abraham, our forefather, discovered in this matter? ²If, in fact, Abraham was justified by works, he had something to boast about—but not before God. ³What does the Scripture say? "Abraham believed God, and it was credited to him as righteousness."

⁴Now when a man works, his wages are not credited to him as a gift, but as an obligation. ⁵However, to the man who does not work but trusts God who justifies the wicked, his faith is credited as righteousness.

Paul has just finished saying that in the matter of having righteousness that avails before God, everyone has to receive it by grace, as a gift. Therefore, boasting in one's own accomplishments is excluded (3:27). But what about Abraham?

Paul begins with the following: "If, in fact, Abraham was justified by works, he had something to boast about." Paul states the case in a hypothetical manner: "If, in fact, Abraham was justified by works, ..." Paul is not conceding that Abraham was justified by works. That may have been the popular opinion; it may look that way to people's view of Abraham's life and conduct, but that's not the important thing. What is the verdict where it really counts—in the eyes of God?

Paul says that *before God,* Abraham has nothing to boast about. How can he know that? Because God in his Word has said so. The Scriptures say, "Abraham believed God, and it [his faith] was credited to him as righteousness." Note that Paul considers the Old Testament to be God's inspired Word. He quotes Genesis 15:6 and treats it as though God himself were speaking. In his book of Genesis, God says that he "credited" Abraham's faith as righteousness.

The apostle draws an example from the workplace to illustrate what God means when he says that he "credits" righteousness to someone. If a person agrees to work for an employer at a stipulated rate of pay, then the wages at the end of the day are something the worker has earned. "Now when a man works, his wages are not credited to him as a gift, but as an obligation." It would be an insult if the employer were to say after the worker had finished the agreed-upon job, "Here, let me give you a gift." The money is not a gift; it's an

obligation owed to the person who did the work. However, if
a person doesn't work and still gets something at the end of
the day, that's a gift being credited to that person.

Paul now transfers this workplace scenario to the spiritual realm: "However, to the man who does not work [for
salvation] but trusts God who justifies the wicked, his faith is
credited as righteousness." If a person hasn't done anything
to earn righteousness for himself, and God gives it to him as
a gift, that's crediting righteousness to someone—and that's
the way God dealt with Abraham. That's the term God uses
in his inspired record: Abraham believed, and it was "credited" to him as righteousness. Conclusion: Abraham received
salvation as a gift by faith, not as a reward by works.

The principle of faith illustrated: David

For the Jewish nation, who were the descendants of
Abraham, Abraham was Exhibit A in demonstrating how
God deals with his people. If Abraham was Exhibit A,
then King David would be Exhibit B. His reign was in
many ways the glory era of Israel's history. King David's
testimony regarding God's dealing with his people, therefore, would also be very important. Paul calls on him
next to provide insight into the matter of how righteousness comes to sinful people.

To believing Abraham, God "credited" righteousness as a
gift. Works were not a factor in his case. Paul now adds the
testimony of King David:

⁶**David says the same thing when he speaks of the blessedness
of the man to whom God credits righteousness apart from works:**

⁷ **"Blessed are they
   whose transgressions are forgiven,
   whose sins are covered.**

⁸ Blessed is the man
whose sin the Lord will never count against him."

The quotation is from Psalm 32. A repentant King David
is speaking as he recalls his own sorry past. Initially stubborn and unrepentant, David tried to minimize and ignore
his sin, but that didn't work. He now admits:

> When I kept silent,
>   my bones wasted away
>   through my groaning all day long.
> For day and night
>   your hand was heavy upon me;
> my strength was sapped
>   as in the heat of summer. (verses 3,4)

Brought to his knees, David resorted to the only thing
that works: looking in faith to the God who justifies the
ungodly. David had no good works to bring, only ungodli-
ness to confess. And he does just that:

> Then I acknowledged my sin to you
>   and did not cover up my iniquity.
> I said, "I will confess
>   my transgressions to the LORD"—
> and you forgave
>   the guilt of my sin. (verse 5)

God forgave the guilt of David's sin. This free forgiveness through faith without the addition of any works or
merit is precisely the same pattern that Abraham had experienced. And it forms the basis for David's cry of joy and
relief, which Paul quotes almost word for word:

> Blessed is he
>   whose transgressions are forgiven,
>   whose sins are covered.

> Blessed is the man
>   whose sin the LORD does not count
>   against him. (verses 1,2)

Righteousness without circumcision

Abraham and David were both richly blessed when God credited their faith as righteousness. This pattern of salvation by grace through faith worked in their cases. Both of them, however, were Jewish. The question might therefore arise as to whether this righteousness is something that works only for the Jewish nation, or whether it is applicable also to others. Recall the mixed readership of this epistle, sent to both Jews and Gentiles at Rome. Hence particularly for the benefit of his non-Jewish readers, Paul asks this question:

⁹Is this blessedness only for the circumcised, or also for the uncircumcised? We have been saying that Abraham's faith was credited to him as righteousness. ¹⁰Under what circumstances was it credited? Was it after he was circumcised, or before? It was not after, but before! ¹¹And he received the sign of circumcision, a seal of the righteousness that he had by faith while he was still uncircumcised. So then, he is the father of all who believe but have not been circumcised, in order that righteousness might be credited to them. ¹²And he is also the father of the circumcised who not only are circumcised but who also walk in the footsteps of the faith that our father Abraham had before he was circumcised.

Again Abraham's example becomes a very important test case as to how God deals with people in the matter of crediting righteousness. The question is, "Under what circumstances was it [righteousness] credited?" Or, to make the question a bit more specific, "Was it after he was circumcised, or before?" And Paul immediately gives the answer: "It was not after, but before!"

A glance at the sequence of events as they are recorded in Genesis will verify the correctness of Paul's answer. In the 12th chapter of Genesis, we are told of God's call to Abraham at age 75, promising him a special land where he would grow to become a great nation in whom all the world would be blessed. From time to time, God repeated this promise to Abraham. One such reassurance to Abraham is recorded for us in Genesis chapter 15. It is this particular repetition of the promise that the Scriptures allude to when they testify, "Abram believed the LORD, and he credited it to him as righteousness" (verse 6).

As you know, God took his time, humanly speaking, to fulfill for Sarah and Abraham the promise of a son, who also was so essential for Abraham's becoming a great nation. When Abraham was 99 years old, God again repeated his promise to Abraham in an incident recorded in Genesis chapter 17. At this time God confirmed his covenant with the patriarch by instituting the rite of circumcision. It was a rite God commanded Abraham to observe himself and to administer to all the male members of his household. It should be noted, however, that observing circumcision did not bring righteousness to Abraham. We have God's testimony that he had credited righteousness to the patriarch already, more than two decades earlier. Circumcision was simply the sign and seal of the righteousness that Abraham already had by faith previous to the rite, "while he was still uncircumcised," as Paul puts it.

Abraham received God's righteousness without having to undergo circumcision. It follows then that circumcision can't be considered a requirement for salvation or an action that earns any kind of merit or favor with God. Since that is the case, Paul can now take the next logical step. If circumcision isn't essential—only faith is—then believing Gentiles, in their state of uncircumcision, are at no disadvantage before a God who credits faith as righteousness. Paul spells out the implications of this with his observation, "So then, he [Abraham] is the father of all who believe but have not been circumcised [Gentiles], in order that righteousness might be credited to them." God shows no favoritism. Believing Gentiles are acceptable, even in their state of uncircumcision.

Consistent with that impartiality, God also accepts Jews who observe circumcision, providing that their observance of the rite is not viewed as something necessary for salvation or done to earn merit with God. They are true children of Abraham if they hold to the faith of their father. Of him, Paul says, "He is also the father of the circumcised who not only are circumcised but who also walk in the footsteps of the faith that our father Abraham had before he was circumcised."

Righteousness without the law

Paul has clearly indicated that God credited righteousness to Abraham before the rite of circumcision became a requirement for the patriarch. Therefore, circumcision wasn't something that Abraham did to gain favor with God. But did he perhaps do something else? Did he fulfill any obligation or keep any law? This too the apostle rules out.

[13]It was not through law that Abraham and his offspring received the promise that he would be heir of the world, but through the righteousness that comes by faith. [14]For if those who live by law are heirs, faith has no value and the promise is worthless, [15]because law brings wrath. And where there is no law there is no transgression.

Becoming "heir of the world" is simply Paul's way of saying that God would make Abraham into a great nation through whom all the world would be blessed. The benefit of using the term *heir* becomes evident when we see how Paul

73

uses that everyday concept to illustrate the spiritual truth he is explaining. The point he's making is that an heir doesn't have to do anything for the stipulation of the will to go into effect. The promise of the one making the will is the determinative factor, not the action of the heir. It would be a travesty of justice for the courts to say to an heir, "Your uncle died and had stated in his will that you're to have this piece of property, but you're going to have to work for it before we let you have it." In such a case, the will would really be of no value for putting into effect the wishes of the maker of the will who promised the property to his nephew.

So it also was with the understanding between God and Abraham. God repeatedly promised to make a great nation from Abraham. If Abraham would have had to work for his "inheritance," then his faith would have been of no value, and God's promise would have been worthless.

Many Jews, of course, felt that having and keeping God's law were essential for them to be God's people. Paul points out that the law doesn't and can't do that, because it brings wrath rather than blessing. In fact, where there is law, the sinner's guilt can actually be said to become worse because he is consciously and intentionally overstepping a clearly drawn line. He is transgressing a known command.

In the previous section (verses 11,12), Paul drew the conclusion that Abraham is the "father of all who believe," circumcised and uncircumcised alike. With his use of "therefore" to lead into the next section, he is drawing a similar conclusion. In the sight of God, Abraham is the father of all believers—regardless of their relationship to the Mosaic Law, or to any other law, for that matter.

¹⁶Therefore, the promise comes by faith, so that it may be by grace and may be guaranteed to all Abraham's offspring—not

only to those who are of the law [Jews] but also to those who are of the faith of Abraham [Gentiles]. He is the father of us all. ¹⁷As it is written: "I have made you a father of many nations." He is our father in the sight of God, in whom he believed—the God who gives life to the dead and calls things that are not as though they were.

Verses 16 and 17 are parallel to verses 11 and 12, in that both speak of Abraham as the father of all believers, both Jews and Gentiles. There is, however, an advance in thought in this latter section. The advance is that God is described as worthy of the trust that faith places in him. He can be trusted for every good blessing because he is a God who can even bring life from death. He clearly showed that ability in his dealing with Abraham and Sarah.

¹⁸Against all hope, Abraham in hope believed and so became the father of many nations, just as it had been said to him, "So shall your offspring be." ¹⁹Without weakening in his faith, he faced the fact that his body was as good as dead—since he was about a hundred years old—and that Sarah's womb was also dead. ²⁰Yet he did not waver through unbelief regarding the promise of God, but was strengthened in his faith and gave glory to God, ²¹being fully persuaded that God had power to do what he had promised. ²²This is why "it was credited to him as righteousness."

Before turning to the content of these verses, a word needs to be said about the translation of the opening verse. The NIV translators have rendered the verse, "Abraham in hope believed *and so became* the father of many nations." That could sound as though the desired outcome was achieved because Abraham hoped hard enough or earnestly enough. Such an understanding could make Abraham's belief and hope look like a good work, something he did to accomplish the goal. Any such notion would obviously be in conflict with the whole line of thought Paul has been developing. A better translation of the sentence would be, "Abraham in hope believed *that he would become* the father of many nations, just as it had been said to him." That translation is not only grammatically defensible but is also in line with Paul's emphasis.

God had repeatedly promised Abraham and Sarah that they would have a son through whom they would become a great nation. Time moved on, however, as Abraham and Sarah waited for the realization of God's promise. In fact, God waited so long that the fulfillment of the promise came to seem not only unlikely but physically impossible. What Abraham in faith hoped for was really "against all hope."

At almost one hundred years old (actually 99 years old, Genesis 17:1), Abraham had to face the fact that as far as procreation was concerned, "his body was as good as dead." Sarah was ten years younger than Abraham (Genesis 17:17), but regarding her situation too, both of them were aware "that Sarah's womb was also dead," as Paul puts it. Humanly speaking, the fulfillment of the promise of having many descendants had become impossible. And yet, Abraham "did not waver through unbelief regarding the promise of God, but was strengthened in his faith and gave glory to God, being fully persuaded that God had power to do what he had promised."

We have previously described saving faith as trust and confidence in God's promises. Note how that definition is supported here. Abraham's faith was essentially his "being fully persuaded that God had power to do what he had promised." Humanly speaking, the chance of Abraham having many descendants seemed impossible, but the more impossible it became from a human point of view, the more Abraham relied on God's promise and his power to do what he had promised.

Abraham reasoned that, if necessary, God could even bring life from the dead—which is, of course, what God in his good time did. Isaac was truly a miracle baby, born from "dead" parents. Abraham's faith, with its disregard for human weakness and its unflinching confidence in God's power, "gave glory to God" and as such "was credited to him as righteousness."

Paul has called Abraham the father of all believers (4:16), whether they are Jews or Gentiles. That includes everyone. But the apostle now personalizes it for his readers when he spells out the full implications of such a sweeping statement.

²³The words "it was credited to him" were written not for him alone, ²⁴but also for us, to whom God will credit righteousness—for us who believe in him who raised Jesus our Lord from the dead. ²⁵He was delivered over to death for our sins and was raised to life for our justification.

Abraham received righteousness by faith, but that blessing was not restricted just to the patriarch. This method of receiving righteousness—and with it eternal salvation—works for every believer in Christ, including the Roman readers "to whom God will credit righteousness."

Paul does not mean to say that the Romans were not righteous at the time they were reading his letter or that they were still awaiting the blessing of righteousness through Christ. The use of the future tense here is simply Paul's logical extension of the promise made to the patriarch carried on to all believers subsequent to the time of Abraham. Every believer of all time is included and will be credited with righteousness.

The reason they can all have righteousness credited to them is because their faith rests on the proper object of faith, namely, the one "who raised Jesus our Lord from the dead." Note again how God's power to raise the dead comes into sharp focus.

Christ "was delivered over to death for our sins." Because we had sinned, we deserved to die. Instead of requiring our death, however, God sent his Son to earth to live the perfect life we could not live and die the death we should have died. By his life he earned righteousness for us, and by his death he paid for our sins. In Christ, God now views us as righteous; in him we have been justified.

The sinner's justification is an accomplished fact, punctuated by Christ's cry on the cross, "It is finished" (John 19:30). And to show that he had accepted his Son's sacrificial death for the justification of all sinners, God raised his Son from death on Easter morning. In doing so, God made a statement to all the world. Paul summarizes this law/gospel statement into a neat, two-line couplet:

> He was delivered over to death for our sins
> and was raised to life for our justification.

We might paraphrase that in this way:

> Christ had to die because we had sinned,
> but he could be raised to life
> because we had been justified by his death.

To the Romans, to us, and to people of all times, our Savior-God bids us look to his finished work and extends the invitation, "Accept what I have done for you; trust in it as your hope of righteousness before God."

The effects of justification

5 **Therefore, since we have been justified through faith, we have peace with God through our Lord Jesus Christ, ²through whom we have gained access by faith into this grace in which we now stand. And we rejoice in the hope of the glory of God. ³Not only so, but we also rejoice in our sufferings, because we know that suffering produces perseverance;**

⁴perseverance, character; and character, hope. ⁵And hope does not disappoint us, because God has poured out his love into our hearts by the Holy Spirit, whom he has given us.

With his introductory word *therefore*, Paul is again inviting us to see an important connection. This time it is the connection between the righteousness received from God (justification) and the effect this righteousness has in the believer's life.

A number of times Paul has spoken of justification as being for *all* people. That teaching is often referred to as *general justification.* The universal aspect of justification, however, is just one side of the picture. The necessary counterpart to this teaching of general justification is a proper understanding also of *subjective justification,* that is, the need for faith in the heart of an individual to receive the blessings that objectively are there for him and for all people by virtue of God's doing. The unbeliever who rejects Christ's righteousness loses the benefit of what is truly there also for him.

It is the former group, namely, believers who are subjectively justified by faith, of whom Paul speaks here. There are great and grand things coming to them in their new life in Christ. The first blessing Paul mentions is *peace.* "Since we have been justified through faith, we have peace with God through our Lord Jesus Christ."

This peace is not just a feel-good kind of emotion in the heart of the believer. This peace has an objective reality. It has an existence entirely separate from the believer because it is a peace that comes from God. He created and provided it, for it is a peace that comes "through our Lord Jesus Christ."

The sinner can do nothing to create that peace. Look a few verses ahead to see how Paul describes us in our natural state. We were "powerless" and "ungodly" (verse 6), "sinners" (verse 8), and "God's enemies" (verse 10). Positive input from us was nil, and our situation was hopeless, but God reconciled us "through the death of his Son" (verse 10). Hence there is now peace because of God's having brought about a reconciliation. Note again that this peace has an objective existence. It is there for the sinner to accept by faith.

In addition to the great gift of peace with God, there is another blessing springing from the sinner's justification, and that is "access" to God. The believer is free to come to God's throne of grace with any and every petition. Paul points out that all of this is possible by our connection with Christ, "through whom we have gained access by faith into this grace in which we now stand."

Instead of hostility or fear and anxiety, there is now a tranquil peace in the life of the believer, marked by continual, unhampered access to God. But that's just the beginning. There's more: a glorious hope for the future. Paul continues, "And we rejoice in the hope of the glory of God." What we have now is just a tiny foretaste of the unspeakably greater joy of sharing in the glories of heaven and of God himself.

This glorious prospect makes bearable the inevitable crosses and difficulties that come into every Christian's life. These crosses, however, not only become bearable, but in the midst of them, the Christian can still rejoice. We can do so because we know that under the loving care of a good and gracious God, even suffering leads to blessings and positive results in the Christian life. Hence Paul can make the bold claim that we rejoice not only in the hope of future glory "but we also rejoice in our sufferings, because we know that suffering produces perseverance; perseverance, character; and character, hope. And hope does not disappoint us, because God has poured out his love into our hearts by the Holy Spirit, whom he has given us."

A number of passages in Scripture set up a sequence, or chain, of virtues.* The order in which the virtues are listed is not always the same, seemingly because each author has a particular point of emphasis he wishes to bring out. Here Paul wants to end with *hope,* which is really a synonym for *faith* in the sense of trust and confidence.

According to Paul's sequence, *suffering* produces "perseverance," the quality of bearing up under adversity. Such *perseverance* produces "character," as seen in the reliability and dependability of the veteran who has withstood and survived some challenging situations. Hence *character* leads to "hope," which is nothing other than trust and confidence.

Hope and confidence, if misplaced, can leave us in the lurch. But that is not the case with the hope Paul speaks of, for it is well placed. Christian hope "does not disappoint us, because God has poured out his love into our hearts by the Holy Spirit, whom he has given us."

This hope is reliable because the one in whom it trusts is trustworthy and reliable. The object of trust is God, and he "has poured out his love into our hearts." The form of the verb used here for "has poured out" makes the point that God has previously done this and the effect of it still continues at the present time. God sent his Holy Spirit into our hearts to bring us to a knowledge of God's love for us. The Spirit has worked in us a faith that reflects a confidence in God's continuing love for us.

But how can this hope be so sure of God's love? Paul urges the reader, Take a look at what God's love was willing to do—even under the most adverse circumstances.

⁶You see, at just the right time, when we were still powerless, Christ died for the ungodly. ⁷Very rarely will anyone die for a righteous man, though for a good man someone might possibly

* Galatians 5:22,23; James 1:2-4; 2 Peter 1:5-7

81

dare to die. ⁸But God demonstrates his own love for us in this: While we were still sinners, Christ died for us.

In the English language, there are widely varying levels of attachment expressed by the solitary verb *love.* We love God; we love our spouses; we love family and friends; we love animals; we love the outdoors; we love chocolate cake.

The Greek language had a number of verbs to differentiate, to some extent at least, between varying levels of affection and attachment. It is important to realize that the word used here for God's love is *agape,* the term indicating a one-way, unreciprocated love coming entirely from God. There were no endearing qualities in rebellious humanity that moved or influenced God. It wasn't like in human friendship where both parties bring endearing qualities to the relationship so that a mutual affection develops. No, in the situation Paul is describing, all the good things originate on God's side of the relationship.

Note first of all the timing. The apostle says, "You see, at just the right time, when we were still powerless, Christ died for the ungodly." In writing to the Galatians, he said, "When the time had fully come, God sent his Son, born of a woman" (4:4). Christ came according to God's timetable, not in response to any human choosing or planning.

Note, furthermore, that Christ came when we were "powerless." Even if we had wanted him to come, which was not the case, we couldn't have done anything positive to bring it about. But the infinitely worse situation was that by nature we didn't want anything to do with God and his promised Savior, because we were "ungodly." And yet, for such ungodly people as us, the Father sent his Son to die. That's one-way love, the kind one can hardly find even the faintest approximation of in the human experience. Note the negative adverbs "very rarely" and "might possibly" when the apostle writes, "Very rarely will anyone die for a righteous man, though for a good man someone might possibly dare to die." This verse has been interpreted in several ways. In the NIV the perceived difference lies between a *righteous* man and a *good* man.

The point is that even if a person has all kinds of legal and logical reasons to expect help and support from others, only very rarely will someone step in to die for him. For a *good* man—that is, one whose position of power or prestige strongly argues that he should be spared for the public good—somebody "might possibly dare" to die. The message in either statement, however, is clear: Don't expect it!

Other interpreters have chosen the linguistic possibility of substituting the meaning "cause" for *man,* particularly in the second instance. The point then being that very rarely will anybody die for a righteousness *person,* but for a good *cause* "someone might possibly dare to die." Examples such as that of a soldier throwing himself on a live grenade to spare the members of his squadron are usually envisioned. Again, that might possibly happen, but don't count on it!

Whichever interpretation one takes, the point is the same, namely, that human love generally doesn't extend to the point of a person's dying for his neighbor. What doesn't happen among people, however, God did. "But God demonstrates his own love for us in this: While we were still sinners, Christ died for us."

Do you want to know if God loves you? Look at what he has been willing to do for you. When you were not just weak and "powerless" but an "ungodly" sinner actively opposed to him, Christ died for you—as he did for everyone. That is God's one-way love in action. It is the love that allows Paul to say that God is a God who "justifies the wicked" (4:5).

Justification is a present reality, bringing the priceless blessings of peace, joy, and hope even now amid sufferings, but it bodes well also for the future.

⁹Since we have now been justified by his blood, how much more shall we be saved from God's wrath through him! ¹⁰For if, when we were God's enemies, we were reconciled to him through the death of his Son, how much more, having been reconciled, shall we be saved through his life! ¹¹Not only is this so, but we also rejoice in God through our Lord Jesus Christ, through whom we have now received reconciliation.

From Paul's use of the future tense ("how much more *shall* we *be saved*"), it is plain that the apostle is taking the long view. God's love, poured out in our hearts, gives us a sure hope for the day of God's eternal and final judgment. Paul supports that confidence with an argument from the greater to the lesser. The logic is, If God did something that's difficult, then surely he'll also do something that's easy. Notice the two negative aspects in the first part of verse 10, the difficult things to work around. We were God's *enemies,* and God's Son hung *dead* on the cross. But God's loving power successfully addressed both of those negatives: We have since become *reconciled* to God, and Christ has been raised to *life.* Paul reasons, "For if, when we were God's enemies, we were reconciled to him through the death of his Son, how much more, having been reconciled, shall we be saved through his life!" As reconciled friends of God with a living Savior, we have every reason to be confident about judgment day.

Paul, however, is a very practical person, much concerned about the real problems besetting his readers in their day-to-day lives. Hence he returns once more to the concerns of the present. He points out that Christian hope is not some pie-in-the-sky future prospect, as some suppose; it brings reconciliation and life even now. He assures them, "Not only is this [hope for the future] so, but we also rejoice in God through our Lord Jesus Christ, through whom we have now [for the present time] received reconciliation."

Summary: Man's unrighteousness brought death; God's righteousness brings life

To follow Paul's line of thought here, it's useful to take a look at the structure of verses 12 to 21. The dominant feature of this whole section is a major comparison Paul sets up using the comparison words "just as . . . so." The complicating feature is that the comparison, begun with "just as" in verse 12, gets interrupted. Note the NIV translators' dash at the end of verse 12. The comparison will be picked up again and completed at verse 18. There we see that what Paul had in mind already in verse 12 was a statement like this: Just as Adam's disobedience brought sin and death to all mankind, so Christ's obedience brings righteousness and life for all mankind.

Fitted between verses 12 and 18 are two asides, or digressions. The first one, verses 13 and 14, speaks of a similarity, or parallel, between what Adam and Christ did. The second digression, verses 15 to 17, points out the great contrast between what the two did, with Christ's gracious gift far overshadowing and offsetting the damage father Adam did to the human race.

¹²Therefore, just as sin entered the world through one man, and death through sin, and in this way death came to all men, because all sinned—¹³for before the law was given, sin was in the world. But sin is not taken into account when there is no law. ¹⁴Nevertheless, death reigned from the time of Adam to the time of Moses, even over those who did not sin by breaking a command, as did Adam, who was a pattern of the one to come.

Paul asserts that through one man (Adam) sin entered into the world. Death, which is the wages of sin, necessarily followed, because "all sinned." At this point, however, Paul is sidetracked by an objection he anticipates. Someone is going to say, Did everybody really sin like Adam? What about those people who lived "from the time of Adam to the time of Moses"? At that time there was not yet a Mosaic Law given from Mount Sinai. Wasn't there a difference between Adam, who had a specific command from God, and those who came after? Could one say of them that "all sinned"? Paul answers in the affirmative: "Before the law was given, sin was in the world."

He then follows with, "But sin is not taken into account when there is no law." To be sure, the record-keeping is different when there are no specific laws to measure people's disobedience. Recall Paul's similar evaluation at 4:15: "Where there is no law there is no transgression." But quite apart from the individual infractions of specific rules, there was something else at work after the fall. That something is what has come to be called inherited sin, or original sin. With his sin Adam gave sinfulness to all people, so that all people are born in a sinful condition. King David finds it necessary to confess, "Surely I was sinful at birth, sinful from the time my mother conceived me" (Psalm 51:5).*

True, before the Mosaic Law was given, the record of individual sins may have looked different, but even so, all people were sinners. We can be sure of that, Paul argues, because all died—the penalty for sin. "Nevertheless, death reigned from the time of Adam to the time of Moses, even over those who did not sin by breaking a command, as did Adam, who was a pattern of the one to come."

* See also Genesis 8:21; Psalm 48:3; John 3:6.

What Adam did had an effect on all people. In this respect Adam is a pattern, or type, of "the one to come," that is, the promised Messiah, the Christ. Paul is very close to resuming his original comparison: "Just as what Adam did had an effect on all people, . . ." But before he returns to completing his statement with the similarity between Adam and Christ, Paul first asserts that there are also some major differences between the two.

¹⁵But the gift is not like the trespass. For if the many died by the trespass of the one man, how much more did God's grace and the gift that came by the grace of the one man, Jesus Christ, overflow to the many! ¹⁶Again, the gift of God is not like the result of the one man's sin: The judgment followed one sin and brought condemnation, but the gift followed many trespasses and brought justification. ¹⁷For if, by the trespass of the one man, death reigned through that one man, how much more will those who receive God's abundant provision of grace and of the gift of righteousness reign in life through the one man, Jesus Christ.

The "gift" Christ brought is not like the "trespass" Adam committed. Christ's gift is far greater and better than anything Adam could ever do to us. Paul brings that out in the next three sentences. Basically the three sentences all say the same thing; repetition reinforces Paul's point. But there are a few distinguishing features in the sentences that we should note. He says, "If the many died by the trespass of the one man, how much more did God's grace and the gift that came by the grace of the one man, Jesus Christ, overflow to the many!" In the original Greek, it is very apparent that in this section, Paul is piling up a variety of terms for *gift* and *grace* to emphasize God's generosity. Note also in these sentences the use of the comparative "more" to show the superiority of Christ's gifts.

This is also a good place to start sensitizing ourselves to Paul's use of the terms *many* and *all*. *Many* simply says that the group is large; it may or may not include *all*. The context has to determine the scope of inclusion in the *many*. When Paul uses the term *all,* he is informing us that the total number of a certain group is being included. The total group, however, need not be large. For example, we might say, "All the 90-year-olds in our congregation are housebound." The group in its totality may very likely be small.

Of the two terms, the more difficult one to understand is Paul's use of *many* (a large group). The important thing to keep in mind is that using *many* does not rule out the possibility that these "many" may actually be one hundred percent of those under discussion. We have an example of that here, when Paul says, "If the many died by the trespass of the one man, . . ." With the rare exception of an Enoch or an Elijah, the mortality rate for humans is one hundred percent. Hence with his statement that "the many died," Paul obviously means that *all* (the total number of) people died.

The significance of this becomes apparent immediately. Paul states that the many who died (that is, all people) are the same "many" to whom God's grace and gift in Christ overflows. In the next sentence, Paul identifies this universal gift for all. It is nothing other than justification.

The apostle continues, "Again, the gift of God is not like the result of the one man's sin: The judgment followed one sin and brought condemnation, but the gift followed many trespasses and brought justification." Adam and Christ bear a similarity to each other in that both did something that has an effect on the whole human race. What Christ did, however, is much greater and far superior. The legacy Adam left followed from one sin committed in the Garden of Eden. What Christ did reverses the effect of thousands of sins. Israel piled up sin upon sin in their disobedience of the Mosaic Law. Add to that the transgressions of the Gentiles sinning against the natural knowledge of God written in their hearts, and one sees tons of transgressions in the history of the world. Adam's *one* sin brought *condemnation* on all, but Christ's gift, following *many trespasses,* brought *justification* for the same group.

Paul adds a third sentence: "For if, by the trespass of the one man, death reigned through that one man, how much more will those who receive God's abundant provision of grace and of the gift of righteousness reign in life through the one man, Jesus Christ."

The comparison—or rather, the contrast—between Adam and Christ moves to its highest level with the discussion of the core issue: the matter of whether life or death will "reign" in people's lives. The wages of sin is death, and by the sin of one man, death "became king," as Paul says literally. But that state is reversible. Death can be dislodged from its throne by the gift of God. What Adam did is serious because it put death in charge. But by God's grace in Christ, all is not lost. Paul exclaims, "How much more will those who receive God's abundant provision of grace and of the gift of righteousness reign in life through the one man, Jesus Christ."

In verse 15 Paul spoke of the universal justification earned for all by Christ's death. It is important to note Paul's change in scope here. He does not say that all will reign in life. That would be the unscriptural teaching of universalism. Paul clearly states that reigning in life comes "through the one man, Jesus Christ." It is believers in him "who receive God's abundant provision of grace and of the gift of righteousness." Salvation is there for all, but only the believers in Christ actually receive it. Christ's earnest warning remains true: "Whoever does not believe will be condemned" (Mark 16:16).

With this discussion of the reign of life or death for the sinner, Paul is now back to the subject matter that introduced this whole section in the first place. Thus at this point he logically completes the comparison that was interrupted after verse 12.

¹⁸Consequently, just as the result of one trespass was condemnation for all men, so also the result of one act of righteousness was justification that brings life for all men. ¹⁹For just as through the disobedience of the one man the many were made sinners, so also through the obedience of the one man the many will be made righteous.

In these two sentences, we see why Paul has put so much emphasis on the transferred effect of Adam's sin. What Adam did had its effect on all the world. Paul has pointed out that even without a Mosaic Law for people to break and thus incur personal and individual guilt by willful sinning, all died because all had been infected with inherited sin. Adam's guilt was passed on to them. We could say that Adam's guilt was imputed, or charged, to them.

The point is important for Paul's comparison here. Just as one trespass on Adam's part brought condemnation to all people, so there is also a blessed counterpart to that. By a similar transfer process, the righteous conduct of one man, Christ, came to be credited to that same world of sinners who had been infected by the one man, Adam. Because of what Christ has done for the world of sinners, God now looks at them as being holy and sinless.

The world of sinners has done nothing to bring about a change. They have not changed themselves so as to actually become holy. It is rather that in Christ, God looks at them as if they were holy. He declares them to be just; he justifies them. Thus, they have a new and changed status before God.

When Paul says that this is a justification "that brings life for all men," we need to take that at face value. What Christ did for sinners truly brings life, but it is a blessing that needs to be accepted by faith. Life and salvation are there for all, but unbelief rejects what is there and thus loses the benefits a gracious God has provided.

Paul continues, "For just as through the disobedience of the one man the many were made sinners, so also through the obedience of the one man the many will be made righteous." This sentence is virtually a repetition of the previous one, with only a few variations. "Many" replaces the "all" of the previous verse, but as already stated, *many* simply means that the group under discussion is large. This is not in conflict with the information of the previous verse but simply states that this large group in fact includes all the world.

Referring to this whole group, Paul says, "the many will be made righteous." Here also, "to make righteous" does not mean that they actually become holy and without sin. Rather, in Christ their sins have been paid for so that God can now look at them as if they were without sin. Being viewed by God as being righteous reflects their new and changed status before him.

Note that verse 18 introduced this section with the adverb *consequently*. When Paul now says that the many "will be made righteous," he is not referring to a future time but rather to the *logical consequence* of Christ's work. That consequence, or connection, is, in fact, the point illustrated and taught by the comparison Paul sets forth. Just as what Adam did had its effect on all people, so it logically follows that a similar effect, or consequence, may be expected from what Christ did. That consequence is that sinners "will be made righteous" in God's sight.

Notable throughout this whole section is the frequent use of terms such as "more" (verses 15,17), "overflow" (verse 15), "abundant provision" (verse 17), and the like. All are terms highlighting the grace and generosity of our Savior-God. It is no surprise, then, that Paul one more time sets up a "just as . . . so" comparison to show that the blessings Christ accomplished by his obedience are greater and more abundant than the damage done by man's disobedience. In this last comparison, Paul moves ahead and includes not just the sin of one man, Adam, but the guilt of everyone who has ever gone contrary to God's holy will as expressed in his law. Adding these "actual" sins to the damning "inherited" sins increases the quantity of guilt to a frightening load. But even this poses no insurmountable problem for a gracious God. As man's sin increased, God's grace in Christ simply increased all the more. The apostle describes this amazing phenomenon with these words:

20The law was added so that the trespass might increase. But where sin increased, grace increased all the more, 21so that, just as sin reigned in death, so also grace might reign through righteousness to bring eternal life through Jesus Christ our Lord.

So great is the love of our Savior-God! So rich his grace to fallen sinners deserving of death! Where sin previously reigned in death, there grace now reigns to bring eternal life through Jesus Christ our Lord. As believers in Christ and beneficiaries of his grace, we might do well at this point to break out in a doxology of praise, as Paul later does:

> Oh, the depth of the riches of the wisdom
> and knowledge of God!
> How unsearchable his judgments,
> and his paths beyond tracing out!
> "Who has known the mind of the Lord?

Or who has been his counselor?"
"Who has ever given to God,
that God should repay him?"
For from him and through him and to him
are all things.
To him be the glory forever! Amen.
(Romans 11:33-36)

PART FIVE

Righteousness in Christian Living: Sanctification
(6:1–8:39)

With chapter 6 of this letter, Paul takes up a new topic. However, before we turn to a discussion of that, it might be useful to retrace our steps to see where Paul's epistle has taken us so far. Actually, we can review Paul's two major points rather easily on the basis of the comparison between Adam and Christ just completed (5:12-21).

What Adam did brought sin and death to the whole world. None of his descendants in their natural state has any righteousness to offer God. Recall how that conclusion was forced on us in Paul's first major section (1:18–3:20). Gentiles and Jews alike have sinned and are therefore lacking God's approval. It makes no difference whether the lack of righteousness was incurred through the coarse immorality of the Gentiles (1:18-32), the self-righteousness of the moralists (2:1-16), or the double standard of the Jews, who boasted in having God's law but didn't keep it (2:17-29). All show the effects of Adam's sin. All are without righteousness; all lack God's approval.

But just as what Adam did had the effect of losing righteousness for the human family, so what Christ did had the effect of regaining righteousness for a sinful world (3:21–5:11). Christ came to earth to live the perfect life sinners couldn't; Christ died the death sinners should have died for their sins. Through the work of this substitute, there is now a righteousness from God, a robe of righteousness to be accepted by sinners through faith.

All believers in Christ receive this "alien righteousness" as Luther called it. It is a righteousness from the outside, credited to the believer without any inner change or moral improvement in the recipient. God declares the believer to be righteous. Hence all of this comes to the believer by grace, purely as a gift from God.

It bears repeating that all of these things come without any change or improvement in the believer. However, subsequent to becoming a child of God by faith and receiving the gift of free and full salvation, there is a marked change and a major transformation that takes place in the life of the believer. It is the change of now leading a life that conforms, more and more, to the will of God. The believer's new life of faith, often called *sanctification,* becomes the focus of Paul's attention in the next three chapters.

It will be immediately evident from Paul's exposition that the driving force behind the believer's ongoing attempts to conform to God's will is that which brought the Christian's new life in the first place. That powerful force is the death and resurrection of Christ. His death and resurrection free the Christian from an old life of disobedience and empower the Christian to now live a new life obedient to God's will. Paul will be treating this newfound freedom in three distinct but somewhat overlapping stages:

> freedom from the clutches of sin (chapter 6);
> freedom from the domination of the law
> (chapter 7);
> freedom from the fear of death (chapter 8).

Freedom from the clutches of sin

6 **What shall we say, then? Shall we go on sinning so that grace may increase? ²By no means! We died to sin; how can we live in it any longer? ³Or don't you know that all of us who were baptized into Christ Jesus were baptized into his death?**

⁴We were therefore buried with him through baptism into death in order that, just as Christ was raised from the dead through the glory of the Father, we too may live a new life.

Paul has made the startling assertion that where sin increased, God's grace in Christ increased all the more (5:20). The apostle anticipates a perverse logic that might reason, If that's the case, then why not go on sinning so that grace will increase even more? Paul heads that thought off in no uncertain terms with his curt response, "We died to sin; how can we live in it any longer?"

But how did we die to sin? Paul answers this question with another question—the answer to which is self-evident. "Don't you know that all of us who were baptized into Christ Jesus were baptized into his death?" he asks. Note the major assumption on Paul's part that Baptism is a means of grace. Baptism is effective in doing something. It accomplishes something. What Baptism does is put the baptized person in touch with Christ, or, to be more specific, it makes the baptized person a partner in Christ's death and burial. "We were therefore buried with him through baptism into death." This close connection with Christ through Baptism is a theme that will be repeated throughout this section. In fact, the prepositional phrase "with him" occurs five times in verses 4 to 8.

A second major assumption on Paul's part is that being connected "with him [Christ]" makes a difference. Through Baptism we were buried *with him* into death "in order that, just as Christ was raised from the dead through the glory of the Father, we too may live a new life." Recall that Christ's death and resurrection were the basis of the righteousness that the Father credited to us to make us children of God, fit for his kingdom.

But Christ's death and resurrection do more. They are also the power enabling the child of God to lead a new life. In this new life of faith, the believer is enabled to do what is pleasing to God. As such, it is a life of faithful obedience to God's will, not rebellion against his commandments by continuing in sin.

⁵If we have been united with him like this in his death, we will certainly also be united with him in his resurrection. ⁶For we know that our old self was crucified with him so that the body of sin might be done away with, that we should no longer be slaves to sin—⁷because anyone who has died has been freed from sin.

When Paul says "*If* we have been united with him . . ." he is using a conditional sentence, but the context makes it clear that the content of this sentence is not hypothetical or "iffy" at all. Hence the sentence could be translated, "*Since* we have been united with him . . ."

The general emphasis of this section is similar to the previous one, that is, our being united *with Christ* in death. But there is also an advance in thought. Paul becomes more explicit as to *what* in us died and *how* it died. In dying with Christ through Baptism, it was "our old self" that was "crucified."

Crucifixion was a grim form of execution reserved for the worst criminals. That kind of death was appropriate for the criminals all of us had become by virtue of following the lead of our first parents, Adam and Eve. Our old self—our "old Adam," as it is often designated—is the evil nature we were born with, which is always inclined only toward evil. It is the sinful human condition God deplored when he made the promise after the flood, "Never again will I curse the ground because of man, even though *every inclination of his heart is evil from childhood*" (Genesis 8:21). Here in his letter to the Romans, Paul refers to this sinful nature as the "body of sin" that needed to "be done away with, that we should no longer be slaves to sin."

Verse 7 adds Paul's rationale for the preceding statement. The translators of the NIV have used a dash to set the verse off as a parenthetical remark. Their translation, "because anyone who has died has been freed from sin" makes it a general statement, true of any deceased person. Death ends any human response to outward stimuli. As such, it is certainly true that a dead person no longer sins.

But an alternate interpretation is possible here. The Greek language had an indefinite pronoun for anyone. That word, however, is not used here. The original simply says, "*the one who died* has been freed from sin." That need not be a generalization referring to anyone who has died; it could refer to a specific person, that is, Christ.

Christ's death is the focus of attention throughout this section and is the enabling cause of the new life in the Christian. Christ's death, appropriated by the believer through Baptism, is critical to the change that needs to take place if there is to be any new life in the child of God.

Furthermore, Christ's being freed from sin by death is not a new or strange concept for Paul. Paul said virtually the same thing in 4:25, that Christ had to die because we had sinned, but he could be raised to life again because by his death he had completely paid for our sins and we were now justified. He is finished with sin, once and for all. If in verse 7 we take Christ to be the one whose death brought release from sin (*our* sin), note how neatly that leads into Paul's next thought:

⁸Now if we died with Christ, we believe that we will also live with him. ⁹For we know that since Christ was raised from the dead, he cannot die again; death no longer has mastery over

him. ¹⁰The death he died, he died to sin once for all; but the life he lives, he lives to God.

If somebody has fallen into a deep sleep and is totally oblivious to what's going on, we might say, "He's dead to the world." To be dead to something means that it makes no impression on us; it has no control or influence over us. That's the situation between Christ and sin.

Christ died for sin. Sin is now paid for, and the sinner has been justified. With the defeat of sin, the wages of sin, which is death, has also been taken care of (1 Corinthians 15:55-57). Death no longer has any hold on Christ. Now and forever he lives a glorious, holy, blissful existence "to God." It is this kind of life Paul has in mind for the Christian when he says, "Now if we died with Christ, we believe that we will also live with him."

Again Paul says, "*If* we died with Christ . . ." Everything said regarding the conditional sentence in verse 5 applies here also. There is no doubt in Paul's mind that through Baptism we are united with Christ in death. Since ("if") that is true, we also partake in his resurrection and therefore are joined to him in a new life. This is the third time Paul refers to our connection with Christ in his death (verses 5,6,8). This time the stress is not only on Christ's death but also especially on his life and on the prospect of our participating in the holy life that Christ now lives to God.

Paul leads into his discussion of a life lived to God with the phrase "in the same way." Christ's life is to find a counterpart in the Christian's new life of faith and gratitude to God.

¹¹In the same way, count yourselves dead to sin but alive to God in Christ Jesus. ¹²Therefore do not let sin reign in your mortal body so that you obey its evil desires. ¹³Do not offer the parts of your body to sin, as instruments of wickedness, but

rather offer yourselves to God, as those who have been brought from death to life; and offer the parts of your body to him as instruments of righteousness. ¹⁴For sin shall not be your master, because you are not under law, but under grace.

After calling attention to Christ's resurrection from death and his subsequent life lived to God, Paul now applies that truth to the believer. The *in order* sequence of events is important here. Christ has gone before. He died; he was raised to a new life that he now lives to God. The Christian, by Baptism, has been joined to Christ in his death and has also been raised with him to life. Note the passive verbs: the Christian *has been joined* to Christ; the Christian *has been raised* with Christ. New life has been given. Everything needed to make a new life for the Christian has been done.

What Paul is leading up to is the Christian's grateful response for everything that has been done for him. What Christ has done *for* the Christian and what he continues to do *in* the Christian now enables the Christian to respond with a life of cheerful obedience to God.

Where this new God-given life exists in the Christian, directives for activity on the part of the "new man" become possible—and are appropriate. Hence Paul now uses imperatives to give guidance and direction to the Christian's new man. Although he uses a number of imperatives, basically they fall into three pairs. *urgent commands*

First Paul addresses the Christian's new outlook, or perception of himself. He says, "Count yourselves dead to sin but alive to God in Christ Jesus." By virtue of his connection to Christ, who died to sin once for all, so also the Christian is now to count himself "dead to sin." And with Christ, who rose from death, so too the Christian now counts himself to be "alive to God."

Such an outlook and frame of mind leads to a life of activity on the Christian's part. A second pair of imperatives encourages negative activity: "Therefore do not let sin reign in your mortal body so that you obey its evil desires. Do not offer the parts of your body to sin, as instruments of wickedness." Resisting sin is a constant activity on the Christian's part. Contrary to what some teach, sin and the temptation to sin remain with the Christian all his life. Paul laments that state of affairs in his own life (Romans 7:18,19), and we dare not feel that we will be exempt either (1 Peter 5:8).

Refusing to "let sin reign" in our lives and not offering our bodies to sin as instruments of wickedness is, however, only part of the Christian life. The third pair of Paul's imperatives is directed toward encouraging the positive activity of putting ourselves into the service of God. Instead of succumbing to evil, Paul urges, "rather offer yourselves to God, as those who have been brought from death to life; and offer the parts of your body to him as instruments of righteousness."

When Paul speaks of offering "the parts of your body," he seems to be using the analogy of an Old Testament child of God bringing an animal sacrifice to God's altar. What Paul is referring to, of course, is the use we make of our hands, feet, eyes, ears, and the like. In chapters 12 to 14, Paul will be bringing some practical examples of how Christians can offer themselves to God in daily lives of love and service.

We have stressed that the sequence of events is important for a proper understanding of Paul's encouragement to live the Christian life. Unconverted people are not able to count themselves dead to sin nor able to do good things pleasing to God. This can happen only *after* Christ's redemptive work has been accepted by faith, thus creating the new life to which Paul is here making his appeal. Simply giving somebody a command, that is, applying the law, will never produce the God-pleasing results that our Lord looks for and that Paul is urging. The apostle himself indicates this when he points to the proper motivation: "Sin shall not be your master, because you are not under law, but under grace." Good works can't be produced by commands or demands. Only appreciation for what God in his grace has done for us is able to provide proper motivation. When such appreciation exists, it will invariably show itself in the good works that spring up and grow in our lives. Such works are truly pleasing to God.

¹⁵What then? Shall we sin because we are not under law but under grace? By no means! ¹⁶Don't you know that when you offer yourselves to someone to obey him as slaves, you are slaves to the one whom you obey—whether you are slaves to sin, which leads to death, or to obedience, which leads to righteousness? ¹⁷But thanks be to God that, though you used to be slaves to sin, you wholeheartedly obeyed the form of teaching to which you were entrusted. ¹⁸You have been set free from sin and have become slaves to righteousness.

The apostle has made the striking statement that sin is not to be the master of his Roman readers. And the reason he gave is that they are not under law but under grace. Admittedly, that approach defies conventional wisdom. Usually people think that rules and regulations are a necessity to keep people in line; otherwise there will be total chaos and anarchy.

In dealing with unregenerate worldlings, that is undoubtedly true. But Paul is speaking to Christians, to those who have come to know their Savior and have received new spiritual life through faith in him. Their new life and activity will be motivated by appreciation for what God's grace has done for them, not by fear of punishment for broken laws.

Paul anticipates, however, that his explanation will not satisfy everybody. He expects an objection from the same kind of thinking that was expressed earlier. Recall Paul's statement that where sin increased, God's grace increased even more (5:20). That drew the question, Then why not continue in sin?

Similar logic is at work here. Some will reason, If we're not under law, if there are no restrictions, then why not continue in sin? Again Paul retorts, "By no means!" Doing so would be sheer folly; that would make you slaves to sin.

It will be helpful to recall Christ's basic teaching on the subject of attachment to a master. Recall first of all that Christ says everyone has a master; neutrality is impossible. "He who is not with me is against me, and he who does not gather with me scatters" (Matthew 12:30). Note also that nobody can serve two masters: "Either he will hate the one and love the other, or he will be devoted to the one and despise the other" (Matthew 6:24).

Paul is operating here with that same principle of attachment to a master. "Don't you know that when you offer yourselves to someone to obey him as slaves, you are slaves to the one whom you obey—whether you are slaves to sin, which leads to death, or to obedience, which leads to righteousness?"

No one is without a master, and no one can serve two masters. But one can change masters. Paul says, "But thanks be to God that, though you used to be slaves to sin, you wholeheartedly obeyed the form of teaching to which you were entrusted. You have been set free from sin and have become slaves to righteousness."

By nature the Romans, like everyone else, were born with the taint of Adam's sin on them. And they added to that guilt by willingly and eagerly committing countless other sins. They were slaves of sin. But what changed that? It was their wholehearted obedience (faith) to the teaching that had been brought to them by faithful gospel preachers. In other words, the change in masters was brought about by nothing other than the message of Christ's substitutionary death for sinners and triumphant resurrection. Trusting Christ put them under a different master—or as Paul says, "You have been set free from sin and have become slaves to righteousness."

¹⁹I put this in human terms because you are weak in your natural selves. Just as you used to offer the parts of your body in slavery to impurity and to ever-increasing wickedness, so now offer them in slavery to righteousness leading to holiness. ²⁰When you were slaves to sin, you were free from the control of righteousness. ²¹What benefit did you reap at that time from the things you are now ashamed of? Those things result in death! ²²But now that you have been set free from sin and have become slaves to God, the benefit you reap leads to holiness, and the result is eternal life. ²³For the wages of sin is death, but the gift of God is eternal life in Christ Jesus our Lord.

Verse 19 is very close to the thought already expressed in verse 13. Paul has returned once more to his third group of imperatives, urging Christians to offer themselves in service to the Lord. It is not an easily understood concept or a particularly inviting prospect that Paul is presenting to them. Hence he strives to explain it to them in the clearest and most engaging way possible. He resorts to an illustration. He says, "I put this in human terms because you are weak in your natural selves."

"Put[ting] this in human terms" means that he's using an illustration from everyday life. He's drawing on a common, well-known aspect of the ancient Greco-Roman world, namely, slavery. It's a useful illustration, as we will see shortly. The institution of slavery, however, had features about it that made it decidedly unpalatable to people, with their natural desire for freedom. We all like to be in charge of our own affairs—to be our own boss. Slavery was just the opposite of that. Being a slave meant losing one's own will and doing someone else's bidding.

In the final analysis, however, that is exactly what Paul (or rather, God) asks of the Christian. The child of God is to become a slave—a slave of righteousness. "Just as you used to offer the parts of your body in slavery to impurity and to ever-increasing wickedness, so now offer them in slavery to righteousness leading to holiness."

Again Paul is making a forceful argument by employing a comparison using a "just as . . . so" line of logic. As eagerly and zealously as the Romans used to surrender their bodies to impurity before their conversion to Christianity, so eagerly are they now to pursue righteousness. It's an arresting thought Paul expresses here—also for us. As zealously as the world pursues evil and self-serving goals, such as power, wealth, fame, or pleasure, so eagerly are we now to be devoted to doing God's will. That's a challenging order, and one not to our old Adam's liking. It means submerging our own will and letting God's will guide and direct us. Giving up one's will to follow that of another is, by definition, slavery. And that's just what Paul calls it when he says, "Offer them [the parts of your body] in *slavery* to righteousness."

Why would anyone want to enter slavery? Paul outlines the alternatives. And remember, Christ indicated there are only two alternatives. On the one hand, everyone has a master. There can be no disinterested neutrality toward God (Matthew 12:30). On the other hand, no one can serve two masters (6:24). Our master is God or someone else. Paul confronts his readers with this inescapable either-or scenario. "When you were slaves to sin, you were free from the control of righteousness. What benefit did you reap at that time from the things you are now ashamed of? Those things result in death!"

Before becoming Christians, the Romans were "free from the control of righteousness." They did not feel the inhibiting force of God's holy will telling them to lead decent, honest, chaste, industrious lives. They were free from the control of righteousness—but were slaves of sin.

"What good did that do you?" Paul asks. The force of the Greek verb here suggests the meaning, What were you able to gain from that lifestyle? In the setting of a wage earner, one might frame the question like this: After all the deductions from your paycheck, what was your take-home pay? Or to return to the spiritual implication of Paul's question, What lasting benefit did you get from your freedom from righteousness?

The answer, of course, is obvious: "Those things [the sins you're now ashamed of] result in death!" It doesn't take a financial wizard to figure out that the rate of return on such an investment, such freedom to sin, isn't very favorable if it results in death.

Paul turns to the alternative. "But now that you have been set free from sin and have become slaves to God, the benefit you reap leads to holiness, and the result is eternal life." It is essential to note the passive verbs here. Paul says, "You *have been set free* . . . and *have become* [or, *have been made*] slaves to God." The Romans didn't choose a new master for themselves. The new master chose them—at tremendous cost to himself. He suffered and died to pay for their sins and thus to free them from their slavery of sin so that they might live under him in his kingdom and serve him in everlasting righteousness. Such "slavery" leads to righteous living now and to eternal life in heaven hereafter.

Which is the better alternative? The answer is obvious even before Paul gives his assessment: "The wages of sin is death, but the gift of God is eternal life in Christ Jesus our Lord."

Just as the two outcomes are different, so the ways in which the result is obtained are different. Death is something sinners can earn by themselves. It is the wages they have coming for their many sins. Eternal life, on the other hand, is the gift of God. It's available only in Christ Jesus our Lord; by faith in him it is an absolutely sure thing, because it is guaranteed by God's promise. What pathetic folly, therefore, to cast one's lot with sin, to accept its slavery and suffer death when there is such a glorious and blessed alternative in Christ.

Freedom from the domination of the law

In the section just completed, Paul urged the Romans, on the strength of their baptismal connection with Christ (6:3-23), to consider themselves dead to sin and free from its slavery. In chapter 7 he will speak of a similar type of liberation—this time, however, it is the Christian's freedom from the law that is under discussion.

We have previously called attention to the fact that the Greek word usually translated as "law" *(nomos)* requires some special attention. The word allows a variety of meanings, and there often is a significant difference indicated by whether it has the definite article or not. When Paul here says, "I am speaking to men who know [nomos]," it's without an article. Hence Paul is not referring to a specific law, but he is using the word in the sense of a general set of laws. Paul is giving his readers credit for knowing how the legal system works.

His progression of thought in this section is as follows: In verse 1 he states the legal principle he wants his readers to focus on; in verses 2 and 3 he gives an example illustrating that principle; and in verse 4 he then makes the connection to the spiritual truth he wishes to teach, namely, the Christian's freedom from any legal requirements for salvation.

7 Do you not know, brothers—for I am speaking to men who know the law—that the law has authority over a man only as long as he lives?

The legal principle Paul sets forth is fairly simple and straightforward. A law—any law—has authority over a person only so long as that person is alive. The law obligates living people; it has no claim on the deceased. The latter are both literally and figuratively "dead to the law." They take no orders; they make no response. The point Paul would have us notice is that death changes a person's relationship to the law.

The apostle now proceeds to illustrate this truth with an example from everyday life. He draws from the marriage laws that regularly are in force in an orderly society.

²For example, by law a married woman is bound to her husband as long as he is alive, but if her husband dies, she is released from the law of marriage. ³So then, if she marries another man while her husband is still alive, she is called an adulteress. But if her husband dies, she is released from that law and is not an adulteress, even though she marries another man.

The point stated theoretically in verse 1 is illustrated practically in these two verses. The death of a spouse allows the surviving partner to remarry. In both cases the point is the same: a death changes things; it breaks the power of the law. Paul now moves on to show that this general legal principle in everyday life has its counterpart in the spiritual realm. There too death changes things. It loosens the law's grip. Paul points out this similarity when he writes:

⁴So, my brothers, you also died to the law through the body of Christ, that you might belong to another, to him who was raised from the dead, in order that we might bear fruit to God.

The Christian has "died to the law." A death has happened, so that the law's hold on the Christian has been broken, making the Christian eligible for a new relationship to be formed, or as Paul puts it, free to "belong to another."

To understand what Paul is saying here, we need to go back and explain a few of the elements Paul has incorporated into this verse. Note first of all that here "law" has a definite article. Therefore, "law" needs to be understood as a specific law, the law of God that has a hold on people and justly requires punishment for every sin. Being subject to the punishing power of this law is the natural state of every man, woman, and child since Adam's fall into sin.

As indicated by Paul's illustration, the only release from the law is the one provided by death. But the marvel of God's plan of salvation is that it provided a way that did not require the sinner to die. Rather, God provided a substitute, his sacrificial Lamb, to die in the sinner's place. This substitute's death was credited to the sinner. Sinners themselves do not actually die, as they rightly deserve for their sins, but instead die "through the body of Christ" on Calvary.

Notice how we're right back to the thought of chapter 6, with its stress on our connection to Christ through Baptism. Through Baptism we died and were buried with Christ (6:3,4). Hence a death has happened—for the Romans and for us—so that Paul can say, "You also died to the law through the body of Christ."

Thus, by the grace of God, the law's hold on us has been broken. That opens up a grand new possibility: "that you might belong to another, to him who was raised from the dead." Like the woman whose husband died, thus making her eligible for remarriage, so the sinner's death to the law and its domination permits a new union, one with "him who was raised from the dead," namely Christ.

Earlier Paul urged his readers, set free from the slavery of *sin,* to live a life that "leads to holiness" (6:22). He says much the same here also to those freed from the domination of the *law.* Christ suffered and died for us to free us from the law, Paul says, "in order that we might bear fruit to God." Living to God, leading a life of holiness, bearing fruit to God—all these are expressions describing the new life of faith and good works that follow upon Christ's freeing us from the demands of the law.

It goes without saying that in our new state of being free from the law, the law can't be the motivating force for bearing fruit for God. In fact, a person subject to the law bears quite different fruit.

⁵For when we were controlled by the sinful nature, the sinful passions aroused by the law were at work in our bodies, so that we bore fruit for death. ⁶But now, by dying to what once bound us, we have been released from the law so that we serve in the new way of the Spirit, and not in the old way of the written code.

Paul is careful to avoid saying that the law of God is something bad. Read his words carefully here to catch his emphasis that it is "the *sinful nature,* the *sinful passions* aroused by the law" that are the problem. They, not the law, result in the sinner's producing "fruit for death." Paul will shortly be saying a great deal about the proper place and role of the law. For the moment he is concentrating on just one point, namely, that the law is not the driving and energizing force that enables the Christian to lead a life of holiness. That ability has to come from a different source. It comes from the Spirit. "But now, by dying to what once bound us [the law], we have been released from the law so that we serve in the new way of the Spirit, and not in the old way of the written code [the law]."

111

When Paul calls this the "new way of the Spirit," we need to realize that it is new only in the sense that it is the follow-up and the successor to the previous, old stage where the law was in control. For a very similar statement regarding the new status of the Christian after being freed from sin, review 6:14. There Paul wrote, "Sin shall not be your master, because you are not under law, but under grace." The Holy Spirit works in the believer an appreciation for God's grace, and that appreciation reflects itself in a new life of love and service to God and our neighbor. Incidentally, this is the first time in the letter that Paul mentions the Holy Spirit. In the next chapter, Paul will be speaking in detail about the Spirit's work.

Paul is aware that some of the things he has said in urging the Christian's freedom from the law could sound negative and uncomplimentary to God's law. Someone might wonder, Is the law perhaps something bad? Paul anticipates such a reaction on the part of his readers and therefore poses the question:

⁷What shall we say, then? Is the law sin? Certainly not!

Perhaps the remark most likely to raise a question would be the apostle's description of the believer's former condition. When we were under the law, Paul says, "sinful passions aroused by the law were at work in our bodies."

If sinful passions were aroused by the law, is the law of God perhaps responsible for sin? Paul stoutly denies that, but it still leaves him with the task of explaining the connection between sin and the law. He proceeds to supply that explanation in the next paragraph. His division of material there is as follows: In verses 7 to 13 he recalls the role of the law in his early life; in verses 14 to 25 he speaks of his present life as a Christian.

Paul begins his defense of God's law with an illustration of the good service it rendered him early in his life. He points to the law's useful function of alerting people to what God's will is so they can know and avoid what is evil.

Indeed I would not have known what sin was except through the law. For I would not have known what coveting really was if the law had not said, "Do not covet."

Paul uses the first person singular throughout this chapter. What he describes is actually true for the life of every person, but seemingly for reasons of tact, Paul restricts his remarks to himself. In that way he is protected against anyone's feeling accused or confronted by what he says about the law. But even more important, it lends credibility to Paul's observations. He knows what he's talking about. He's been there!

As an illustration of the service the law rendered to him, Paul chooses the example of coveting. The word he uses for "coveting" is a neutral term, meaning simply "desire." It could be a good desire, as in the case of Jesus' use of the term on Maundy Thursday evening when he says to his disciples, "I have eagerly desired to eat this Passover with you before I suffer" (Luke 22:15).

But the term also allows a wide range of evil desires. It often includes the idea of lust, as well as the more common English meaning of "covet" in the sense of the Ninth and Tenth Commandments, namely, having a strong desire to obtain what belongs to one's neighbor.

Paul no doubt had learned early in life that stealing was wrong. However, he would not have known the full extent of God's will. He would not have realized that not only is *taking* a neighbor's property wrong, but it's wrong even *to want* to take or to entertain thoughts of getting a neighbor's property.

The law did Paul a service by pointing out to him something that was wrong and harmful, much as the park ranger does us a service when he warns us of a steep drop-off next to the path on which we're hiking.

Hence the law in itself was something good that served Paul well—until the scoundrel Sin appeared on the scene and misused God's good law!

⁸But sin, seizing the opportunity afforded by the commandment, produced in me every kind of covetous desire. For apart from law, sin is dead. ⁹Once I was alive apart from law; but when the commandment came, sin sprang to life and I died.

Paul says, "Apart from law, sin is dead." Twice previously Paul has expressed a similar thought (4:15; 5:13). His point is not that sin is totally lacking or nonexistent when the law isn't spelled out. Rather, the activity of sin is different when there is no specific commandment to transgress. We might paraphrase the verse as follows: Apart from law, sin is *dormant.* Sin is there, but it needs a line in the sand to step over in order to show itself as sin. The law draws that line in the sand, and sin incites the sinner into stepping over it. In a manner of speaking, the law, or commandment, provides the "opportunity." It did that in Paul's life, and he has to admit, "Sin, seizing the opportunity afforded by the commandment, produced in me every kind of covetous desire."

If a freshly painted park bench has a WET PAINT sign on it, as surely as night follows day, people will go up and touch the paint to see if it really is wet. The fault lies not with the sign but with the perversity of the passersby. The end result, however, can easily be that the thing that which intended to be helpful and protective now appears to be the problem. The sign on the park bench that was intended to be helpful can appear to be the cause of paint-stained hands and ruined clothes. So it was in Paul's life. When the commandment stating God's will became known to him, dormant sin "sprang to life."

¹⁰I found that the very commandment that was intended to bring life actually brought death. ¹¹For sin, seizing the opportunity afforded by the commandment, deceived me, and through the commandment put me to death. ¹²So then, the law is holy, and the commandment is holy, righteous and good.

Sin is the villain, not God's law. Sin serves up all kinds of deceptive rationalizations: it will be enjoyable; everyone is doing it; nobody will be hurt by it; it's necessary for survival in a dog-eat-dog world; and so on. Sin offers all kinds of deceptive encouragement to step over the line—until the sinner has fallen into the trap. Then it turns on him and confronts him with the death penalty, the just consequences of disobeying God's will as spelled out in the law. Hence Paul can tell the Corinthians, "The power of sin is the law" (1 Corinthians 15:56), and the law shows its power when it thunders, "The wages of sin is death" (Romans 6:23). Thus the law that was given to be helpful actually ends up bringing death.

Is the law, then, the problem? Not at all! Follow the simple line of thought in verse 11. Stripped of its modifiers, the sentence reads, "Sin . . . deceived me, and . . . put me to death." Sin is the villain, not the law. "So then, the law is holy, and the commandment is holy, righteous and good."

The law may be good, but what about its death-dealing aspect? That certainly is a feature that can't be ignored. Paul addresses that issue with a theoretical question:

¹³Did that which is good, then, become death to me? By no means! But in order that sin might be recognized as sin, it produced death in me through what was good, so that through the commandment sin might become utterly sinful.

There is no denying that the law condemns the sinner to death, but even that verdict of death serves a useful purpose. It shows how serious sin is and thereby becomes a call to repentance. When I see the slippage between what God asks of me in his law and what I do in my life, I then realize how utterly sinful I am and what trouble I'm in. I need help; I need a Savior. Fortunately, that Savior is there for all of us in the person of Christ Jesus.

The need for a Savior from sin doesn't disappear when a person becomes a Christian. Conversion to faith in Christ doesn't just give us a start so that we can become good enough to be acceptable to God on our own. No, faith in Christ accepts the perfect righteousness Christ has earned for us. God credits that righteousness to the believer. God looks at the believer as perfectly holy. He declares the believer to be just and holy. Hence justification is one hundred percent completed.

The new life of faith, however, the Christian's walk with God, is in a constant state of becoming. The Christian's life of holiness, often called *sanctification,* grows and matures as the Christian experiences continually new outpourings of grace and goodness from a loving God.

The very fact that one needs to speak of growing and maturing indicates that the Christian's sanctification is an ongoing thing; it's never completed here in this life on earth. The Christian life, in fact, is marred by frequent lapses into sin that call for repentance and forgiveness. The first of Luther's Ninety-five Theses began with that thought when it stated, "When our Lord and Master Jesus Christ said, 'Repent' [Matt. 4:17], he willed the entire life of believers to be one of repentance."*

That sin continues to surface in our lives should not surprise us, because even the great apostle Paul had to admit to the continuing force of sin in his life.

---

* *Luther's Works,* American Edition, Volume 31, page 25.

14We know that the law is spiritual; but I am unspiritual, sold as a slave to sin. 15I do not understand what I do. For what I want to do I do not do, but what I hate I do. 16And if I do what I do not want to do, I agree that the law is good. 17As it is, it is no longer I myself who do it, but it is sin living in me.

There has been considerable discussion among Bible students as to what Paul means when he says, "I am unspiritual, sold as a slave to sin." Some feel that such a strong statement could not be made of a Christian. Therefore they assume Paul is still speaking of his preconversion days, the time referred to in the previous section (verses 7-13) when Paul first learned the full meaning of God's law.

It seems more likely, however, that the key to Paul's thought here lies in understanding the dual nature of the Christian—what Luther speaks of when he describes the Christian as being "saint and sinner at the same time." What that means is that at all times the new self of faith is beset by the old sinful nature, the old Adam. Both old and new self remain active in the Christian throughout this earthly life.

Seeing both an old self and a new self active in the Christian's life accords well with what Paul described to the Galatians. He wrote to them about the "conflict" going on within every child of God. He told them, "So I say, live by the Spirit, and you will not gratify the desires of the sinful nature. For the sinful nature desires what is contrary to the Spirit, and the Spirit what is contrary to the sinful nature. They are in conflict with each other, so that you do not do what you want" (5:16,17).

The view that the Christian is a combination of both the old and new self is the interpretation assumed here in Romans. Hence it is Paul the Christian who in verses 17 to 24 laments the fact that he still keeps on sinning every day. We should note, however, that while the old and new self are found side by side in the Christian, they do not hold an equal place. The Christian's real identity lies with the new self. Not the old sinful nature but the new self is the true "I" Paul refers to when using the first person singular pronoun in this section. Where that is not the case, as in verse 18, Paul alerts us to the change.

Because there is an "unspiritual" component in him by virtue of the sinful nature clinging to him (as it is with every Christian), Paul has to admit that he continues to sin daily. In fact, so tenacious is the old Adam's hold that Paul can describe himself as being "sold as a slave to sin." This does not mean that Paul is under the control of sin. Remember that sin's domination has been broken by Christ's death, a death the believer shares through Baptism. Sin is not the master of Paul's life, but, time and again, his old sinful nature spoils even Paul's best intentions. He has to concede, "I do not understand what I do. For what I want to do I do not do, but what I hate I do."

The translation "I do not understand what I do" is perhaps a bit misleading. Paul understood full well what he was doing—or rather *not* doing. The problem in translating this verse lies in the fact that we're again dealing with a verb that allows a number of meanings, depending on its context. Literally, the apostle wrote, "I do not know what I do." The verb for "know," however, is not restricted simply to having knowledge about something. Very often the word contains the idea of knowing by personal experience, of knowing intimately, of knowing with affection and approval. Hence we might translate here, "I do not *approve of* what I'm doing, because what I want to do, I don't do, but what I don't want, that I keep right on doing."

Recall that Paul is in the midst of making a defense for God's law, which he has described as "holy, righteous and good" (verse 12). Paul is addressing that point when he now continues, "If I do what I do not want to do, I agree that the law is good." The NIV translators have reproduced verse 16 literally, but our English idiom is a little different from the Greek here. We might catch the force of Paul's logic a little more easily if we invert the English word order and say, "If I really don't want to do what I'm doing, then I agree that the law is good."

That line of logic can be illustrated from the life of a person who unfortunately has become addicted to drugs. His life is a mess: he's become unemployable; he's on the verge of losing his house; his children are suffering and his wife is threatening to leave him. Remorsefully, he looks at the situation and says, "I don't want to go on like this. The law of the land is right when it forbids the misuse of the drugs I've gotten into." Paul is in the same frame of mind. When he doesn't want to do the bad things God forbids, he's actually agreeing with God that God's laws and commands are good and right.

But how, then, can Paul's continuing in sin be explained when he knows God forbids it and has to agree that God is right in forbidding it? Paul answers, "As it is, it is no longer I myself who do it, but it is sin living in me."

This is not a cop-out on Paul's part but an accurate assessment of his situation. We have noted that the Christian retains an old sinful nature throughout this earthly life. That nature lives alongside his new and real self, which was created by the Holy Spirit when the Spirit brought that person to faith in Christ. This new self is totally in sync with God's will. It wants to do the things God wants done. So it is also in Paul's case. His new self, his "inner being" (7:22), delights in God's law. Hence the problem does not lie with the Christian's new self or with God's law. The villain is sin, which operates through the old sinful nature, which still clings to every Christian.

¹⁸I know that nothing good lives in me, that is, in my sinful nature. For I have the desire to do what is good, but I cannot carry it out. ¹⁹For what I do is not the good I want to do; no, the evil I do not want to do—this I keep on doing. ²⁰Now if I do what I do not want to do, it is no longer I who do it, but it is sin living in me that does it.

Verses 18 to 20 are a close parallel to verses 15 to 17, with one difference. Note that in these verses Paul is not identifying himself with the new self but rather is talking about the old Adam when he refers to his "sinful nature."

It would not be correct to say, "Nothing good lives in the Christian." To the extent of having the new self, a Christian is perfectly holy, as acceptable to God as his own Son, whose righteousness he sees when he looks at the believer. It's the other part of the combination, the sinful nature, which Paul brings into the picture in these verses.

Summary

Paul now proceeds to evaluate the situation in which he finds himself (along with every other Christian):

²¹So I find this law at work: When I want to do good, evil is right there with me. ²²For in my inner being I delight in God's law; ²³but I see another law at work in the members of my body, waging war against the law of my mind and making me a prisoner of the law of sin at work within my members. ²⁴What a wretched man I am! Who will rescue me from this body of death? ²⁵Thanks be to God—through Jesus Christ our Lord!

We have noted at a number of places the care required to catch the proper meaning of the Greek noun *nomos*. It occurs five times in verses 21 to 23, and each time our translators have rendered it "law." That's not impossibly bad, but Paul seems to intend three slightly different slants on the word.

Distinguishing those meanings will enhance our understanding of Paul's emphasis. Let's look at the five instances individually, to determine the meaning that fits in each context, and then reassemble the section.

Paul says, "I find this [nomos] at work." The apostle has indicated in the previous verses that the combination of old Adam and new self within him is not something he can change. It's a fixed principle that sets a pattern, or scheme, in his life. Hence Paul sees in his life the *pattern* that although he wants to do good, evil is right there with him.

That pattern causes a tension in Paul's life because, as he says, "in my inner being I delight in God's [nomos]." Here the term unquestionably refers to the holy will of God that has been revealed in his Word. Let's leave the standard translation of *law* for this instance.

There is a guiding principle, or pattern, in Paul's life that has him wanting to do God's will. The apostle, however, continues, "but I see another [nomos] at work in the members of my body." Alongside the positive impulse, or pattern, there is another *pattern*. This one, unfortunately, is negative.

This negative pattern is "waging war against the [nomos] of my mind." Before addressing this version of the term, we need to take another concept into consideration. It's Paul's use of terminology for what we have come to call the believer's "new self." Paul expresses that concept in various ways. In the previous verse, he used the term "my inner being." In this verse and the next, he refers to his new self, or inner being, as his "mind."

Hence Paul now speaks of a negative pattern at work in him that battles against the nomos of his new self. Here Paul is using the term in a third sense (alongside "pattern" and "law"). Here it refers to the force, or *control,* that Paul's new self attempts to exert in the struggle against temptation. Unfortunately, the efforts of the new self all too often fall short, and Paul succumbs to the evil at work in the members of his body. Then he becomes a "prisoner of the [nomos] of sin at work within my members." As in the previous clause, so here too the sense of control fits the context, only this time it is the control exerted by sin.

Let's go back and reconstruct the sentence, substituting the italicized words from the above commentary wherever forms of *nomos* occur in the Scripture text. Paul would then be saying, "So I find this *pattern* at work: When I want to do good, evil is right there with me. For in my inner being I delight in God's *law;* but I see another *pattern* at work in the members of my body, waging war against the *control* my new self tries to exert and making me a prisoner of sin's *control* at work within my members."

In a Christian the real "I" is the new self. This new self delights in the law of God and wants to do God's will. But sin keeps getting in the way and spoiling the Christian's best efforts. It is a terrible frustration, one that makes Christians totally miserable. With Paul we cry out, "What a wretched man I am! Who will rescue me from this body of death?" But for us, as for Paul, there is a solution to the problem. It's the forgiveness of sin earned by Christ's perfect sacrifice.

As one who trusts that promise of full and free forgiveness, Paul exclaims, "Thanks be to God—through Jesus Christ our Lord!" The apostle raises a very similar shout of triumph in his letter to the Corinthians, where we hear him say, "Thanks be to God! He gives us the victory through our Lord Jesus Christ" (1 Corinthians 15:57).

Paul is not despairing. He does, however, close his summary paragraph with a realistic description of himself and every Christian:

So then, I myself in my mind am a slave to God's law, but in the sinful nature a slave to the law of sin.

Perfect sanctification is not possible here on earth; that will happen only in heaven.

Freedom from the fear of death

Paul closed the previous chapter with the sobering statement that sin at all times remains a factor in the life of a Christian. Sin, however, has been paid for by the innocent blood of Christ, our substitute. Because that sacrifice has earned the forgiveness of sins, Paul can optimistically continue his letter to the Romans with a "therefore."

8 **Therefore, there is now no condemnation for those who are in Christ Jesus, [2]because through Christ Jesus the law of the Spirit of life set me free from the law of sin and death. [3]For what the law was powerless to do in that it was weakened by the sinful nature, God did by sending his own Son in the likeness of sinful man to be a sin offering. And so he condemned sin in sinful man, [4]in order that the righteous requirements of the law might be fully met in us, who do not live according to the sinful nature but according to the Spirit.**

For believers in Christ there is no condemnation for sin because a force greater and stronger than sin has appeared on the scene. Through Jesus Christ "the law of the Spirit of life" set us free from "the law of sin and death."

We are again confronted (twice in this verse) with the flexible word *law (nomos)*. In both of these instances, the meaning of "control" will fit nicely. Using that meaning for nomos, we might paraphrase the sentence like this: Through Christ Jesus the *control,* or rule, of the Holy Spirit, who gives life, set me free from the *control* of sin that brings death.

How does sin bring death? Answer: by invoking God's holy law. To the Corinthians, Paul wrote, "The sting of death is sin, and the power of sin is the law" (1 Corinthians 15:56); he says in this letter to the Romans, "The wages of sin is death" (6:23).

But now Paul says he has been set free from the control of sin that brings death. How did this change come about? Not through the law, which sin calls upon to mete out the death penalty on sinners, but through the work of the Holy Spirit, who brings people to faith in Christ and thus gives them life.

Notice that we are now speaking of law as the expression of God's holy will as revealed in the Bible. That is the sense in which Paul also uses it here in verse 3 when he says, "What *the law* was powerless to do in that it was weakened by the sinful nature, God did by sending his own Son in the likeness of sinful man to be a sin offering. And so he condemned sin in sinful man."

The law is indeed powerful. It is the voice of God pointing out right from wrong, and it severely punishes those who disobey its commands. But despite its great power, in the final analysis the law is powerless to make people do what is right. The sinful nature people are born with has the awesome power to rebel against God and thumb its nose at his just demands. Man can break God's law. Thus weakened by the sinful nature, the law could never bring mankind to true righteousness before God.

But what the law could not accomplish in our lives, God stepped in and did for us "by sending his own Son in the likeness of sinful man to be a sin offering." God's own Son took on human flesh so that he would be able to suffer and die as a sin offering. And what did that sacrifice accomplish? Paul uses the striking terminology that in Christ, God "condemned sin" in sinful man. Sin is always quick to accuse and condemn. After it has lured and enticed the sinner into committing wrong, sin hauls out the law and reads all the law's condemnations to the guilty sinner. Sin is quick to condemn, but God turned the tables on sin. In Christ, God "condemned sin." God tells accusing sin to be quiet. It no longer has any legitimate complaint against the sinner, because in Christ,

God's gracious purpose has been accomplished. He sent his Son "in order that the righteous requirements of the law might be fully met in us." Christ's holy and sinless life earned for us the righteousness we couldn't attain, and his innocent death paid for every sin we would ever commit. Hence God now looks at us as righteous; sin no longer has any grounds for complaint against the believer. A just God can throw the case out of court because the righteous requirements of the law have been fully met in us.

But there is a second purpose God had in mind when he credited Christ's righteousness to us, namely, that we would ever more fully become people "who do not live according to the sinful nature but according to the Spirit." After all, the Spirit of life has set us free from the control of sin that leads to death.

In what very easily could have been set up as two parallel columns, Paul goes on to show the great difference between the mind-set of "those who live according to the sinful nature" and "those who live in accordance with the Spirit" (verse 5).

⁵Those who live according to the sinful nature have their minds set on what that nature desires; but those who live in accordance with the Spirit have their minds set on what the Spirit desires. ⁶The mind of sinful man is death, but the mind controlled by the Spirit is life and peace; ⁷the sinful mind is hostile to God. It does not submit to God's law, nor can it do so. ⁸Those controlled by the sinful nature cannot please God.

At first glance the negatives in verses 7 and 8 do not appear to have positive counterparts, as the previous two verses do. However, the positive mind-set, which is Paul's chief concern and emphasis, follows in verses 9 and 10:

⁹You, however, are controlled not by the sinful nature but by the Spirit, if the Spirit of God lives in you. And if anyone does not have the Spirit of Christ, he does not belong to Christ. ¹⁰But

if Christ is in you, your body is dead because of sin, yet your spirit is alive because of righteousness. ¹¹And if the Spirit of him who raised Jesus from the dead is living in you, he who raised Christ from the dead will also give life to your mortal bodies through his Spirit, who lives in you.

At various places we have expended some effort in trying to determine the precise shades of meaning for the flexible word *law (nomos)*. There is a somewhat similar but less vexing flexibility to the Greek word *pneuma*. It is regularly translated as "spirit," but here the task is to determine whether it should be with a capital *S* or a lowercase *s*. With a capital *S* it refers to the Holy Spirit. With a lowercase *s* it refers to the "spirit" within a person—we might say "heart," or "mind," or even "mind-set."

The two meanings (with lowercase or uppercase) are closely related when used in reference to Christians. In their case *pneuma* refers to the new heart and mind they have received, their spiritual nature.

As we well know, however, there can be no spiritual life in anyone unless the Holy Spirit has created that life. Therefore, in such cases where the discussion centers on spiritual life worked by the Holy Spirit, one wouldn't go far wrong using either the capital or lowercase *s*. The resulting sense will be very similar. But there is a rule of thumb that is often helpful. If there is a contrast in the sentence between "flesh" (usually translated by the NIV as "sinful nature") and "spirit," it is likely that the apostle intends the use of the lowercase "spirit." In that case he will be referring to the Christian's spiritual nature as opposed to the sinful nature—in other words, the new self as distinguished from the old Adam.*

---

* Many translators, including those for the NIV, tend to overuse the uppercase "Spirit." For places where the NIV appropriately uses the lowercase "spirit," see verse 16 of this chapter, as well as verses 15 and 10.

In verse 9 we have this contrast between flesh ("sinful nature") and spirit. Therefore, it would be appropriate to reflect that contrast with a translation such as, "You, however, are controlled not by your sinful nature but by your spiritual nature, if the Spirit of God lives in you." In the second use of *pneuma* ("the Spirit of God"), the capital *S* is, of course, proper. Not only is the pneuma specifically identified as the Spirit of God, but there can be no spiritual life in a person unless the Holy Spirit has first worked such spirituality. Paul calls attention to this important work of the Spirit by adding, "And if anyone does not have the Spirit of Christ, he does not belong to Christ." Regarding the designation "Spirit of Christ," more will be said at verse 11.

Notice that each of the four sentences that make up verses 9 to 11 is a conditional sentence. The Greek construction, however, makes it plain that these sentences are not at all hypothetical or iffy. They are so certain, in fact, that one could substitute *since* or *because* for "if" to get Paul's intended meaning.

The observation regarding the certainty of these conditional sentences is important particularly in verses 10 and 11, which carry the key emphasis for this section. Recall that we have entitled this chapter "Freedom from the fear of death." A very important freedom the Holy Spirit gives Christians is the freedom from death—both spiritual and physical. Paul treats them in that order, beginning with freedom from spiritual death. He says in verse 10, "But if Christ is in you, your body is dead because of sin, yet your spirit is alive because of righteousness."

There is no doubt in Paul's mind that Christ is dwelling in the hearts of his readers through faith worked by the Holy Spirit. Hence he can operate on the assumption that they have spiritual life. He can say, "Your spirit [pneuma] is alive."

That is a marked change from the former state of things. Previously, their whole being and existence, separated from God as they were since the fall, was one of spiritual darkness and death. Now the Spirit (capital *S*) has given them a new spirit (lowercase *s*). He has given them spiritual life by leading them to accept the merits of Christ. They have spiritual life already now, a life that will last for all eternity "because of righteousness," namely, Christ's righteousness credited to them by faith.

But there is more: "And if the Spirit of him who raised Jesus from the dead is living in you, he who raised Christ from the dead will also give life to your mortal bodies through his Spirit, who lives in you."

In verse 9, Paul spoke of the "Spirit of Christ." In the present verse he refers to the Holy Spirit as the Spirit of "him who raised Jesus from the dead," that is, God the Father. Note how the confession we make in the Nicene Creed agrees with these two verses, for there we say that we believe the Holy Spirit "proceeds from the Father and the Son."

Note also that although the term *triune God* doesn't occur in Scripture, here we have a clear reference to all three persons in the same sentence. This triune God is the giver of the future physical life that will be ours by a resurrection comparable to what the Father did for his Son on Easter morning.* And all of this is possible "if [or rather *because*] the Spirit of him who raised Jesus from the dead is living in you."

Sons and heirs

¹²**Therefore, brothers, we have an obligation—but it is not to the sinful nature, to live according to it. ¹³For if you live according**

---

* The evangelist John expresses a parallel sequence of thought in the fifth chapter of his gospel: verses 24 to 27 speak of present spiritual life; verses 28 and 29 speak of future physical life.

to the sinful nature, you will die; but if by the Spirit you put to death the misdeeds of the body, you will live, ¹⁴because those who are led by the Spirit of God are sons of God.

Paul's "therefore" invites us, his brothers and sisters in the faith, to draw a conclusion. The Holy Spirit has freed us from death and has given us life—both spiritual and physical. What kind of life should that now be? The answer, of course, is obvious: It is a life lived in close connection with the Spirit, who has given us our life.

In forming such a response, Paul's line of thought, however, veers off to another related gift of the Spirit. The NIV translators have given us some help in following the shift in Paul's train of thought by inserting a dash here. The simple and straightforward response would have been like this: Therefore, brothers, we have an obligation *to live by the Spirit's leading.*

But before getting to that positive "obligation," Paul interrupts by pointing out that which is not under our obligation. When he later returns to the positive aspect of the situation, he doesn't dwell on the obligation but rather moves right on to another blessing the Spirit (capital *S*) provides for our spirit (lowercase *s*), namely, sonship.

In first stating the negative, Paul says, "Brothers, [you do not have an obligation] to the sinful nature, to live according to it. For if you live according to the sinful nature, you will die." Paul has not forgotten the thrust of the previous chapter in which he lamented the fact that he still continues to sin daily. Paul's new self fights valiantly against sin; sin isn't allowed to run rampant or to be in charge. Paul isn't living "according to the sinful nature." Or to reach ahead and borrow a term from the next verse, he isn't being "led by" the sinful nature. To allow it to rule would be to revert to the death from which the Spirit freed him. It would be a denial of the faith, a fall from grace. It would mean losing the righteousness Christ died to win for him.

On the other hand, "if by the Spirit you put to death the misdeeds of the body, you will live, because those who are led by the Spirit of God are sons of God." In the opening words of this sentence, we have an example of a use of *pneuma* that could readily be understood with either an uppercase or a lowercase "spirit." Literally, Paul says, "But if by [pneuma] you put to death the misdeeds of the body, you will live." Since there is a contrast with the preceding "sinful nature," one could very easily understand *pneuma* here as the "spiritual nature" of the Christian, which puts to death the misdeeds of the body. Recognizing, however, that such a spiritual nature is possible only because of the Holy Spirit's activity, one would not be wrong in thinking of the Christian's activity of putting to death the misdeeds of the body as being done by the Holy Spirit, who lives in us. The NIV translators have chosen this latter interpretation.

To be sure, Paul touches on the obligation Christians have to curb the "misdeeds of the body." But this is not viewed as a burdensome thing, something we now have to do. Rather, Paul hurries on to provide the proper gospel motivation and the right reason for doing so.

[15]**For you did not receive a spirit that makes you a slave again to fear, but you received the Spirit of sonship. And by him we cry, "*Abba*, Father." [16]The Spirit himself testifies with our spirit that we are God's children. [17]Now if we are children, then we are heirs—heirs of God and co-heirs with Christ, if indeed we share in his sufferings in order that we may also share in his glory.**

The four instances of *pneuma* in these verses again present us with an interesting mix of uppercase and lowercase uses. When Paul says in verse 14 that "those who are led by the Spirit of God are sons of God," *pneuma* unquestionably calls for a capital S. In the next verse, however, it seems more likely that Paul intends both instances of *pneuma* to be the lowercase usage. Literally, the apostle writes, "You did not receive a [pneuma] of slavery again to fear, but you received a [pneuma] of adoption as sons." The two uses are on the same level; both should be translated with a lowercase *s,* "spirit."

Note first of all what Paul here rules out with the words, "You did not receive a spirit that makes you a slave again to fear." The majority of the Roman Christians were of a gentile, pagan background. Paul is taking them back to those miserable days when they had worshiped false gods before coming to know Christ. They had felt obligated to try and earn favor from harsh and demanding gods by bringing the right offerings and living the right kind of lives. When they had failed, they feared the wrath of the offended deities.

With the work of the Holy Spirit in their hearts, all of that had become a thing of the past. They now know a gracious God who has done everything for them and who has given them everything as a gift through Christ.

Now they have the heart and mind not of a slave, but of a son. Paul tells them, "You received the [s]pirit of sonship. And by [it] we cry '*Abba,* Father.'" *Abba* is simply the Aramaic word for "father." It is the type of address a child would use to go up to a parent and ask for something. Children don't stop and wonder whether this would be a convenient time to interrupt what their parents are doing. No, they confidently ask for whatever they need whenever they want it. That is the kind of confidence the Holy Spirit instills in believers, so that they approach God "as boldly and confidently as dear children ask their dear father," to use Luther's comparison (The Lord's Prayer, "The Address").

How do believers know they may do this? The apostle answers, "The Spirit himself testifies with our spirit that we are God's children." Such confidence isn't arrogance or presumption. It is permissible and proper because we're *children* and God is our heavenly *Father.* Through the means of grace, through Word and sacrament, the Holy Spirit works in our hearts, in our "spirit," the conviction and the assurance that we are children of God (see 1 John 4:13).

Being children of God, who are permitted to call God *our Father,* has some absolutely mind-boggling implications. If we are "God's children," then the Son of God is our brother by virtue of having the same Father, and what's more, we are in line for all the blessings the Father accords to his Son. Paul attempts to give us a hint of what that means when he says, "Now if we are children, then we are heirs—heirs of God and co-heirs with Christ."

Everything the risen, triumphant, ascended Christ has received from his Father belongs also to us. Everything serves his church, and it therefore protects and sustains us even now. But the full realization of that will come only in heaven—only after the trials and tribulations of this world are permanently replaced with the glories of heaven. Then we will see with our eyes the inheritance we now have by faith. Hence Paul can say that we are "heirs of God and co-heirs with Christ, if indeed we share in his sufferings in order that we may also share in his glory."

Again we have a conditional sentence, but the Greek construction makes plain that the matters under discussion are not in doubt. Our inheritance is a sure thing—as is the certainty that we also will have to suffer if we follow the Spirit's lead in a sinful and perverse world. And yet, the inevitability of suffering is not a cause for concern. The sufferings of this present life are no match for the glorious future that awaits all believers in Christ.

¹⁸I consider that our present sufferings are not worth comparing with the glory that will be revealed in us. ¹⁹The creation waits in eager expectation for the sons of God to be revealed. ²⁰For the creation was subjected to frustration, not by its own choice, but by the will of the one who subjected it, in hope ²¹that the creation itself will be liberated from its bondage to decay and brought into the glorious freedom of the children of God.

The glory awaiting us in heaven is something that "will be revealed in us." As such, it lies off in the future. It is, to a great extent, an unknown quantity to Paul and us. We can't know or comprehend it fully. And it can't be adequately described for us, because we have no experience with anything like it. Paul doesn't attempt to describe it here either. Rather, he gives us a feel for the greatness and glory of heaven by showing the keen anticipation and eager expectation it causes not only in the children of God but in all creation, animate and inanimate alike. He says, "The creation waits in eager expectation for the sons of God to be revealed."

There are a number of difficulties that confront the interpreter here. We have already noted above that we are dealing with prophecy here. Paul is speaking of things coming in the future. The broad outline is clear, but the details are still lacking.

A second factor is that Paul here is using a figure of speech called personification. He ascribes personal qualities and characteristics, such as thinking and feeling, to things other than people. Creation "waits in eager expectation" (verse 19); creation "has been groaning" (8:22). How creation does this and how Paul knows about it are not revealed to us. A mitigating factor in all this is that we really don't need to have answers to these questions. Nor is Paul's main purpose here to give us a detailed description of creation's "attitude" during its career in a sin-stained world. The apostle's emphasis becomes clear in verse 23, where the believer's anticipation of glory becomes the real focus of attention for this section.

Paul tells us that creation is waiting "for the sons of God to be revealed." In the everyday world, it is impossible to tell with certainty who is a child of God. True, open idolatry and rank godlessness may make it fairly clear that some are not on the road to salvation. But there are many honorable and upstanding people of whom no such determination can be made. Who is and who is not among the "sons of God" will become public knowledge only on judgment day. Then Jesus will formally separate the sheep from the goats.

Paul says creation is eagerly awaiting judgment day, when the believers will be identified, because that day correlates closely with its own release from "frustration." The apostle writes, "For the creation was subjected to frustration, not by its own choice, but by the will of the one who subjected it, in hope that the creation itself will be liberated from its bondage to decay and brought into the glorious freedom of the children of God."

Creation is described as being frustrated because its original goodness and bounty became diminished by man's fall into sin. Ever since that time, there has been a constant deterioration. Creation is in "bondage to decay." A further frustration is that creation really didn't have this coming, as we might say. The downturn didn't happen to creation "by its own choice," or as it might also be translated, "because of its own *willfulness*." No, it was God's will to curse the earth and have it produce thorns and thistles. In this way it became hard to work and as such served as a constant reminder to Adam and his descendants of the seriousness of their sin (see Genesis 3:17-19).

But now Paul gives us a little glimpse into what the future holds for creation. He says it was subjected to its present state of frustration "in hope that the creation itself will be liberated from its bondage to decay and brought into the glorious freedom of the children of God."

Scripture speaks clearly about a new heaven and a new earth in which righteousness will dwell (2 Peter 3:13; Revelation 21:1-4). It does not, however, settle for us with certainty whether the new heaven and new earth will be made of new material or whether the existing world will be recycled and restored. Paul's way of speaking here inclines one toward thinking in terms of restoration. Passages such as 2 Peter 3:10-13 allow more room for the thought of the present world being destroyed and replaced with another. The point is interesting but not essential for us to know. Nor is it Paul's main emphasis here, as we see when he now turns to the real focus of attention, namely, the lot of believers.

²²We know that the whole creation has been groaning as in the pains of childbirth right up to the present time. ²³Not only so, but we ourselves, who have the firstfruits of the Spirit, groan inwardly as we wait eagerly for our adoption as sons, the redemption of our bodies.

Without going into any additional details, Paul asserts that the whole creation has been groaning in eager anticipation for things to be set right on judgment day. When he continues with "Not only so, . . ." he is using a shortened expression for the fuller statement: *Not only does creation groan in this way,* "but we ourselves . . . groan." Paul has now come to the point that he wishes the Roman Christians to focus on, namely, patient endurance under suffering as they wait for God's great day.

The first step in building up their fortitude for waiting patiently for their inheritance is to call attention to what they have already received. He does that by referring to them as people "who have the firstfruits of the Spirit." In Old Testament times, God commanded his people to offer the first of the harvest to him (Exodus 23:19; Deuteronomy 26:1-11). For the believers to cheerfully offer the first of the crop to the Lord implied their trust and confidence that God would be giving them more later on. As such, the "firstfruits" came to be looked at as a pledge, a token, God's down payment, assuring that God would give them the rest of the harvest also.

Paul uses that picture when he speaks of the Holy Spirit as being God's firstfruit. God's sending the Holy Spirit into their hearts is God's down payment assuring them that he will also give them the rest of what he has promised.

What the Romans were eagerly waiting for, and what God had promised to give them, was their "adoption as sons." This is the same term Paul used previously in verse 15, but with a different meaning. There it meant being taken into God's family, becoming his sons and heirs. Here Paul is talking of the full realization of what God had promised in making them sons and heirs. Hence Paul defines what "adoption as sons" means here by adding "the redemption of our bodies." That redemption will take place in the final resurrection when the believers are raised with glorified bodies to live with God forever. That glorious hope is to strengthen the Roman Christians, and us, who groan inwardly in eager anticipation of God's great day.

The fact that Christians live in hope for a fulfillment of God's promises that they don't see yet during their lifetimes shouldn't surprise us. Hope is, after all, an integral part of

God's plan of salvation. Faith alone saves, but faith, which is essentially trust and confidence in God's promises, also gives the Christian a basis for sure, confident hope.

²⁴For in this hope we were saved. But hope that is seen is no hope at all. Who hopes for what he already has? ²⁵But if we hope for what we do not yet have, we wait for it patiently.

Faith and hope combine to work patience in Christians as they wait for God's good time to come. But faith often wavers, and hope tends all too easily to wane as the time gets long, particularly in suffering. Aware of this, the apostle introduces a second, and infinitely greater, defense against weariness. He returns to the central figure of this chapter, the Holy Spirit.

²⁶In the same way, the Spirit helps us in our weakness. We do not know what we ought to pray for, but the Spirit himself intercedes for us with groans that words cannot express. ²⁷And he who searches our hearts knows the mind of the Spirit, because the Spirit intercedes for the saints in accordance with God's will.

Just as hope proves to be a buffer against weariness and discouragement in times of suffering, so the Holy Spirit helps us in our weakness when we don't know what we ought to pray for. Time and again Christians find themselves at their wits' end, wondering what the will of God is for them in this or that situation. They find themselves lamenting, "If only I knew what the Lord wanted me to do; if only I knew what to pray for." At such times the Holy Spirit steps in and does for us what we're at a loss to do for ourselves. "The Spirit himself intercedes for us with groans that words cannot express."

In verse 23 it was the children of God who were groaning; here it is the Holy Spirit. Bible interpreters are divided as to

137

whether the Holy Spirit's petitions are framed without words, that is, unspoken, or are spoken in words that surpass human speech. The point becomes unimportant when we realize that the petitions are understood perfectly by him for whom they are intended, regardless of their form. God the Father, who searches our hearts, "knows the mind of the Spirit, because the Spirit intercedes for the saints in accordance with God's will."

The "saints" for whom the Holy Spirit intercedes are not some especially pious and good Christians but are those who are holy by their faith in Christ—in other words, all believers. Therefore, help in prayer is a service the Holy Spirit renders to all Christians. That does not release us from God's command and encouragement to pray, but it does cover for us when we do it poorly or too little. And unlike many of our bumbling prayers, the Holy Spirit's prayers for us are always on target, always "in accordance with God's will."

More than conquerors

We have noted at several places that a single Greek word can have a number of meanings. Flexible words like *law (nomos)* and *spirit (pneuma)* are examples. The choice of meaning will affect one's understanding of the passage. There also are other causes of variation, however. Variation in the text can occur when a slight change in the form of a word, caused by hand copying, changes its construction in the sentence. For example, the difference of one letter can change the subject of a verb into its object. Under God's providential hand, such variations in the text have not caused false doctrine, but they do give a slightly different slant to the sentence in which they occur.

We have an example of such a variation in verse 28. The NIV translators have rendered the passage this way:

²⁸And we know that in all things God works for the good of those who love him, who have been called according to his purpose.

As a footnote they print the rendering we are perhaps more familiar with: "And we know that all things work together for good to those who love God." The footnote rendering has manuscript support every bit as strong as the other reading and could just as well have been retained in the main text. Either reading reflects basically the same thought.

The connecting link to the previous verse is that no anxiety while we are waiting for judgment day and no gaps in our prayer life—or any other problem, for that matter—can seriously threaten our spiritual status, because we are objects of God's love, chosen from eternity. Whether the text reads "in all things God works for the good" or "all things work together for good," the favorable outcome is sealed and certain.

But of whom is Paul speaking? For whom is this true? When Paul says things will work out for the good of those who love God, that tends to make us uneasy. We immediately ask ourselves whether we love God enough to fit into such a category. But the apostle at once sets our hearts at ease when he points out that in all of this, it is not what *we* do but what *God* has done for us that makes all the difference. All things work for the good of those "who have been called according to his [God's] purpose."

Believers in Christ can and should rest assured that everything involving their salvation has been taken care of by a gracious God. From eternity he has been active in their salvation. Paul lines up a chain of events that makes the child of God's promised inheritance absolutely sure and certain.

²⁹For those God foreknew he also predestined to be conformed to the likeness of his Son, that he might be the firstborn among

many brothers. [30]And those he predestined, he also called; those he called, he also justified; those he justified, he also glorified.

The sequence of events referred to here covers the time from eternity past to the present and on into the eternal future. Paul opens the series with the statement, "Those God foreknew, he also predestined." In the commentary on Romans 7:15, we noted that the Greek verb *know* is not restricted merely to having information. It implies much more. It implies an intimate knowledge gained by personal experience, reflecting approval and acceptance of the thing or person known. Note how that force comes through, albeit in the negative, when Jesus states that he will say to false teachers, "I never knew you. Away from me, you evildoers!" (Matthew 7:23). Jesus is not saying that he was unaware of these false teachers' activities. He knew exactly what they were teaching. The point is that he will never acknowledge them as being his own. Hence rejection is the logical consequence of Jesus' not "knowing" or approving of them.

Exactly the opposite is true of those whom God knows with approval and acceptance. They are his own, his chosen ones. But Paul is saying something more significant than merely that God knows his own. Rather, God "foreknew" us from eternity, that is, by his grace God chose us in advance, from eternity, before we ever had a chance to lift a finger or do anything to win his favor and approval. That's grace! Paul spells out this doctrine of grace more fully when he writes to the Ephesians, "Praise be to the God and Father of our Lord Jesus Christ, who has blessed us in the heavenly realms with every spiritual blessing in Christ. For he chose us in him before the creation of the world to be holy and blameless in his sight. In love he predestined us to be adopted as his sons through Jesus Christ, in accordance with his pleasure and will" (Ephesians 1:3-5; see also 2:8-10).

What was God's goal or objective in choosing the elect? Paul says God "predestined [them] to be conformed to the likeness of his Son, that he might be the firstborn among many brothers." God's gracious goal and intention was to bring the elect into conformity with Christ. He wanted believers to share in the boundless blessings that now are the rightful possession of Christ. In bringing the elect into his family, in making them *sons of God,* the Father honored Christ, the *Son of God,* by giving him many siblings.

"And those he [God] predestined, he also called." From eternity God predestined the elect to share in the blessing of his Son. In order to bring that about, he called them in their time on earth. Through the means of grace, through Word and sacraments, he invites them to accept the righteousness of Christ and thus become sons of God and heirs of heaven.

"Those he [God] called, he also justified." God's call comes through the means of grace. The Holy Spirit, working through these means, works the faith through which the believer accepts the righteousness Christ earned for all the world. Recall that we have previously distinguished between general justification and personal justification (also called objective justification and subjective justification). Here in this chain of events, Paul is talking about personal acceptance of the righteousness Christ earned, whereby God declares the individual believer to be just and holy, acceptable as a son and an heir.

"Those he [God] justified, he also glorified." Believers, fully justified and secure under the protecting care of a gracious God, are already sharing in God's glory. The full realization of that, however, will not come on this side of judgment day. The believer's full glorification will come only in heaven. However, what God has promised is as good as done. Hence Paul can use a past tense of the verb ("glorified") here in adding the last link of the chain of unbreakable certainties that mark the whole course of a Christian's existence.

God has done absolutely everything necessary for our salvation. In his mercy he foreknew us, predestined us, called us, justified us, and glorified us. How are we now to respond to such love and grace from our Savior-God? Paul provides the answer in the next few verses: Respond with confident trust that has no fear—no fear of condemnation despite accusations from our foes (verses 31-34), no fear of separation from God despite whatever circumstances may confront us in life (verses 35-39).

³¹What, then, shall we say in response to this? If God is for us, who can be against us? ³²He who did not spare his own Son, but gave him up for us all—how will he not also, along with him, graciously give us all things? ³³Who will bring any charge against those whom God has chosen? It is God who justifies. ³⁴Who is he that condemns? Christ Jesus, who died—more than that, who was raised to life—is at the right hand of God and is also inter- ceding for us.

Paul asks the question, "What, then, shall we say in response to this?" And he then answers his own question with a half dozen more questions, the answers to which are all perfectly obvious.

"If God is for us, who can be against us?" Once again, the conditional sentence is not iffy. One could just as read- ily translate it this way: *Since* God is for us, who can be against us? The answer, of course: No one! With God on our side, there is no one who could possibly be successful against us.

"He who did not spare his own Son, but gave him up for us all—how will he not also, along with him, graciously give us all things?" Here the argument is again from the greater to the lesser. If (or rather *since*) God did the greater thing of giving his own Son into death to win salvation for us, won't he now also do all the lesser and easier things to see to it that we actually get that salvation?

In the next two questions, Paul shifts to a courtroom scene. He asks, "Who will bring any charge against those whom God has chosen? It is God who justifies." The Greek word underlying the term *chosen* is *eklekton,* "the elect." They are the ones whom God foreknew and predestined, and whom he justified in time. Who could possibly oppose God in regard to that choice?

"Who is he that condemns? Christ Jesus, who died—more than that, who was raised to life—is at the right hand of God and is also interceding for us." The accusations of Satan that we should be condemned would carry a great deal of weight in any court of justice—if it were not for three things. Christ Jesus died to pay for those sins; the debt has been canceled. What's more, the Father has accepted the payment, as proven by the fact that he raised his Son on Easter morning. And third, far from agreeing with Satan that the Father should condemn justified sinners, Christ sits at the Father's right hand. He has the Father's full attention, and he is interceding on our behalf. With that kind of attorney pleading our case before a favorable judge, there's no chance of the case being decided against us or of an unfavorable verdict coming down on us.

So Satan's vicious frontal attack at the courtroom level can be dismissed. It will be unsuccessful. But what about the wear and tear of everyday Christian living? Isn't it possible, even likely, that we'll grow weary and lose heart over the long haul? What about persecution and hardship? Might they not take their toll on us? It's a serious concern, and Paul addresses it with these questions:

³⁵**Who shall separate us from the love of Christ? Shall trouble or hardship or persecution or famine or nakedness or danger or sword? ³⁶As it is written:**

> **"For your sake we face death all day long;
>   we are considered as sheep to be slaughtered."**

Paul doesn't give the Romans, or us, any assurance that things like trouble, hardship, persecution, or famine won't happen. Rather, he operates with the assumption that they will happen. He cites Scripture to support his point. With his quotation he's saying, Our situation is exactly like the one the psalmist wrote about in Psalm 44:22: We're like sheep being led to slaughter. Nor should that surprise us. Jesus told his disciples: "If anyone would come after me, he must deny himself and *take up his cross* and follow me" (Matthew 16:24).

The situation looks desperate, but will it separate us from our Savior-God? Paul answers:

³⁷**No, in all these things we are more than conquerors through him who loved us. ³⁸For I am convinced that neither death nor life, neither angels nor demons, neither the present nor the future, nor any powers, ³⁹neither height nor depth, nor anything else in all creation, will be able to separate us from the love of God that is in Christ Jesus our Lord.**

Far from being overcome, we are the ones who will overcome and be the conquerors. In fact, Paul promises even more! Literally, he says that we will be "hyper-victorious," or "super-conquerors." That, however, is no credit to us, because it will not come about by anything we do. It will not be accomplished by our love and devotion for the Lord. Rather, it is entirely the other way around. We're conquerors "through him who loved us." When it is his love that carries the day, then nothing in all creation "will be able to separate us from the love of God that is in Christ Jesus our Lord." No evil forces (death/demons) and no dimension (height/depth) can offset, or counterbalance, the love God has for us. Wherever we go and whatever our circumstances, God's love is there to protect us (see Psalm 139). Such is the love the tri-une God has lavished on us and continues to lavish on us. He chose us from eternity; now in time he calls us to faith; and he will keep us in that faith until we reach eternal glory.

PART SIX

God's Righteousness in Dealing with "Israel"
(9:1–11:36)

Paul closed chapter 8 with the firm assurance that nothing can separate the believer in Christ from God's love. Christians may rest secure knowing that they are the objects of God's loving care, chosen by him from eternity for eternal life.

As comforting as that truth was for Paul's Roman readers, it was also bound to raise a serious question. Paul's mixed readership of Jews and Gentiles was certainly aware that, in general, the Christian church was growing through the addition of *gentile* converts. The Jewish nation tended to stay aloof from Christianity or to be openly hostile toward it. One needs only to look into the book of Acts to see the vigor and persistence of Jewish opposition. Peter and the Twelve experienced it in Jerusalem (Acts 5:17,18), as did Paul and his coworkers in their worldwide mission outreach (Acts 9:23-25; 13:6-8; 17:5-14).

But if the Jews in their rejection of Christ were largely outside of the Christian church and its blessings, what about their status as God's chosen people? What about his Old Testament promises to them? Paul addresses that issue in his next major section, chapters 9 to 11.

God's free choice

When Paul proclaimed Jesus of Nazareth as the Christ, the Promised Messiah, he was preaching a message that was not at all congenial to the Jewish way of thinking. Viewing Jesus as the fulfillment of the Old Testament, with its carefully prescribed rituals and ceremonies, seemed to pose a threat to traditional Jewish ways and customs. In fact, when Paul returned to Jerusalem after completing his third missionary journey, James and the Christian brothers in Jerusalem warned Paul of the danger to his life from his Jewish enemies. Paul was perceived by the orthodox Jewish community as being hostile to Jewish customs and virtually anti-Semitic (Acts 21:17-21). Actually, nothing could have been farther from the truth, as the apostle himself strongly asserts.

9 **I speak the truth in Christ—I am not lying, my conscience confirms it in the Holy Spirit—²I have great sorrow and unceasing anguish in my heart. ³For I could wish that I myself were cursed and cut off from Christ for the sake of my brothers, those of my own race, ⁴the people of Israel. Theirs is the adoption as sons; theirs the divine glory, the covenants, the receiving of the law, the temple worship and the promises. ⁵Theirs are the patriarchs, and from them is traced the human ancestry of Christ, who is God over all, forever praised! Amen.**

Far from being anti-Semitic in his dealing with the members of the Jewish race, Paul suffers "great sorrow and unceasing anguish" in his heart because of their rejection of the Promised Messiah. Paul emphasizes that thought with a triple assertion: I am speaking the truth; I'm not lying; the Holy Spirit has instructed my conscience.

But the real proof of his love for the Jewish nation comes in his next statement. Recall that after the incident involving Israel's worship of the golden calf, God threatened to destroy the rebellious Jewish nation and make a great people from Moses (Exodus 32:9,10). Reminiscent of Moses' offer (Exodus 32:31,32), Paul now says, "I could wish that I myself were cursed and cut off from Christ for the sake of my brothers, those of my own race, the people of Israel." If it were possible, Paul would prefer that he himself would be eternally lost and condemned if only the "brothers" of his own race, the people of Israel, might be saved. So earnestly Paul longed for their salvation.

Nor is their salvation an unrealistic hope. Look at all the advantages God gave them. For example, "Theirs is the adoption as sons." Of all the nations on earth, it was only regarding the Jewish people that God declared, "When Israel was a child, I loved him, and out of Egypt I called my *son*" (Hosea 11:1).

"Theirs [is] the divine glory." Paul seems here to be referring to *the glory of the Lord,* that unique phenomenon whereby God made his presence known among the Israelites. This glory of the Lord is referred to in numerous places in the Old Testament. A representative example occurs in Leviticus chapter 9. There, after prescribing which animals were to be brought for sacrifice, Moses tells the people, "Today the LORD will appear to you" (verse 4). Then the account continues: "They took the things Moses commanded to the front of the Tent of Meeting, and the entire assembly came near and stood before the LORD. Then Moses said, 'This is what the LORD has commanded you to do, so that the glory of the LORD may appear to you.' Moses and Aaron then went into the Tent of Meeting. When they came out, they blessed the people; and the glory of the LORD appeared to all the people. Fire came out from the presence of the LORD and consumed the burnt offering and the fat portions on the altar. And when all the people saw it, they shouted for joy and fell facedown" (verses 5,6,23,24). Among no other nation did the "glory of the LORD" appear in this way.

"[Theirs are] the covenants." God struck numerous covenants with his chosen people—with Abraham (Genesis 15:17,18), with Moses (Exodus 19:5,6), with David (2 Samuel 7:8-16), through Jeremiah (31:31-40), through the prophet

149

Romans 9:1-5

Ezekiel (34:25-31). By their very nature these covenants made a special people of Israel.

"[Theirs is] the receiving of the law." Israel had the advantage of knowing precisely what God expected of them, both through the Ten Commandments given on Mount Sinai (Exodus 20:1-17) and through the five books of Moses (Deuteronomy 31:24-28).

"[Theirs are] the temple worship and the promises." Other nations followed the natural knowledge of God within their hearts to devise ways of worshiping their gods. Israel not only had divinely given, God-pleasing forms of worship, but their worship had true content! It offered the comfort that only the promise of a Savior from sin could give.

"Theirs are the patriarchs, and from them is traced the human ancestry of Christ, who is God over all, forever praised!" Other nations had their philosophers and sages, but only Israel had heroes of faith like Abraham, Isaac, Jacob, Judah, David, and Solomon, who not only believed and proclaimed God's promises but were themselves bearers of the Promised Seed. Jesus was born a Jew according to his human nature, a direct descendant of the patriarchs. But he was also more, much more! He was the promised Christ "who is God over all, forever praised!"

Paul is not biased against his own kinship, the members of the Jewish race. Far from it! Rather, he accords them a premier place in the world. They are, in reality, the nation that is at the center of all world history by virtue of their being the bearer of the promised Messiah. But with all this national prestige and with all these God-given advantages, why are so few of them in step with what is happening through the worldwide spread of the Christian church? Paul first heads off a wrong notion and then gives his answer.

150

⁶It is not as though God's word had failed. For not all who are descended from Israel are Israel. ⁷Nor because they are his descendants are they all Abraham's children. On the contrary, "It is through Isaac that your offspring will be reckoned." ⁸In other words, it is not the natural children who are God's children, but it is the children of the promise who are regarded as Abraham's offspring. ⁹For this was how the promise was stated: "At the appointed time I will return, and Sarah will have a son."

If many of the Jews are not in the Christian fold, Paul states that it is not because God wasn't in earnest when he extended his Word and promise to them. Israel as a nation retains the many advantages he previously listed. The promises are still good. The problem is not with God and his Word. The problem is that, by and large, the individual members of the Jewish race have rejected and spurned those promises in unbelief. This is what the apostle means with his paradoxical statement that not all who are descended from Israel are Israel.

"Israel" is the name God gave the patriarch Jacob after he wrestled with God and by faith prevailed (Genesis 32:28). Hence all of Jacob's physical descendants came to be called Israelites. But as Paul hints already here, and as he will be illustrating more fully later on, not all of Jacob's descendants are true Israelites. True Israelites are those who in faith cling to the Savior promised to Jacob by God. The "true Israel," therefore, is a *spiritual* Israel, the believers looking in faith to the promised Messiah found in Christ. Sadly, the majority of Paul's compatriots did not accept Jesus of Nazareth as the promised Messiah. Therefore, Paul has to say, Not all physical Israelites are the true (spiritual) Israel—the way we might say, Not all Christians are true Christians. Simply holding membership in a Christian congregation is no guarantee of faith or spiritual life residing in the heart.

Not all of Jacob's (Israel's) descendants are true Israelites. Moving back two generations, from Jacob to Abraham, Paul repeats that same thought when he says, "Nor because they [members of the Jewish race] are his descendants are they all Abraham's children."

When Abraham was 75 years old, God promised to make him into a great nation. Ten years later he still had no children. In an ill-advised attempt to help God fulfill his promise, Sarah suggested that Abraham take her Egyptian servant woman as a substitute wife. The result of this relationship was the birth of Abraham and Hagar's son, Ishmael.

The conniving of Sarah, Abraham, and Hagar had indeed produced a child, but this child was not God's way of fulfilling his promise. Paul makes the observation, "It is not the natural children who are God's children, but it is the children of the promise who are regarded as Abraham's offspring." Ishmael was a natural child of Abraham, but he was not God's choice. We might say God had not "elected" to fulfill his promise through this child. Rather, God's choice rested on a descendant of Abraham and Sarah. Quoting Genesis 18:10,14, Paul says, "For this was how the promise was stated: 'At the appointed time I will return, and *Sarah* will have a son.'" By God's choice, or election, this statement would be true: "It is through Isaac that your offspring will be reckoned."

Keep in mind that Paul has brought up the case of Isaac and Ishmael to illustrate the matter of God's election. Paul senses that some among his readers might take a logical shortcut and come to a wrong conclusion. The mistaken conclusion he wants to head off is the thought that there is some reason discernible to the human mind as to why God does what he does—in other words, that God's election is in response to what people do or don't do. Paul debunks that notion with a second example, also from the life of the patriarchs.

¹⁰**Not only that, but Rebekah's children had one and the same father, our father Isaac. ¹¹Yet, before the twins were born or had done anything good or bad—in order that God's purpose in election might stand: ¹²not by works but by him who calls—she was told, "The older will serve the younger." ¹³Just as it is written: "Jacob I loved, but Esau I hated."**

In looking at the case of Isaac and Ishmael, it would be very easy for someone to reason as follows: Of course God wouldn't choose Ishmael. He didn't have the right mother. He was born of an Egyptian slave girl. Isaac had the advantage of being born of Sarah, the patriarch's real wife.

To take away the possibility of seeing merit in the life and actions of an individual as the basis for God's election, Paul now turns to the case of Jacob and Esau. God's dealing with them will make it very plain that his election comes about "not by works but by him who calls"—that is, not by people's doing or merit but by God's sovereign choice.

Isaac, chosen over Ishmael by God to be the bearer of the messianic line, married Rebekah, and God blessed them with twins, Jacob and Esau. Actually, Esau was born first (Genesis 25:25) and would normally have been expected to receive priority. "Yet, before the twins were born or had done anything good or bad—in order that God's purpose in election might stand: not by works but by him who calls— she was told, 'The older will serve the younger.'"

Receiving the birthright of the firstborn involved advantages in family leadership and inheritance of property, but in the case of the patriarchal family, there was another factor involved. The choice of Jacob over Esau included the great distinction that Jacob, not Esau, would be the bearer of the promise and an ancestor of the Savior. Why did these distinctions go to Jacob? Not because of any inherent worth or value in Jacob but because God wanted it that way. It was his sovereign choice.

Paul quotes the prophet Malachi (1:2,3) to show just how sharp a distinction God made between the two. He says the matter is "just as it is written: 'Jacob I loved, but Esau I hated.'" Bible interpreters have struggled with this quotation. Rather often the explanation is given that *hate* is to be understood here as "to love less." The problem with this interpretation is that when one arbitrarily softens the meaning of *hate* to something less, the degree of its opposite partner, *love,* is also called into question. Can *love* mean less than total devotion? If so, how does that affect "God so loved the world . . ."?

A better explanation is to let both terms have their full meaning and see in them the twofold quality exhibited by a loving and merciful God who is also just and holy. As a just and holy God, he is rightly angry with sin and hates the sinner. And who are the sinners whom God hates? Recall how convincingly Paul made the point earlier that all people are sinners lacking the righteousness that avails before God. By nature all of them are under his wrath. But God is also a loving and merciful God—so unalterably opposed to the sin he hates that in love he gave his very Son to die as the only acceptable payment for the sins of all the world.

Both these statements are therefore true: God hates the sinner; God loves the sinner. In the final analysis of this Malachi quotation, we have the tension that exists between law and gospel. The law thunders God's hatred of sin and the sinner, voiced when the psalmist says of God, "The arrogant cannot stand in your presence; you hate all who do wrong" (Psalm 5:5). But the same God who cannot tolerate sin also solemnly asserts, "As surely as I live, . . . I take no pleasure in the death of the wicked, but rather that they turn from their ways and live" (Ezekiel 33:11). This is also the God of whom Paul has said, "God demonstrates his own love for us in this: While we were still sinners, Christ died for us" (Romans 5:8).

The Lord hates sin and sinners, and the Lord dearly loves sinners and wants them saved. The resolution to this seeming paradox is found in the cross of Calvary, where Christ's perfect sacrifice once and for all made it possible for a just and holy God to accept sinners—believing sinners with forgiven sins.

However, if we are totally candid, it is likely that such an answer still may not entirely satisfy us, nor answer to our satisfaction the rationalizing question, Why Jacob rather than Esau? We too may want to ask the question Paul expects from his readers.

[14]What then shall we say? Is God unjust? Not at all! [15]For he says to Moses,

**"I will have mercy on whom I have mercy,
and I will have compassion on whom I have compassion."**

[16]It does not, therefore, depend on man's desire or effort, but on God's mercy.

In any discussion on the doctrine of election, it is almost inevitable that the question will be asked, Is God being fair? More specifically, Is it fair for God to condemn people in some far off continent who haven't heard the gospel or who haven't had the same advantages he has given us?

In addressing such questions, a couple of things need to be kept in mind. Note first of all that the Bible speaks only of an election to salvation. It never speaks of a double election, where some are designated from eternity for condemnation, thus creating a situation where they never had a chance to be saved. Verses 18 and 22 of this chapter have been misunderstood that way by some, and these verses will be discussed later in context.

Second, note that the real conundrum here—the area where one could more legitimately question God's rightness and fairness—is, Why should God be *merciful* to anyone? After all, punishing the evildoer is simple justice. And keep in mind, in the first three chapters, Paul established beyond the shadow of a doubt that by nature *all* are under God's wrath and thus deserve his punishment.

Gentiles have the natural knowledge of God written in their hearts, but they rebelliously suppress that knowledge. Hence "the wrath of God is being revealed from heaven against all the godlessness and wickedness of men who suppress the truth by their wickedness, since what may be known about God is plain to them, because God has made it plain to them" (Romans 1:18,19). The self-righteous moralists who think they are in God's good graces because their outward conduct is a little better than that of others have to hear God's verdict, "You, therefore, have no excuse, you who pass judgment on someone else, for at whatever point you judge the other, you are condemning yourself, because you who pass judgment do the same things" (2:1). And the Jews who pride themselves on having the law are solemnly warned, "You who brag about the law, do you dishonor God by breaking the law? As it is written: 'God's name is blasphemed among the Gentiles because of you'" (2:23,24).

All have sinned and should justly be punished for their disobedience. That makes sense. That we can understand. What we can't comprehend is why God should still be merciful to such sinners. And yet that's the quality he reveals about himself when he says to Moses, "I will have mercy on whom I have mercy, and I will have compassion on whom I have compassion." From God's declaration about himself, Paul draws the inescapable conclusion, "It does not, therefore, depend on man's desire or effort, but on God's mercy."

This statement forces us to wrestle with some very weighty concepts, such as mercy and grace. "I'm saved by grace." We say it easily; it rolls off our lips. But stop and think of what that really means: "I did absolutely nothing to qualify for being saved. I was as bad as the next person. God did it all. It is a pure gift." Paul is right in telling the Ephesians, "It is by grace you have been saved, through faith—and this not from yourselves, it is the gift of God—not by works, so that no one can boast" (2:8,9).

And what is the "gift" that God's grace has given us? Paul gave the answer to that question in the opening sentence of his letter to the Ephesians: "Praise be to the God and Father of our Lord Jesus Christ, who has blessed us in the heavenly realms with every spiritual blessing in Christ. For he chose us in him before the creation of the world to be holy and blameless in his sight. In love he predestined us to be adopted as his sons through Jesus Christ, in accordance with his pleasure and will" (1:3-5).

From eternity, "before the creation of the world," God chose us to be his children. And why did he do it? Because it was "in accordance with his pleasure and will." In other words, he did it because he wanted to.

Nor is this simply Paul's analysis of the situation. James says the same thing in a passage that the King James Version nicely translated as, "Of his own will begat he us" (James 1:18). We might paraphrase it, "Because he wanted to, he made us his children." What child ever decided to be conceived and born? It just doesn't work that way—neither in the biological world nor in the spiritual world. Our spiritual life, our becoming children of God, "does not, therefore, depend on man's desire or effort, but on God's mercy."

God's sovereign will, reflected by his underlying mercy, is going to be accomplished. Everything that happens in this world is guided and controlled by him in the interest of his elect. Even the evil things that wicked people perversely do are used by a merciful God to accomplish his gracious purpose. A case in point is God's dealing with Pharaoh at the time of the exodus.

¹⁷For the Scripture says to Pharaoh: "I raised you up for this very purpose, that I might display my power in you and that my name might be proclaimed in all the earth." ¹⁸Therefore God has mercy on whom he wants to have mercy, and he hardens whom he wants to harden.

Reread verse 17, carefully noting what it says and what it does not say. The point of emphasis is God's *mercy* in action. God acts to display his power so that his name "might be proclaimed in all the earth." God's deliverance of Israel was a gracious display of his power, intended to win many to trust in him as their Lord or to strengthen weak faith by letting believers see his loving care of them. And it certainly accomplished that gracious purpose. God's victory over Pharaoh not only was commemorated in the songs of deliverance sung by Moses (Exodus 15:1-18) and by his sister Miriam (verse 21), but its display of God's powerful protection became a recurring theme throughout the whole Old Testament that strengthened many a fainting spirit.

Note also what verse 17 does *not* say. We do not hear God saying that he raised Pharaoh for the purpose of condemning Pharaoh. But what about verse 18: "Therefore God has mercy on whom he wants to have mercy, and he hardens whom he wants to harden"? Doesn't that have a negative twist to it? Indeed it does, but one that becomes more understandable if we take into account the force of the Greek verb used here. The translation "God has mercy on whom he wants to . . . , and he hardens whom he wants to . . ." here sounds arbitrary, almost capricious. It would help to retain the Greek verb's emphasis on God's will. One could reflect that with a translation such as "Therefore God has mercy on whom it is his will to have mercy, and he hardens whom it is his will to harden."

In discussing God's will, we need to distinguish between what has been termed God's *antecedent will* and his *consequent will.* Using technical terms like these doesn't help to explain why God does what he does, but it does help us to focus on *what* he does.

Scripture is filled with statements that clearly tell us it is God's will that all people be saved. Through the prophet Ezekiel, God says, "As surely as I live, . . . I take no pleasure in the death of the wicked, but rather that they turn from their ways and live" (Ezekiel 33:11). A New Testament counterpart would be Paul's clear testimony to Timothy, "God our Savior . . . wants all men to be saved and to come to a knowledge of the truth" (1 Timothy 2:3,4). Clearly it is God's basic, or antecedent, will that all come to faith in his Son and thus be saved eternally.

Sinful and perverse people, however, retain the awesome power to resist God's grace. In stubborn unbelief they can reject the righteousness Christ has won for them. A just and holy God cannot let such wickedness and rebellion go unaddressed. Hence alongside the sweet gospel promise "Whoever believes and is baptized will be saved" stands the stern law declaration "but whoever does not believe will be condemned" (Mark 16:16). The condemnation of the wicked is also God's will, but in this case it's his consequent will, following upon the sinners' rebellion and rejection.

It is the consequent will of God we see directed against Pharaoh. To be sure, the miracles and wonders God enabled Moses and Aaron to do were signs for the children of Israel

159

indicating that Moses was indeed God's designated leader. But in the final analysis, the miracles and plagues were really a message for Pharaoh and his advisors (Exodus 7:1,2). God was revealing himself to Pharaoh and inviting Pharaoh to accept him. Pharaoh had to respond. And respond he did—by repeatedly rejecting God and hardening his heart against God. Here too the Hebrew text is very helpful in the verb forms it employs. First it uses forms indicating that Pharaoh hardened his heart (Exodus 8:15,32). When, however, it came to the stage where his time of grace had run out, we are then told that God hardened Pharaoh's heart (Exodus 9:12; 10:1,20,27).

It was not God's antecedent will that Pharaoh should be lost, but it was God's consequent will that Pharaoh's stubborn unbelief be punished. And it is worthy of note that in this matter, through it all, God's good and gracious will was served, in that God's power was displayed and his name proclaimed in all the earth for the encouragement and strengthening of many faithful believers throughout the ages. Furthermore, the case of Pharaoh serves to illustrate the assurance Paul had earlier given the Romans: "We know that in all things God works for the good of those who love him, who have been called according to his purpose" (8:28).

If God's good and gracious purpose is served even when he punishes evildoers like Pharaoh, in reality aren't all people playing into God's hand? Instead of evildoers being blamed for resisting God's will, shouldn't they really be credited with advancing his cause? Paul anticipates this kind of question.

¹⁹One of you will say to me: "Then why does God still blame us? For who resists his will?"

It's an impertinent question. It deserves—and gets—a sharp rebuke from the apostle. Curtly he says, in effect, "Mind your mouth, mister!"

²⁰But who are you, O man, to talk back to God? "Shall what is formed say to him who formed it, 'Why did you make me like this?'" ²¹Does not the potter have the right to make out of the same lump of clay some pottery for noble purposes and some for common use?

Paul replies, "A creature has no right to talk like that to its Creator! As little as the clay can make decisions for the potter, or a board argue with the carpenter, so is it likewise inappropriate for a human to question God's action." Paul's approach is in harmony with God's declaration spoken through the psalmist: "Be still, and know that I am God" (Psalm 46:10). All that God does is good and right because he is God. Period!

But to this brusque rebuke Paul adds a more reasoned response, one calculated to give the questioner some food for thought. He poses two rhetorical questions with answers so obvious that he doesn't have to give them.

²²What if God, choosing to show his wrath and make his power known, bore with great patience the objects of his wrath—prepared for destruction? ²³What if he did this to make the riches of his glory known to the objects of his mercy, whom he prepared in advance for glory—²⁴even us, whom he also called, not only from the Jews but also from the Gentiles?

To catch Paul's line of thought in these two questions, we need to be clear on three important points. Let's first treat those points separately and then try to reassemble this section in an expanded translation or paraphrase.

First, note the repeated introduction to the two questions. Both are introduced with "What if . . . ?" These questions are the curt kind of rebuttal we can express with the defensive retort "So what if . . . ?" For example, an employee comes in late for work one morning. When his boss speaks to him about it later in the day, he defends himself by saying, "So what if I was a little late? I got all the work done, didn't I?" His point is, Did I really do something seriously wrong if . . . ? That same defensive tone is the point of Paul's question. "Is God doing something wrong if . . . ?"

Second, take a look at what action on God's part the critic is being asked to evaluate. Follow the main clause of the sentence and you hear Paul ask, "Did God do something wrong when in great patience he bore with the objects of his wrath?" Of course, the answer is, Absolutely not! The next verse has a parallel line of logic: "Did God do something wrong if he acted in such a way as to make the riches of his glory known to the objects of his mercy?" Again there can be but one answer: Certainly not!

Third, we need to understand who the "objects" of God's attention are. Both are described in the NIV translation as "prepared." Using the modifier *prepared* in both instances is a most unfortunate choice, because it leaves the impression that both groups are dealt with in the same manner. Both seem to have had something done to or for them. That is not the case. The NIV translators are using the same English word, *prepared,* to translate two different Greek verbs—*katartidzo* and *pro-hetoimadzo,* respectively. Furthermore, the second verb has the prefix *pro,* meaning "to do in advance," which the former verb does not have.

Thus, with the second group, the "objects of his [God's] mercy," we are clearly told that God prepared them in advance for glory. This is God's choice of the elect, his eternal election to salvation as described in Ephesians 1:3-6.

The former group, the ones with whom God is angry, were not prepared by him from eternity for condemnation. Their case is parallel to Pharaoh's. Though it was God's earnest intent (antecedent will) to save them, they refused. Like

Pharaoh, they hardened their hearts and thereby left a just and holy God no alternative but to show his anger and exercise his consequent will to punish evildoers. By their own doing they became "objects of his wrath" and are thus "prepared for destruction."*

But even though they are deserving of punishment, and even though it is God's consequent will to show his wrath against them, yet he "bore with great patience the[se] objects of his wrath." Hence Paul asks, Was God's action inappropriate? Is it wrong for him to show patience?

Let's now try to incorporate these thoughts into an expanded translation or paraphrase. In a general way, the words in italics reflect the editorial expansions.

> Verse 22: *Is God blameworthy* if with great patience he puts up with objects that are under his wrath, that is, people who *by their unbelief and rejection of him* are fit for destruction, *even though it is his consequent will* to show righteous wrath *against such people* and to make his power known?

> Verse 23: And *is it wrong* if he acts in such a way as to make known the greatness of his glory to the objects of his mercy, people whom he *by an act of his own will (James 1:18)* has previously— *in fact, from eternity (Ephesians 1:4)*—prepared for glory?

> Verse 24: When I speak of "objects of his mercy," I'm referring to us, *the ones who are righteous by faith in Christ* (9:30,31), *the true Israel,* whom he has called not only from among the Jews but also from among the Gentiles.

---

* For a parallel situation in Romans, note the many active verbs describing the unbelievers' rebellion against God (1:21-23). Only after they have rejected God do we hear, "Therefore God gave them over . . ." (1:24,26,28).

A major concern on Paul's part throughout chapters 9 to 11 is the lost condition of his kinfolk, the members of the Jewish nation. Their wholesale rejection of Christ and Christianity deeply disturbs him. Hence he feels compelled to point out that just because they are descendants of Abraham by birth and by blood, and thus physical members of the nation God chose to bear the Savior, does not mean that all of them are automatically on the road to heaven. If they reject the Messiah, the Savior born of their own race, they will die in their sins and be lost eternally, despite their heritage and their genes.

That is the point Paul was making earlier in this chapter when he said, "Not all who are descended from Israel are Israel" (verse 6). Not every Jew is a true Israelite in the sense of being a child of God. (For a similar thought, see 2:28,29). True Israelites are those who accept the Savior and in this way follow in the steps of their spiritual father Abraham.

It follows then that if salvation is by faith and not by birth, then the true Israel is to be found also among believing Gentiles. They too are among the elect whom God has prepared in advance for glory. Paul indicates that clearly when he specifically states, " . . . even us, whom he [God] also called, not only from the Jews *but also from the Gentiles.*"

Paul now draws on Scripture to substantiate his contention regarding the true Israel's dual citizenry. Hosea serves to illustrate the inclusion of Gentiles; Isaiah indicates that not all of Abraham's physical descendants are among the saved, but only a "remnant." Paul begins with two quotes from the prophet Hosea.

25As he [God] says in Hosea:

**"I will call them 'my people' who are not my people;
and I will call her 'my loved one' who is not my
loved one,"**

²⁶**and,**

> **"It will happen that in the very place where it was said
>   to them,
>   'You are not my people,'
> they will be called 'sons of the living God.'"**

Although in their original setting Hosea's words were spoken to the Jewish nation, Paul here adapts them to serve as an illustration of God's gracious and unmerited love shown to Gentiles. Verse 25 draws on Hosea 2:23; verse 26 reflects Hosea 1:10. The point of both quotations is the same: Gentiles who at one time were foreign to God and did not at all seem to be chosen by him have at this time become his beloved people and "sons of the living God."

Meanwhile the Jewish nation, so highly favored by God, has largely squandered God's grace. Here the prophet Isaiah must sound an entirely different note.

²⁷**Isaiah cries out concerning Israel:**

> **"Though the number of the Israelites be like the sand by
>   the sea,
>   only the remnant will be saved.
> ²⁸ For the Lord will carry out
>   his sentence on earth with speed and finality."**

God kept his promise to Abraham and made of him a great nation, with descendants as numerous as the sand by the sea and the stars in the heavens. But not all who descended from Abraham and Jacob (Israel) are true Israelites. In fact, the prophet leads us to understand that the majority of physical Israelites is not in the blessed camp of spiritual Israel. Only a *remnant* will be saved, says the apostle, quoting Isaiah 10:22,23. In fact, Paul goes a step further and, with Isaiah, compares the majority of physical Israel to the doomed cities of Sodom and Gomorrah.

²⁹**It is just as Isaiah said previously:**

> **"Unless the Lord Almighty**
> **had left us descendants,**
> **we would have become like Sodom,**
> **we would have been like Gomorrah."**

In this negative comment, it is important to also note the positive element. God has "left us descendants." Also for the Jewish nation, there is salvation in Christ, if only they will accept it.

The necessity of faith and the guilt of unbelief

Paul has spoken of Gentiles as being the new people of God, whereas the Jewish race, historically chosen as God's people, has been reduced to a "remnant." "What then shall we say?" Paul asks. What conclusions can be drawn of the basis of the widely differing status in which these two groups now find themselves? Paul supplies the proper answer for both.

³⁰**What then shall we say? That the Gentiles, who did not pursue righteousness, have obtained it, a righteousness that is by faith; ³¹but Israel, who pursued a law of righteousness, has not attained it. ³²Why not? Because they pursued it not by faith but as if it were by works. They stumbled over the "stumbling stone."
³³As it is written:**

> **"See, I lay in Zion a stone that causes men to stumble**
> **and a rock that makes them fall,**
> **and the one who trusts in him will never be put to shame."**

"What then shall we say [about the Gentiles]?" Paul asks. He answers, "[We should say] that the Gentiles, who did not pursue righteousness, have obtained it, a righteousness that is by faith."

At no time in history was there ever a major repentance or a general change of heart among Gentiles that led God to say that it was now time to bring in the Gentiles and have them become a major component in his church. No, they were going on their merry way with no special concern for earning righteousness with God. They were not looking for God. It was entirely the other way around! God found them. From eternity God in his grace had already chosen them. Now in time God sent messengers of the gospel to them to proclaim the righteousness Christ had earned by his perfect life and his innocent death on the cross. In Christ, God proclaimed forgiveness to Gentiles for the sins they were wallowing in. By the working of the Holy Spirit, he led them to repent of their sins and in faith to accept the gift of God's forgiveness. They accepted this righteousness from God as their only claim to stand before a just and holy Judge. The Gentiles did nothing good; they brought nothing of value. They merely accepted salvation as a gift from God.

Paul then moves on to the next group. "What then shall we say [about Israel]?" He answers, "[We should say that] Israel, who pursued a law of righteousness, has not attained it. Why not? Because they pursued it not by faith but as if it were by works. They stumbled over the 'stumbling stone.'"

In contrast to the moral indifference and carelessness of the Gentiles, the Jews were very concerned about righteousness. They pursued it vigorously. But they went about it in the wrong way: "They pursued it . . . as if it were by works." They felt *they needed to do* what God required in his holy law. Hence they tried very hard to serve him with a law-righteousness. But, unfortunately, they tried to the degree that they felt that they had kept God's law and were therefore acceptable to God on the basis of their own merit; they rejected the idea of needing a redeemer or savior from sin. They resented the suggestion that they needed help from the outside. When Jesus confronted them with their sin and demanded that they

167

repent, they were incensed. When he said, "I am the way and the truth and the life. No one comes to the Father except through me" (John 14:6), they took offense. When he claimed to be the bread of life come down from heaven that had to be eaten (accepted by faith), they said, "This is a hard teaching. Who can accept it?" (John 6:60), and as a result "many of his disciples turned back and no longer followed him" (verse 66). For them, Christ and his teachings had become a "stumbling stone."

Such rejection, however, should not come as a total surprise to Paul's Roman readers. After all, the prophets had foretold it in the case of unbelieving Israel, as Paul points out by putting together two quotations from Isaiah. Combining Isaiah 8:14 and 28:16, he writes, "They stumbled over the 'stumbling stone.' As it is written: 'See, I lay in Zion a stone that causes men to stumble and a rock that makes them fall, and the one who trusts in him will never be put to shame.'"

The NIV translation, which speaks of God's setting up Christ as a stone "that *causes* men to stumble," could be misleading, as though God's intention from the start was that people should stumble over the stone and be lost. As indicated earlier, Scripture does indeed speak of God choosing people from eternity for salvation, but it never says that God elected others for damnation. And we don't have that thought in Isaiah, either—even though at first sight it might seem that way.

It helps to know that in the Greek original, the same two words for "stumbling stone" are used in both verses 32 and 33. Literally, the phrase in question is the two-word expression for "stone of stumbling." That's well translated in verse 32 as "stumbling stone," and that translation could have been retained in verse 33, "See, I lay in Zion a [stumbling] stone" rather than "a stone that causes men to stumble."

168

A similar two-word expression occurs also in the next line—dubiously translated as "a rock that *makes them fall*." Here the two-word expression literally means "rock of offense." Hence Christ is described as a rock people take offense at and therefore trip over.

Before we attempt a paraphrase of the complete Isaiah quotation, let's look at one more thing. We noted that Paul is actually combining two passages from Isaiah. The second *and* (first word of the last line in verse 33) is the connecting word that joins the two quoted passages. However, this word is not connecting two *parallel* thoughts, but it is expressing a *contrast* between the two parts of the Isaiah quotation. Hence the connecting word would be translated better as *but* rather than *and.*

Incorporating these ideas into a paraphrase or expanded translation, we hear God say through Isaiah:

> See, I am setting Christ up in my church as a
>   stone people stumble over and a
>   rock they take offense at and trip
>   over (Isaiah 8:14),
> but the one who trusts in him will never be
>   put to shame (Isaiah 28:16).

Paul's question was, What then shall we say? His twofold answer: The Gentiles, without any effort on their own part, have been brought into God's fold purely by his grace, through faith in Christ. The Jews, on the other hand, have lost their favored status because in blind unbelief they have insisted on trying to gain salvation on their own terms, through keeping the law, rather than trusting in Christ's merit.

Unsatisfactory as it is to human reason and logic, the inescapable truth the apostle is sharing with us is that if we are saved, it is solely by the grace of God. If we are lost, it is our own fault, the result of our unbelief.

Israel's unbelief

Returning specifically to the case of Israel, God's Word has not failed nor have his promises expired. There still is hope. But, as Paul points out next, the matter of Israel's guilty unbelief needs to be addressed.

10 **Brothers, my heart's desire and prayer to God for the Israelites is that they may be saved. ²For I can testify about them that they are zealous for God, but their zeal is not based on knowledge. ³Since they did not know the righteousness that comes from God and sought to establish their own, they did not submit to God's righteousness. ⁴Christ is the end of the law so that there may be righteousness for everyone who believes.**

The opening verse of chapter 10 is very similar to the opening paragraph of chapter 9. There Paul solemnly asserted that he had "great sorrow and unceasing anguish" in his heart because of the lost condition of his "brothers, . . . the people of Israel." Here he says much the same thing: "My heart's desire and prayer to God for the Israelites is that they may be saved."

Some of our problems and faults are so delicate and sensitive an issue that "only your best friend will tell you about them," as the saying goes. Paul is being a best friend by plucking up the courage to say some uncomfortable but much needed things about Jewish spiritual life. Although as a national group they were very "zealous for God," that zeal was sadly misplaced and misdirected.

Paul's analysis of their situation is outlined in verse 3. He again uses the rather flexible Greek verb for "to know," which we've talked about a number of times. Its use here isn't limited to knowing in the sense of having knowledge about something, but it implies "knowing *with approval and acceptance.*" Paul says of the Jews, "Since they did not know [approve of and accept] the righteousness that comes from God . . . , they did not submit to God's righteousness." Rather, they "sought to establish their own [righteousness]." That attempt was both impossible and inappropriate.

Establishing their own righteousness was impossible because it required perfect obedience to God's holy law. Anything less would not do. But less than perfect performance is all that sinful, fallen humanity is capable of. Thus, instead of earning righteousness for themselves, sinners can earn only God's wrath and punishment.

The attempt to keep God's law was also foolish and inappropriate. It was attempting to do all over again what Christ had already done for them. By his perfect life of obedience, Christ had already fulfilled all the requirements of God's holy law, so that Paul can now say, "Christ is the end of the law." Paul's compatriots, however, were operating as though keeping the law was still the requirement for salvation.

Paul goes on to show the marked difference between the two approaches to salvation: the way of the law involves doing; righteousness by faith is simply received.

5Moses describes in this way the righteousness that is by the law: "The man who does these things will live by them." 6But the righteousness that is by faith says: "Do not say in your heart, 'Who will ascend into heaven?'" (that is, to bring Christ down) 7"or 'Who will descend into the deep?'" (that is, to bring Christ up from the dead). 8But what does it say? "The word is near you; it is in your mouth and in your heart," that is, the word of faith we are proclaiming: 9That if you confess with your mouth, "Jesus is Lord," and believe in your heart that God raised him from the dead, you will be saved. 10For it is with your heart that you believe and are justified, and it is with your mouth that you confess and are saved.

It is often said that there are really only two religions in the world, two plans for obtaining salvation. One is to be saved by earning it. The other is to receive it as a gift. Paul puts attempting to keep the law into that first category when he quotes Leviticus 18:5, "The man who does these things will live by them."

To be sure, if a person could keep God's law and do what it requires, then salvation could indeed be achieved that way. But if a person falls short of the law's requirements, as every sinner does, then the law turns on the would-be earner of salvation with a curse. Deuteronomy 27:26 minces no words: "Cursed is the man who does not uphold the words of this law by carrying them out." (See also Galatians 3:10.) That road leads to disaster!

Attempting to earn "righteousness that is by the law" is a totally unworkable option. The alternative Paul presents is "the righteousness that is by faith." Using the literary device of personification, Paul ascribes the power of speech to righteousness. When righteousness speaks, it first issues a disclaimer. It tells us what not to do: "Do not say in your heart, 'Who will ascend into heaven?' (that is, to bring Christ down) or 'Who will descend into the deep?' (that is, to bring Christ up from the dead)."

Using expressions drawn from Deuteronomy 30:12-14, righteousness by faith says, Don't embark on a course of action where you try to set up a savior by yourself—as though you had to go up to heaven and bring Christ down to earth. Or do not presume that you have to go to the underworld to bring Christ back from the dead. Trying to create your own savior is a foolish and impossible task.

But what does righteousness by faith advocate? What is the proper plan to obtain salvation? It is that which trusts in a message, that which clings to a promise. It is having the righteousness gained by trust and confidence in the gospel message, the message proclaimed in the Word as taught by Paul and his peers.

Paul asks, "But what does it [righteousness by faith] say?" Answer: "'The word is near you; it is in your mouth and in your heart,' that is, the word of faith we are proclaiming: That if you confess with your mouth, 'Jesus is Lord,' and believe in your heart that God raised him from the dead, you will be saved."

Salvation is not a matter of doing and earning, but of receiving. It is confessing with the mouth that Jesus is Lord and confidently believing that God raised him from the dead as our Savior and substitute.

Jesus came down to earth to live the perfect life sinners could not live; he kept the law for them. He lived a perfect life to earn the righteousness that sinners needed. What's more, he died the death sinners deserved for their many transgressions. With his lifeblood he paid for their lack of keeping the law. By his perfect obedience he earned the righteousness necessary for our salvation.

Christ has done everything. The Word proclaims this glorious truth to us, and that same Word also works faith in the heart to believe and accept Christ's righteousness. The Word creates the confidence that can say, "This Jesus is *my* Lord."

Once again drawing from Deuteronomy 30:14, Paul says that Word "is near you; it is in your mouth and in your heart." In practice, the order of heart and mouth is reversed from what Paul uses here. The Word first penetrates the heart and creates faith there. Then faith, if it is true and living faith, shows itself in the confession of believing lips. Paul uses the chronological sequence of heart and mouth when he repeats this great truth in verse 10: "For it is with your heart that you believe and are justified, and it is with your mouth that you confess and are saved."

april

¹¹As the Scripture says, "Anyone who trusts in him will never be put to shame." ¹²For there is no difference between Jew and Gentile—the same Lord is Lord of all and richly blesses all who call on him, ¹³for, "Everyone who calls on the name of the Lord will be saved."

When Paul alludes here to what "Scripture says," he is going back once more to Isaiah 28:16, which was also quoted at the close of chapter 9. As previously noted in this chapter, theoretically there can be only one of two possible approaches to salvation. It is through either deeds or faith, merit or grace, doing or receiving.

The Word is near you, Paul says, and that Word declares, "Anyone who trusts in him [Christ] will never be put to shame." When the final reckoning has been made, when the dust has settled, the verdict will always be favorable to those who have trusted in God's mercy as shown in Christ. Believers will not be left holding the bag, embarrassed and ashamed because they have foolishly trusted in someone who was unreliable. No, they will never be put to shame for trusting God's promises.

It will be that way because salvation does not depend on human input but on God's grace and mercy. Paul can confidently and boldly declare the truth that "there is no difference between Jew and Gentile—the same Lord is Lord of all and richly blesses all who call on him."

God has done everything. Man has done nothing and needs to do nothing. It remains for us merely to receive God's great gift by accepting and believing God's promises—or as Paul says, by calling on the name of the Lord.

But bringing stubborn and rebellious sinners to despair of their own merit and to trust solely in Christ's righteousness is a significant hurdle to cross. Even that, however, a good and gracious God has taken care of. Through a series of four interlocking questions, Paul now outlines the steps undertaken by a gracious God to lead people to "call on" him.

¹⁴How, then, can they call on the one they have not believed in? And how can they believe in the one of whom they have not heard? And how can they hear without someone preaching to them? ¹⁵And how can they preach unless they are sent? As it is written, "How beautiful are the feet of those who bring good news!"

In reverse order Paul lists the steps necessary for leading people to call on the name of the Lord. He asks four rhetorical questions. In each case the negative answer is self-evident. How will people confidently call on the Lord if they don't trust and believe in him? Obviously, they can't— and won't. And how can they come to believe and trust in the Lord unless they hear the message of God's grace in Christ? Again, they can't believe the message unless they hear it. And how will they hear that message without someone preaching it to them? And how will those people preach unless they're sent?

With these four scenarios, Paul makes the point that everything necessary has been done. God himself took care of it. God not only gave the general directive that Christians should share the gospel, but he also specifically established the public ministry. He sent out the apostles and their coworkers—and still sends out called workers today—to preach the message of God's love in Christ. That message has been heard. Its life-giving power is evident in the hearts and lives of those who hear, for the heard Word works the faith that enables believers to call on the name of the Lord.

God has done everything to get his message out, a message that leads people to call on the name of the Lord. Two verses later, Paul summarizes the process when he says,

"Consequently, faith comes from hearing the message, and the message is heard through the word of Christ" (verse 17).

God has done everything necessary on his part, but there still is a problem. Keep in mind that in this section, beginning with chapter 9, Paul is addressing the disturbing situation involving the Jewish nation. They were God's chosen nation. From them the Messiah came in fulfillment of prophecy. But the majority of Paul's fellow Jews were not in the Christian fold. How are Paul and his readers to understand that? Has God's Word failed? Has God reneged on his promise?

Paul makes it unmistakably clear: God is *not* at fault. He has done all things well. He has made the good news of salvation known. Messengers with "beautiful" feet (Isaiah 52:7) have proclaimed and shared the good news of Christ's salvation. No, the fault does not lie with God. The problem lies in quite another area.

¹⁶But not all the Israelites accepted the good news. For Isaiah says, "Lord, who has believed our message?" ¹⁷Consequently, faith comes from hearing the message, and the message is heard through the word of Christ. ¹⁸But I ask: Did they not hear? Of course they did:

> **"Their voice has gone out into all the earth,
> their words to the ends of the world."**

Paul states categorically that the fault lies not with God, who had his saving message proclaimed, but rather with the Jewish people, the vast majority of whom refuse to accept the good news.

Nor was this just a problem of recent development at Paul's time. Already in his day the prophet Isaiah complained, "Who has believed our message?" (Isaiah 53:1). This is not a question for information; it's a plaintive commentary on the reception, or rather non-reception, the prophet's message was getting. He is saying, Virtually nobody believes our message.

Recall what Isaiah's message in chapter 53 is. He is talking about God's Suffering Servant, the Messiah, who was going to be rejected in person just as the prophet's message about him was being rejected. Speaking prophetically, Isaiah says, "He [Christ] was despised and rejected by men, a man of sorrows, and familiar with suffering. Like one from whom men hide their faces he was despised" (53:3).

What Isaiah foretold happened precisely as the prophet had predicted it would when Christ came to his people some seven hundred years later. The evangelist John summarizes Jewish rejection of the promised Messiah with the terse comment, "He [Christ] came to that which was his own, but his own did not receive him" (John 1:11).

Paul experienced the same blend of apathy and antagonism toward his gospel message. He expresses that with a deliberate understatement when he says, "Not all the Israelites accepted the good news." What he means, of course, is that very few Jews came to faith in Christ.

How did that happen? Could it be that the majority of Jews didn't know about the fulfillment of God's messianic promise? To follow up that possibility with his readers, Paul continues, "But I ask: Did they not hear?" And he goes right on to answer his own question, "Of course they did."

Drawing from the wording of Psalm 19:4, he asserts:

"Their voice has gone out into all the earth,
    their words to the ends of the world."

In the original context, the psalmist was talking about the *heavens* declaring the glory of God and the *skies* proclaiming the works of his hands. Paul uses the same terminology but transfers it to gospel proclamation. He asserts that the gospel's good news of forgiveness in Christ is indeed something that has gone out into all the world. Hence Paul's fellow Jews cannot excuse themselves on the grounds of not having heard the message.

Tactfully Paul pursues yet another possibility with his readers. Could it be that the Jews didn't grasp the meaning of the gospel they heard?

[19]**Again I ask: Did Israel not understand? First, Moses says,**

> **"I will make you envious by those who are not**
> **a nation;**
> **I will make you angry by a nation that has**
> **no understanding."**

[20]**And Isaiah boldly says,**

> **"I was found by those who did not seek me;**
> **I revealed myself to those who did not ask for me."**

[21]**But concerning Israel he says,**

> **"All day long I have held out my hands**
> **to a disobedient and obstinate people."**

Did Israel not understand? Paul answers that question with a line of logic that proceeds from the lesser to the greater. The apostle's point is that if even the lightly regarded Gentiles could understand and accept the gospel message, then surely the more highly favored Jewish nation should also be able to grasp it.

Paul develops his line of logic by quoting Scripture. In Deuteronomy chapter 32, Moses cautions Israel against forsaking the Lord who has led them out of Egypt. Through Moses, God warns them that he will punish any unfaithfulness to him by allowing Israel's heathen neighbors to gain the advantage over them. That is the frame of reference when God threatens in verse 21,

> "I will make them envious by those who are
>   not a people;
> I will make them angry by a nation that
>   has no understanding."

By comparison to their own most-favored-nation status, Israel tended to view Gentiles as "those who are not a nation." And because God had chosen to reveal himself directly to Israel and even to record his holy will in written form for them at Mount Sinai, Israel could easily feel that they had the spiritual advantage. By comparison, Gentiles appeared to be "a nation that has no understanding."

But lo and behold, these supposedly second-rate Gentiles have understood and accepted the gospel. Speaking about the Gentiles, God says through Isaiah, "I revealed myself to those who did not ask for me; I was found by those who did not seek me" (Isaiah 65:1).

The less favored Gentiles have understood and accepted the message, but concerning Israel, with all its advantages, the prophet must regretfully report, "All day long I have held out my hands to an obstinate people" (verse 2).

Paul's question was, "Did Israel not understand?" The inescapable conclusion he has come to is that if even the Gentiles could understand the message and be saved, then surely Israel could also. Sadly, he must conclude that his compatriots are a disobedient and obstinate people who deliberately refuse to accept what they have heard and understood.

God's gracious plan

As Paul showed in chapter 10, Israel as a nation had to be characterized as a disobedient and obstinate people, firmly committed to their opposition to the gospel. Humanly speaking, the situation looked bleak, even hopeless. And so it would have been for humans, if not for a gracious God.

179

Paul turns our attention to the marvelous grace of a loving God who is determined in his faithfulness to save stubborn and rebellious Israel—even if it would be only a remnant.

Israel's present status

11 **I ask then: Did God reject his people? By no means! I am an Israelite myself, a descendant of Abraham, from the tribe of Benjamin. ²God did not reject his people, whom he foreknew. Don't you know what the Scripture says in the passage about Elijah—how he appealed to God against Israel: ³"Lord, they have killed your prophets and torn down your altars; I am the only one left, and they are trying to kill me"? ⁴And what was God's answer to him? "I have reserved for myself seven thousand who have not bowed the knee to Baal." ⁵So too, at the present time there is a remnant chosen by grace. ⁶And if by grace, then it is no longer by works; if it were, grace would no longer be grace.**

⁷What then? What Israel sought so earnestly it did not obtain, but the elect did. The others were hardened, ⁸as it is written:

> **"God gave them a spirit of stupor,**
> **eyes so that they could not see**
> **and ears so that they could not hear,**
> **to this very day."**

⁹And David says:

> **"May their table become a snare and a trap,**
> **a stumbling block and a retribution for them.**
> **¹⁰May their eyes be darkened so they cannot see,**
> **and their backs be bent forever."**

From Paul's description it is obvious that Israel as a nation was in serious trouble. Should Paul perhaps give up on them? Or a more pertinent question: Has God given up on them? Paul answers with a resounding no!

First, Paul offers himself and his own situation as Exhibit A. If in principle God had ruled Jews out of heaven, then Paul himself would have been disqualified. He says, "I am an Israelite myself, a descendant of Abraham, from the tribe of Benjamin. God did not reject his people, whom he foreknew." Furthermore, many of Paul's peers, including Peter and the other apostles, were also Jews. Obviously, God had not rejected his people.

As Exhibit B, demonstrating God's ability to work his saving will under difficult circumstances, Paul reminds his readers of the situation at the time of Elijah (1 Kings 19). Despite Elijah's God-given success against the prophets of Baal, Israel as a nation did not rally behind him. Instead, they aided and abetted the enemy. In this sorry state of affairs, Elijah unburdens himself with the complaint, "Lord, they have killed your prophets and torn down your altars; I am the only one left, and they are trying to kill me."

Despite Elijah's pessimistic outlook, a remnant of true Israel remained in the physical Israel. No less than seven thousand remained faithful to the Lord. Paul makes a comparison to the situation of his own day. He says, "So too, at the present time there is a remnant chosen by grace. And if by grace, then it is no longer by works; if it were, grace would no longer be grace."

That remnant, like all true believers, exists because of God's grace. It does not exist because some have worked for their salvation and earned it. It is purely a gift of God, received by faith, without works. In fact, to do otherwise and bring works or merit into the picture is to ruin God's free gift and lose his favor.

Thinking that they had to earn salvation by keeping God's holy law was the mistake Israel as a nation was so prone to fall into. Recall Paul's earlier analysis of the situation involving Jews and Gentiles: "What then shall we say? That the Gentiles, who did not pursue righteousness, have obtained it, a righteousness that is by faith; but Israel, who pursued a law of righteousness, has not attained it. Why not? Because they pursued it not by faith but as if it were by works" (9:30-32).

To be sure, Israel earnestly sought righteousness, but they tried to acquire it in the wrong way and therefore did not obtain it. When Israel insisted on going it alone, without God's grace, they put themselves in an impossible situation. Drawing from the wording in Deuteronomy 29:4 and Isaiah 29:10 for verse 8 and quoting Psalm 69:22,23 for verse 9, the apostle writes: "What Israel sought so earnestly it did not obtain, but the elect did. The others were hardened, as it is written: 'God gave them a spirit of stupor, eyes so that they could not see and ears so that they could not hear, to this very day.' And David says: 'May their table become a snare and a trap, a stumbling block and a retribution for them. May their eyes be darkened so they cannot see, and their backs be bent forever.'"

When people refuse to accept God's grace, it eventually reaches the stage where they no longer can receive or accept it. Then spiritual hardening sets in. (See the case of Pharaoh, discussed in connection with 9:16-18. See also Isaiah 6:9,10).

Engrafted branches

Unrepentant and unregenerate humans cannot reject God's grace with impunity. Judgment will follow upon such a course of action. Scripture clearly warns, "Whoever does not believe will be condemned" (Mark 16:16). But is that God's choice? Is it God's preferred option that the sinner be lost? Paul now addresses that question in detail.

[11]Again I ask: Did they stumble so as to fall beyond recovery? Not at all! Rather, because of their transgression, salvation has come to the Gentiles to make Israel envious. [12]But if their transgression means riches for the world, and their loss

means riches for the Gentiles, how much greater riches will their fullness bring!

Paul asks, Was it God's intent to get rid of stubborn and disobedient Israel? Was it in his plans that they should fall?*

With its stubborn resistance to the gospel, Israel had made itself grievously guilty. Paul flatly calls their rejection of the gospel a "transgression." It was an offense that should once and for all have canceled them out of God's book of life. But marvel of marvels, God can use even human sinfulness and perversity to advance his gracious cause! Paul points to two positive results of Israel's disobedience when he says that "because of their transgression, salvation has come to the Gentiles to make Israel envious."

The first great blessing God brought about through Israel's spurning of the gospel is that "salvation has come to the Gentiles." Recall how that truth is illustrated by an incident from Paul's first missionary journey as recorded in Acts chapter 13. Paul preached the gospel of Christ to a mixed audience of Jews and Gentile converts in the synagogue of Pisidian Antioch. This receptive audience invited Paul and Barnabas to speak to them again on the next Sabbath. Luke records the response: "On the next Sabbath almost the whole city gathered to hear the word of the Lord. When the Jews saw the crowds, they were filled with jealousy and talked abusively against what Paul was saying. Then Paul and Barnabas answered them boldly: 'We had to speak the word of God to you first. Since you reject it and do not consider yourselves worthy of eternal life, we now turn to the Gentiles'" (Acts 13:44-46; see Acts 18:6 for a parallel incident in Corinth).

---

* In the translation "fall beyond recovery," *beyond recovery* is not in the original Greek. Its addition by the NIV translators is acceptable as long as the idea is not inferred that numerically every member of Israel as a nation will eventually be "recovered." Paul always speaks in terms of a "remnant" being saved. Additional discussion follows at verses 14 and 25.

Picking up the concept of envy previously brought into the picture by the allusion to Deuteronomy 32:21 in 10:19, Paul now calls his readers' attention to an astounding thing. God's intention, he tells them, is that when Israelites see the blessings of the gospel that have come to believing Gentiles, they should become "envious." That is, they should stop to reassess the situation and hopefully accept the gospel, so that in this way they also might share in the great blessings of life and salvation that by default have become the Gentiles' possession by faith in Christ.

A bit later, in verses 33 to 36, Paul will break into a full-blown doxology, or song of praise, marveling at God's grace and wisdom in devising a plan so creative and ingenious. For the moment he simply wonders aloud: If God can get such blessings from Israel's "transgression," what more will he be able to accomplish through an obedient and believing Israel! In awe he exclaims, "But if their transgression means riches for the world, and their loss means riches for the Gentiles, how much greater riches will their fullness bring!"

¹³I am talking to you Gentiles. Inasmuch as I am the apostle to the Gentiles, I make much of my ministry ¹⁴in the hope that I may somehow arouse my own people to envy and save some of them. ¹⁵For if their rejection is the reconciliation of the world, what will their acceptance be but life from the dead? ¹⁶If the part of the dough offered as firstfruits is holy, then the whole batch is holy; if the root is holy, so are the branches.

At first reading, verses 13 to 16 might seem to be essentially a repetition of the thoughts expressed in verses 11 and 12. And they do have much in common. The "transgression" of verse 11 is picked up by the "rejection" spoken of in verse 15. The "riches for the Gentiles" of verse 12 finds its counterpart in the "reconciliation of the world" in verse 15.

The "greater riches" occasioned by Israel's "fullness" (verse 12) are compared to nothing less than a resurrection, a "life from the dead" (verse 15).

But Paul's words here are not mere repetition. He is now changing the focus somewhat in his discussion. Verses 11 and 12 were general remarks addressed to the mixed audience of Jews and Gentiles comprising the Roman readership. Paul now narrows that scope somewhat by turning his attention more directly to the Gentile readers. Addressing them in the second person, he says, "I am talking to you Gentiles. Inasmuch as I am the apostle to the Gentiles, I make much of my ministry in the hope that I may somehow arouse my own people to envy and save some of them. For if their rejection is the reconciliation of the world, what will their acceptance be but life from the dead?"

Much of this section repeats the rationale previously outlined. But here Paul is personalizing it to show the Gentiles where they fit into God's strategy. Called by God to be the preeminent missionary to the Gentiles, Paul zealously pursued his ministry to non-Jews in order to win absolutely as many Gentiles as possible for Christ. The greater the number of Gentiles converted, the greater—humanly speaking—would be the Jewish reaction. Almost as a backlash, they would be attracted to the blessings they saw going more and more to their gentile Christian neighbors. Out of envy they too would then be drawn to Christ and his blessings.

Paul earnestly desires the salvation of all his own people and avidly participates in God's "reverse psychology" plan. However, he never loses sight of the realism instilled by God's Old Testament prophets when they spoke of only a remnant being saved. Paul is totally committed to gentile outreach, also hoping it will at the same time "arouse my own people," as he puts it. But he realizes that, at best, his efforts to arouse Jewish "envy" will result in the salvation of only "*some* of them." The apostle never envisions the mass conversion of all the biological descendants of Abraham.

That realism, however, doesn't mean that God has gone back on his promises to Israel or that he is not serious about wanting them to be saved. In explaining where Gentiles fit in God's plan, Paul once more asserts the priority of Israel.

Paul uses two illustrations to describe the status of Israel. The first is drawn from the Old Testament ceremonial laws. A portion of the first grain harvested was to be baked into a loaf and offered to the Lord. God told Moses to command the people, "Present a cake from the first of your ground meal and present it as an offering from the threshing floor" (Numbers 15:20). Offering the firstfruits to the Lord sanctified the rest of the harvest, or as Paul states here, "If the part of the dough offered as firstfruits is holy, then the whole batch is holy."

In our context, however, Paul is using these words not to speak of a God-given grain harvest but of God's chosen people. If the firstfruits (Abraham and the patriarchs) are holy, then the whole batch (the descendants of Abraham) are also holy. This is not to say that every Israelite was personally "holy," but that God was seriously concerned about providing "holiness" to all of them through his promised Messiah.

Paul's second illustration comes from the horticultural world. He says succinctly, "If the root is holy, so are the branches." The picture here is parallel to the previous illustration. The priority of the root over the branches and the connection between root and branches suggests to Paul another way of looking at the relationship between God's chosen patriarchs and their descendants, the Jewish nation. This second, briefer illustration the apostle expands into an extended metaphor, a figure of speech in which he likens "branches" not only to the Jews but also to the Gentiles.

Warning to the Gentiles

¹⁷**If some of the branches have been broken off, and you, though a wild olive shoot, have been grafted in among the others and now share in the nourishing sap from the olive root, ¹⁸do not boast over those branches. If you do, consider this: You do not support the root, but the root supports you. ¹⁹You will say then, "Branches were broken off so that I could be grafted in." ²⁰Granted. But they were broken off because of unbelief, and you stand by faith. Do not be arrogant, but be afraid. ²¹For if God did not spare the natural branches, he will not spare you either.**

The overarching theme of chapters 9 to 11 has been Paul's loving concern for his fellow Jews, who by and large have refused to accept Paul's gospel. God had fulfilled his Old Testament covenant, but many Jews—in fact, the majority—were insisting on continuing under the Old Testament regulations. They remained preoccupied with keeping the Mosaic regulations as they still awaited the Messiah, who had already come. Disheartening and depressing as this was for Paul, he never lost sight of the fact that God's grace was retaining a remnant for salvation. Furthermore, that remnant would increase in number when many Jews would join the Christian ranks out of envy over seeing Gentiles receiving God's gospel blessings.

Before returning to that optimistic thought regarding Israel, however, Paul first delivers a stern warning to the Gentiles. He tells them not to become arrogant in the favorable circumstances in which they now find themselves, as though they were somehow superior to Israel. He keeps them in their place by expanding the previously introduced illustration of a tree's roots and branches.

According to Paul's figure of speech, God's chosen people, Israel, could be compared to an olive tree in an orchard.

The patriarchs are the roots, and their descendants, the rank-and-file Jewish nation, are the branches. Because of individual unbelief and unfaithfulness in the chosen people, many "branches" of the tree have been broken off by God.

But amazingly, God has taken Gentiles, branches from a *wild* olive tree not in the orchard, and has grafted them into the cultivated olive tree representing God's people. Therefore, considering their lowly origin, Gentiles have no basis on which to boast about the remarkable upturn in their current fortunes. Hence Paul warns, "If some of the branches have been broken off, and you, though a wild olive shoot, have been grafted in among the others and now share in the nourishing sap from the olive root, do not boast over those branches."

If Gentiles are inclined to boast, they not only are forgetting their "wild" and lowly origin but are misreading their present status as well. They are failing to realize their continuing indebtedness and their dependence on blessings God has delivered through the Jewish nation. Christian gentile branches are still dependent on Jewish roots. Jesus, himself a Jew, said it very plainly when he told the Samaritan woman at Jacob's well, "Salvation is from the Jews" (John 4:22).

Hence in his warning against Gentile pride and arrogance, the apostle makes two points. He says first of all: You Gentiles are not contributors, but receivers. Branches don't support the root. It is the other way around. You gentile branches are drawing strength and nourishment from what is essentially a *Jewish* blessing.

The second point is startling in its bluntness and directness. Paul alerts the Gentiles to the sobering fact that God can break them off as easily as he did the unfaithful members of the Jewish nation. Paul declares, "If God did not spare the natural branches, he will not spare you either."

The basis for that sobering observation lies in the nature of God's plan of salvation. There the central feature is the individual's acceptance or rejection of Christ. Unfaithful Israel refused to accept Christ and was broken off "because of unbelief," whereas Gentiles now "stand by faith." The presence or absence of faith in Christ makes all the difference before our Savior-God.

Paul now invites his readers to reflect on the twofold implication of what he has just said about God. For Gentiles, Paul's description of God is to serve as the grounds for fear (verse 20)—or more appropriately, "reverent awe"—but for Israel it is also the basis of *hope.*

²²Consider therefore the kindness and sternness of God: sternness to those who fell, but kindness to you, provided that you continue in his kindness. Otherwise, you also will be cut off. ²³And if they do not persist in unbelief, they will be grafted in, for God is able to graft them in again. ²⁴After all, if you were cut out of an olive tree that is wild by nature, and contrary to nature were grafted into a cultivated olive tree, how much more readily will these, the natural branches, be grafted into their own olive tree!

In this paragraph Paul calls attention to two noticeably different attributes of God. He is a just and holy God who, to be true to himself, must necessarily punish all sin and wickedness. God is at the same time, however, also a loving and gracious God moved by his merciful heart to give every benefit and blessing to undeserving sinners.

In writing to his Roman readers, the apostle here uses shorthand terms to speak of these two qualities in God. He says, "Consider therefore the kindness and sternness of God." Like every faithful spokesperson for this just yet merciful God, Paul needs to proclaim both qualities clearly. He needs to proclaim both law and gospel, as Christ did when he said,

"Whoever believes and is baptized will be saved, but whoever does not believe will be condemned" (Mark 16:16).

Paul considers this either-or status before a just yet merciful God when he describes the contrasting states of unfaithful Jews and believing Gentiles. Referring to their quite different situations, he speaks of "sternness to those who fell [Jews], but kindness for you [Gentiles], *provided that you continue in his kindness.*"

The last clause is critical. God's kindness, not Gentile merit, is the sole basis for the Gentiles' blessedness. If they ever lose sight of that and begin to boast in themselves, then they too will be cut off. Such is the sternness of him who is currently showing them his unlimited kindness.

Conversely, the holy and righteous God who presently is showing his sternness toward Jewish stubbornness and unbelief is also the loving and gracious God who dearly wants them to be saved. He would like nothing better than to shower his kindness on them. Paul can continue, "And if they do not persist in unbelief, they will be grafted in, for God is able to graft them in again."

The thing keeping Jews separate from God's blessings is their own unbelief—not a lack of kindness on God's part. If Jews will in faith accept the Messiah whom God has sent in the person of Jesus of Nazareth, he will "graft them in again."

God is both willing and able to do that. In fact, he is not only able, but it would be easy for him to save Jews—easier, Paul hints, than it was to save Gentiles. Paul supports this rather bold way of speaking by noting what is standard practice in the horticultural world. "After all, if you [Gentiles] were cut out of an olive tree that is wild by nature, and contrary to nature were grafted into a cultivated olive tree, how much more readily will these [Jews], the natural branches, be grafted into their own olive tree!"

The standard practice is to take hardy, wild rootstock and graft good, domestic, fruit-bearing branches onto it. But God did it the other way. To bring Gentiles to salvation, he took these wild branches and grafted them into a cultivated olive tree. If God can go "contrary to nature" and accomplish the salvation of "wild" Gentiles by grafting them in, "how much more readily will these [Jews], the natural branches, be grafted into their own olive tree" and be brought back to salvation.

God's mystery expounded

²⁵**I do not want you to be ignorant of this mystery, brothers, so that you may not be conceited: Israel has experienced a hardening in part until the full number of the Gentiles has come in.** ²⁶**And so all Israel will be saved, as it is written:**

> **"The deliverer will come from Zion;**
> **he will turn godlessness away from Jacob.**
> ²⁷**And this is my covenant with them**
> **when I take away their sins."**

The Greek word *mysterion,* generally translated as "mystery," is not an uncommon word in the New Testament. It occurs three times in the gospels, twice in Romans, about a dozen and a half times in the rest of Paul's letters, and four times in Revelation. Its basic meaning in virtually all of these passages is not that it speaks of something "mysterious" in the sense of something that can't be understood. Rather, it speaks of something human beings would never have figured out or understood by themselves if God had not revealed it to them. Once revealed, it can readily be apprehended by the human mind.

At its most basic level, this "mystery" is the plan of salvation itself, in which a loving heavenly Father sent his only Son to be the Savior of all the world. Sin-darkened humanity could never have devised such a plan or even thought it possible had God not revealed it. Representative of this meaning of *mystery* would be Paul's use of the term as he describes his ministry in relationship to the people in Laodicea. He tells the Colossians, "My purpose is that they [the Laodiceans] may be encouraged in heart and united in love, so that they may have the full riches of complete understanding, in order that they may know the mystery of God, *namely, Christ,* in whom are hidden all the treasures of wisdom and knowledge" (2:2,3).

Another example of *mystery* understood as God's originally hidden wisdom now revealed is located in Ephesians. There the mystery revealed is the inclusion of Gentiles in the New Testament Christian church. That mystery, revealed to Paul, is now being shared by him. He writes to the Ephesian congregation, "Surely you have heard about the administration of God's grace that was given to me for you, that is, the mystery made known to me by revelation, as I have already written briefly. *This mystery is that through the gospel the Gentiles are heirs together with Israel, members together of one body, and sharers together in the promise in Christ Jesus*" (3:2,3,6).

The meaning of mystery as the Jews and Gentiles joining together in the Christian church yields a very workable interpretation of the Romans passage currently under discussion, and we will be returning to it in our exposition. There is, however, another variation of *mystery* that needs to be kept in mind here. That possibility is that the mystery spoken here by Paul is the explanation of the "hardening" that has taken place in Paul's Jewish compatriots. Specifically, Paul says, "Israel has experienced a *hardening in part.*" The latter concept needs explanation, and we will be returning to it also.

A proper understanding of Paul's term *mystery* is critical for this section of Romans because of the conclusion Paul bases on it when he says, "And so [in this way] all Israel will be saved." Basically, three interpretations have been advanced to explain what the term "all Israel" might mean:

a. "All Israel" refers to the nation descended from Abraham (hence all people of Jewish extraction will eventually be saved).

b. "All Israel" refers to the Christian church, the sum total of all God's elect, both Jews and Gentiles.

c. "All Israel" refers to God's elect from among the Jewish nation, with all of this Jewish remnant being saved.

The interpretation of "all Israel" being every Jewish person could seem at first sight to be the logical understanding of this passage. The context of Romans, however, does not allow for that meaning to stand. A number of Paul's statements rule out this interpretation. Note, for example, that in 9:27 the apostle cites the verdict of Isaiah regarding unfaithful Israel. The prophet laments, "Though the number of the Israelites be like the sand by the sea, only the remnant will be saved." The term *remnant* leaves no room for the idea of a mass conversion of all Jews. Or recall that in 11:13,14 Paul speaks of God's gracious intent to make Israel envious of the blessings going to the Gentiles. He says, "Inasmuch as I am the apostle to the Gentiles, I make much of my ministry in the hope that I may somehow arouse my own people to envy and save some of them." When he says "some," there is no thought of winning them all.

The second interpretation—that "all Israel" refers to the sum total of all God's elect, both Jews and Gentiles, united in the Christian church—is a defensible interpretation. It is a possible interpretation because it does not strain Paul's language nor yield a sense that conflicts with the rest of Scripture.

Paul himself compels us to take a closer look at the term *Israel* if we are to understand 9:6. There he says that "not all who are descended from Israel are Israel." Paul is not guilty of double-talk here. What he means is that not every person who is born of the nation of Israel is a true Israelite in the sense of being a believer who is truly a child of God. The next verse repeats that same idea, using slightly different terminology. He continues, "Nor because they are his descendants are they all Abraham's children." Hence *Israel* can have a wide or a narrow meaning.

Narrowing the terms *Israel* and *Israelite* to refer to believing Jews also seems to underlie the commendation Jesus gave Nathanael when he said of him, "Here is a true Israelite, in whom there is nothing false" (John 1:47).

In his letter to the Galatians, Paul lumps together believing Gentiles with believing Jews as the true Israel when he closes that letter with the summary statement, "Neither circumcision nor uncircumcision means anything; what counts is a new creation. Peace and mercy to all who follow this rule, even to the Israel of God" (6:15,16).

Add to this the fact that in writing to the Ephesians, Paul calls attention to this same combination of Jews and Gentiles when he explains the term *mystery* to them. There he declares that the mystery he was sent to proclaim was that Gentiles and Jews stand at the same level in Christ's New Testament church. Hence the understanding of "all Israel" being saved here in Romans could be referring to the sum total of all God's elect, Jews and Gentiles, united in the Christian church.

The setting and context of our Romans passage under consideration, however, seem to slightly favor the third interpretation, namely, that "all Israel" refers to all elect Jews. Recall that since verse 17, Paul has been issuing strong warnings to the highly favored Gentiles not to gloat over the seemingly less fortunate Jews. In verse 18 he warned, "Do not boast." In verse 20 he advised, "Do not be arrogant, but be afraid." In verse 22 we heard him say, "Continue in his [God's] kindness. Otherwise, you also will be cut off."

Now Paul continues with a parallel warning against conceit. Note that he brings up the subject of the "mystery" to head off conceit on the part of his Gentile readers. He tells them, "I do not want you to be ignorant of this mystery, brothers, so that you may not be conceited: Israel has experienced a hardening in part until the full number of the Gentiles has come in."

In effect, Paul is saying, "Just a minute before you Gentiles jump to any wrong conclusions regarding the Jews! True, Israel has experienced a hardening, but it is only *in part*." Taken out of context, the expression *in part* could allow for two possible interpretations. It could seemingly mean that all Israelites have become partially hardened. This would leave open the logical conclusion that when this partial hardening that afflicts all Jews is removed, then all Israel—that is, every Jew—is going to be saved. Some do indeed understand it that way. But we have already shown that by his reference to God restoring only a "remnant" and "saving *some*," the apostle himself has ruled out a mass conversion of all Jews.

Rather, with the expression "Israel has experienced a hardening in part," Paul is saying that not every member of the Jewish nation has been hardened, only some of them. To be sure, there are many who have adamantly set themselves against Christ and his gospel and will therefore not be saved, but the Gentiles are wrong if they think that's the case with *all* Jews. No, there *are* those among the Jewish nation whom the gospel will yet win into the fold. These people may not be believers just yet. They may, in fact, currently be enemies of the gospel, but by God's grace *some* of them will come into the fold of believers. God's mill is turning. A process is going on. Individually, one by one, Jews will turn to Christ "until the full number of the Gentiles has come in."

The coming in of Gentiles is surely a distinguishing feature of the New Testament Christian church. And that will continue until the end of time, when all elect Gentiles have been brought in. In fact, one of the signs of the end times is the gospel's having been preached to the far corners of the earth inhabited by gentile nations. Jesus prophesied, "This gospel of the kingdom will be preached in the whole world as a testimony to all nations, and then the end will come" (Matthew 24:14).

The mystery Paul is here sharing with his gentile Roman readers is that during the whole New Testament era, Jews are indeed going to be brought into the Christian church alongside Gentiles—despite all appearances to the contrary. Observing that ongoing process, Paul says, "And so all Israel will be saved." Or, to paraphrase it, In this way the sum total of God's elect among the Jewish nation will be brought into the Christian church, even though at present it might look as though God has cut them off.

To repeat what was said earlier, it would not be scripturally incorrect to understand "all Israel" as the sum total of all God's elect, both Jews and Gentiles. Here, however, the focus of attention seems to be on the elect from among the Jews. That focus is retained and even strengthened by the passage from Isaiah that the apostle presents in support: "As it is written: 'The deliverer will come from Zion; he will turn godlessness away from Jacob. And this is my covenant with them when I take away their sins.'"

Considering the setting in which Isaiah spoke, the "Jacob" from whom godlessness would be taken away seems best understood as referring to the believing remnant of Israel.

That the prophet is not referring to every single member of the Jewish nation but rather to the elect becomes clear if we look at the whole line of Isaiah's prophecy. The full statement in Isaiah 59:20 reads, "The Redeemer will come to Zion, to those in Jacob *who repent of their sins.*" Sadly, not everyone will repent, but the elect will.

That Paul's focus is on the elect Jews and not primarily on the Gentiles is reinforced also by the way the apostle continues. Addressing the Gentiles, Paul speaks about elect Jews when he says the following:

²⁸As far as the gospel is concerned, they are enemies on your account; but as far as election is concerned, they are loved on account of the patriarchs, ²⁹for God's gifts and his call are irrevocable. ³⁰Just as you who were at one time disobedient to God have now received mercy as a result of their disobedience, ³¹so they too have now become disobedient in order that they too may now receive mercy as a result of God's mercy to you. ³²For God has bound all men over to disobedience so that he may have mercy on them all.

These verses contain little that Paul hasn't talked about previously. He is summarizing his argument as he brings this section to a close. Basically he is drawing together the main points of the mystery that has been the object of his attention and scrutiny in this section.

Paul reminds us that the vast majority of Jews have become "enemies" of the gospel. As a result, God has, generally speaking, taken his gospel from them and given it to the Gentiles. Hence Israel's rejection of the gospel has been a tremendous blessing, a literal godsend, for the Gentiles who now find themselves enjoying the blessings of God's New Testament Christian church. This turn of events, Paul tells his gentile Roman readers, was "on your account," that is, for their benefit.

But Gentiles are not God's only concern. God has not cast off his chosen people or gone back on the promises he made to them as early as his dealings with the patriarchs Abraham, Isaac, and Jacob. God has remained true to himself and his promises. Hence "as far as election is concerned, they [Jews] are loved on account of the patriarchs, for God's gifts and his call are irrevocable."

Like the man in the parable who prepared a great banquet and then time and again sent his servants out into the highways and byways to bring in guests (Matthew 22:1-14; Luke 14:15-24), God is dedicated to receiving a response to his gracious invitation. God has a plan, and that plan includes Jews as well as Gentiles. The apostle makes that clear when he writes, "Just as you [Gentiles] who were at one time disobedient to God have now received mercy as a result of their disobedience, so they [Jews] too have now become disobedient in order that they too may now receive mercy as a result of God's mercy to you."

As a result of Jewish "disobedience," the gospel came to Gentile listeners, who themselves "were at one time disobedient to God." Disobedient Gentiles were not looking for God when, almost by default, the gospel came to them. The Gentiles brought nothing; they had no inherent worth or merit. There was no reason, other than God's boundless mercy, why they should have received the gospel. But God sent his Holy Spirit into their lives to lead them to repent of their gross sins and turn in faith to the righteousness Christ had earned also for them. In this way they received the blessings of forgiveness of sins, peace with God, and the joy of rendering loving service to God and their neighbors.

Paul personalizes these great blessings to Gentiles by speaking to his Roman readers in the second person. All of these things have come, he says, "as a result of God's mercy to you." God's mercy is the sole factor for their current good fortune. That mercy, however, has a twofold effect: precious blessings for the gentile Christians, but envy among Jews who see God's mercy in Christ going to Gentiles. As a result, Jews are being led to reconsider their foolish disobedience that is causing them to lose God's blessings. Such reconsideration leads to a willingness to look anew at God's gracious gifts and to think in terms of accepting them as gifts of God's mercy, not as rewards for personal status or worth.

Such an ongoing process in the heart and mind of the Jewish nation, Paul says, is exactly what God intended all along. All of this is happening by God's design so that "they [Jews] too may now receive mercy as a result of God's mercy to you."

Mercy is the only avenue of hope for people who have no merit—and disobedient people obviously have no merit. By God's holy law, Jews and Gentiles have both been convicted of disobedience. But a guilty verdict has been handed down for a most gracious purpose. Paul says, "God has bound all men over to disobedience so that he may have mercy on them all." Such inclusiveness does not mean that all people will actually accept Christ and his merit as their hope of salvation, even though God desires that outcome (1 Timothy 2:3,4). Paul is not preaching universalism, as though all people will eventually be saved whether they accept Christ or not. Paul is rather saying that God's good and gracious intent, his mercy, extends to all in spite of their disobedience.

On the backdrop of that great truth, one could summarize Paul's line of argument in chapters 9 to 11 as follows: Since everything comes by God's mercy to those who accept Christ and his merit, believing Gentiles have no basis therefore on which to boast of their favorable circumstances, and believing Jews, on the other hand, have no need to despair, as bleak as their current situation may appear.

God's mercy in Christ is in charge! The realization of that great truth can draw but one response: a doxology of praise.

[33] Oh, the depth of the riches of the wisdom and knowledge of God!
How unsearchable his judgments,
and his paths beyond tracing out!

God's plan is a mystery in the sense that we would never have been able to plan or devise anything like it. And even after God in his infinite wisdom devised it, we would never have been able to figure it out if he had not graciously revealed it to us. And even after he revealed it to us, we would never have been able to believe and accept it had he not sent his Holy Spirit into our hearts to work that faith. God's ways far transcend our puny human capabilities.

[34] "Who has known the mind of the Lord?
Or who has been his counselor?"
[35] "Who has ever given to God,
that God should repay him?"

Reflecting the thinking of Isaiah (40:13) and Job (41:11), Paul poses three rhetorical questions, each of which leads us to acknowledge that absolutely no one gave God any help with devising the marvelous plan of salvation where mercy predominates. Hence there is but one possible reaction, and that is to give all glory to the triune God.

[36] For from him and through him and to him are all things.
To him be the glory forever! Amen.

PART SEVEN

Righteousness Practiced
(12:1–15:13)

Beginning with chapter 12, Paul picks up a somewhat different emphasis in his letter to the Romans. There are some who tend to divide all of Paul's letters into two parts, a "doctrinal" section followed by a "practical" section. These people would say that chapter 12 starts the second major part of his letter, the practical portion dealing with sanctification, or Christian living.

Such a division is not necessarily wrong or even inappropriate. Paul here is indeed picking up the practical subject of sanctification. That, however, is not exactly a new topic. Recall that Paul spoke of sanctification—righteous conduct in the life of the believer—already in chapters 6 to 8. There, however, he spoke of it in more abstract terms. He treated it in its doctrinal aspect as the counterpart to the doctrine of justification, that is, how the sinner obtains the righteousness that avails before God.

At this stage in Paul's letter, after finishing the three-chapter digression dealing with Israel's place in God's economy of things, Paul now directs the Romans' attention to the important matter of everyday Christian living. As a broad outline of the material to be treated, one could say that the apostle first asks his readers to take a look at their use of the gifts and talents God has given them (chapter 12). Then he directs them to examine their attitudes toward government and authority (chapter 13). And finally, he addresses the always delicate matter of how strong Christians are to treat their weaker brothers and sisters (chapters 13 and 14).

Use of gifts and talents

12 Therefore, I urge you, brothers, in view of God's mercy, to offer your bodies as living sacrifices, holy and pleasing to God—this is your spiritual act of worship. ²Do not conform any longer to the pattern of this world, but be transformed by the renewing of your mind. Then you will be able to test and approve what God's will is—his good, pleasing and perfect will.

Paul concluded the previous section with a statement about the amazing scope of God's mercy. He made the bold assertion that God had "bound all men over to disobedience so that he may have mercy on them all" (11:32). This mercy of God has reached into the lives of the Roman readers. If they are Gentiles, it was God's mercy that transferred the gospel from disobedient Jews to them as undeserving Gentiles. God richly blessed the preaching of the gospel to Gentiles so that Jews in turn, when they saw God's boundless mercy to Gentiles, would themselves also turn to the gospel and thus become recipients of the same mercy God had shown to Gentiles.

To all his readers, Jew and Gentile, Paul now says, "I urge you, brothers, *in view of God's mercy,* to offer your bodies as living sacrifices, holy and pleasing to God." Their motivation is not to be that of fulfilling any legal requirements in order to gain favor with God. Rather, their motivation is to be one of grateful response to what God's mercy has done for them.

In Old Testament times, God asked his people to bring him animal sacrifices in a variety of settings and situations. These animals would be ceremonially killed and formally presented to the Lord. The sacrifices thus symbolically became the Lord's property.

Paul now asks the Romans and us, as New Testament Christians, to bring ourselves as living sacrifices. Note the radical differences from the Old Testament: not something else brought as a substitute, but Christians bringing themselves; not a dead sacrifice, but living sacrifices that are able to respond to God's mercy with service that is "holy and pleasing" to him. Such service, done from the heart and not just in outward motions, Paul calls our "spiritual act of worship."

An initial attempt on the apostle's part to identify and describe such service to God involves both a negative and a positive. First, he says, "Do not conform any longer to the pattern of this world." Conforming to the world is all that unregenerate worldlings know. It is their usual pattern to rebel against God and go their own way. And in their better moments, when they try to serve God, they do it badly, for they try to earn favor with God and influence him by buying their way into his good graces.

Like all unregenerate sinners, Paul's readers had lived as such. But now Paul says, No more of that! Don't conform any longer to the world but "be transformed by the renewing of your mind." Essentially, Paul is describing the new state of heart and mind that follows upon what we call conversion, or regeneration. It is the change of heart and mind that takes place when a person has come to know Christ as Savior and Redeemer. To the Corinthians Paul wrote, "If anyone is in Christ, he is a new creation" (2 Corinthians 5:17). That new creation, involving believers' outlook and attitude, enables them to "test and approve what God's will is—his good, pleasing and perfect will."

Testing and approving the will of God again involves a negative and a positive, as Paul points out when he continues:

³For by the grace given me I say to every one of you: Do not think of yourself more highly than you ought, but rather think of yourself with sober judgment, in accordance with the

measure of faith God has given you. ⁴Just as each of us has one body with many members, and these members do not all have the same function, ⁵so in Christ we who are many form one body, and each member belongs to all the others.

In keeping with the "grace," or gift, of the public ministry given to Paul, he now shares a useful piece of advice with his readers. Negatively, he says, "Do not think of yourself more highly than you ought." Then turning that into a positive, he says, "Think of yourself with sober judgment, in accordance with the measure of faith God has given you."

The second half of that positive response poses some difficulty. Scripture nowhere speaks of saving faith as being given in different measures to different people. Saving faith saves. One person is not more saved than the next by virtue of having received more faith.

A factor contributing to the difficulty of this verse lies in the translation quoted above. The NIV and other translations that use a rendering such as "the measure of faith" convey the idea that faith is being measured. The original language, however, allows the words "of faith" to be understood as a possessive: *faith's measure* or *the measure that faith uses*. With the latter understanding, Paul's twofold advice would then read as follows: Do not think of yourself more highly than you ought, but rather think of yourself with sober judgment, in accordance with the measure, or standard, that your God-given faith uses.

What standard, or measure, does faith use to assign proper worth and value to the individual Christian's role? Paul suggests that a Christian's role in the church is analogous to the role individual parts or members play in the human body. "Just as each of us has one body with many members, and these members do not all have the same function, so in Christ we who are many form one body, and each member belongs to all the others." "Each member belongs to all the others." That is the harmonious relationship that exists among Christians when each one uses an individual God-given gift or talent for the common good.

⁶We have different gifts, according to the grace given us. If a man's gift is prophesying, let him use it in proportion to his faith. ⁷If it is serving, let him serve; if it is teaching, let him teach; ⁸if it is encouraging, let him encourage; if it is contributing to the needs of others, let him give generously; if it is leadership, let him govern diligently; if it is showing mercy, let him do it cheerfully.

Paul enumerates seven gifts: prophesying, serving, teaching, encouraging, contributing, exercising leadership, showing mercy. He could have made his point listing fewer than seven. He no doubt could have extended the list beyond these seven, had he wanted to. Paul's point is simply this: Don't think too highly of yourself; on the other hand, don't disparage or neglect the gifts God has given you. Rather, employing sound judgment, faithfully use the various gifts God has given you for the common good.

While we need not dwell on each individual gift in the list, the first one, prophesying, has occasionally raised some questions. First of all, prophesying does not necessarily mean foretelling the future. As used in Scripture, it means declaring God's will, which may have been fulfilled already in the past or could be fulfilled yet in the future. Hence "prophesying" basically means making God's will known.

The second part of the apostle's encouragement regarding prophecy also needs some clarification. As translated by the NIV and others, it sounds similar to the "measure of faith" statement previously discussed. Specifically, our translation reads, "If a man's gift is prophesying, let him use it *in propor-tion to his faith*." We need to note that the original does not have the possessive *his* but simply uses the article *the*. Fur-thermore, Scripture does not restrict *faith* to the meaning of "trust and confidence on the part of an individual believer." *Faith* can also refer to the message that is believed, namely, the gospel. That is unquestionably the sense found in Gala-tians when we are told that the Christian church in Judea did not personally know Paul but simply had heard that "the man who formerly persecuted us is now preaching *the faith* he once tried to destroy" (1:23). Paul was preaching the gospel. Hence Paul's encouragement in Romans could be rephrased as such: If a person's gift is prophesying (publicly proclaim-ing the Word), then let that proclamation be in accord with the faith (in agreement with the gospel).

Love

Faithful use of the God-given gifts listed so far seems to deal with activity that takes place rather publicly in the Christian congregation. "By the grace given [him]" (12:3), Paul now moves on to give additional advice and encour-agement in a slightly wider area. All of the directives now added fit under the general heading of showing "brotherly love" (verse 10) to "God's people" (verse 13).

⁹Love must be sincere. Hate what is evil; cling to what is good. ¹⁰Be devoted to one another in brotherly love. Honor one another above yourselves. ¹¹Never be lacking in zeal, but keep your spiritual fervor, serving the Lord. ¹²Be joyful in hope, patient in affliction, faithful in prayer. ¹³Share with God's people who are in need. Practice hospitality.

Again we see the pairing of a negative and a positive ele-ment. In a section that urges love, it is almost startling to hear the apostle say, "Hate what is evil." That, however, is merely the logical counterpart to the other half of the equation: "Cling to [love] what is good."

There is another aspect of this section that features a rather noticeable style, one found in the original and not lost in the translation. Note the short, choppy sentences. The Greek language was admirably suited for putting together long, balanced sentences through the use of connecting words. For independent clauses to stand alone without connecting words was a highly unusual feature. That, however, is the literary form Paul uses from here until the end of the chapter. The result is short, staccato sentences, which some people have called "miscellaneous encouragements"—individual statements set next to each other somewhat like a bulleted list or the subpoints of an outline. The five items listed in verses 12 and 13 are a typical example:

- Be joyful in hope,
- patient in affliction,
- faithful in prayer.
- Share with God's people who are in need.
- Practice hospitality.

Continuing with this style in the next section, Paul relates more short, individual directives:

[14]Bless those who persecute you; bless and do not curse. [15]Rejoice with those who rejoice; mourn with those who mourn. [16]Live in harmony with one another. Do not be proud, but be willing to associate with people of low position. Do not be conceited.

In the previous two sections, Paul gave his Roman readers advice on how to use their gifts publicly and privately *among believers.* When he now includes advice on how to react to "those who persecute you," he is obviously moving out into the wider scope of society in general, including the non-Christian element that neither understands nor appreciates Christianity. Altogether, he gives eight positive and negative encouragements:

- Bless those who persecute you;
- bless and do not curse.
- Rejoice with those who rejoice;
- mourn with those who mourn.
- Live in harmony with one another.
- Do not be proud,
- but be willing to associate with people of low position.
- Do not be conceited.

None of the things in this list are possible for unregenerate people in their natural state. The things urged by Paul are decidedly *Christian* virtues. They are not things done to gain God's favor. Instead, they are a result of the favor God has already shown in and through Christ to the believer. Recall that the apostle started this chapter by directing his readers to what alone can motivate and produce proper, God-pleasing activity. He urged his readers "in view of God's mercy" to offer their bodies "as living sacrifices, holy and pleasing to God" (verse 1).

None of the virtues urged by the apostle are particularly easy for the Christian. The problem is that the believer continues to be hampered by the old Adam, that evil nature, which clings to the child of God all life long.

Although, as stated above, none of the things directed by Paul are easy for the Christian, an especially difficult virtue is reacting properly to the persecution and opposition that come because of our faith in Christ. And yet Paul says, "Bless those who persecute you; bless and do not curse." So radical is this advice that Paul, in the midst of a section that has been marked by short, clipped sentences, devotes the next five verses to expanding upon this theme and motivating his readers to show a proper response to the unchristian opposition that will inevitably come to them.

¹⁷Do not repay anyone evil for evil. Be careful to do what is right in the eyes of everybody. ¹⁸If it is possible, as far as it depends on you, live at peace with everyone. ¹⁹Do not take revenge, my friends, but leave room for God's wrath, for it is written: "It is mine to avenge; I will repay," says the Lord. ²⁰On the contrary:

> **"If your enemy is hungry, feed him;**
> **if he is thirsty, give him something to drink.**
> **In doing this, you will heap burning coals on his head."**

²¹Do not be overcome by evil, but overcome evil with good.

Note first of all that Paul urges the Romans not to be vindictive, not to be the ones making trouble. Rather, "If it is possible, as far as it depends on you, live at peace with everyone." Paul's saying "*If* it is possible . . ." makes it immediately evident, however, that living at peace with everyone will not always be possible. The devil and the wicked world will see to that. They will confront us with situations that simply must be opposed.

But even when trouble and controversy are unavoidable, when situations occur in which we suffer harm and loss, Paul says, "Do not repay anyone evil for evil. . . . Do not take revenge."

From where is the Christian to draw the strength necessary for such a response? First there is not only the example, but especially the enabling power, of Christ. Recall that even as he was being nailed to the cross, Jesus interceded for his executioners with the prayer, "Father, forgive them, for they do not know what they are doing" (Luke 23:34).

Paul adds to this a second consideration: There is a just and holy God in charge even when evil people do evil things. Christians are not called upon to set everything right in the world. They are not to repay the evildoers in kind or to take revenge. That will all eventually work itself out in God's eternal court of justice. Hence drawing on Deuteronomy 32:35, the apostle can say, "Do not take revenge, my friends, but leave room for God's wrath, for it is written: 'It is mine to avenge; I will repay,' says the Lord."

But there is yet a third consideration that urges blessings and kindly treatment for enemies and evildoers. That motivation is the hope of bringing them to repentance and thereby winning them for Christ and his gospel. After telling the Romans not to avenge themselves, Paul says, "On the contrary: 'If your enemy is hungry, feed him; if he is thirsty, give him something to drink. In doing this, you will heap burning coals on his head.'"

When an enemy of Christianity has vented wrath on a Christian and done harm to the Christian, it may go against expectations and cause this person to reflect on his course of action if the Christian responds with kindness. If the evildoer in turn now sees the error of his ways and regrets his ill-conceived course of action against the Christian, his sorrow and remorse over his evil actions will make him feel as though he is carrying "burning coals on his head" (Proverbs 25:22). In this way the Christian's "good" will have overcome an enemy's "evil," and the goal intended by Paul will have been reached. To be sure, things will not always turn out that favorably, but this nonetheless is to be the Christian's goal, as

Paul indicates when he closes this section with the general application "Do not be overcome by evil, but overcome evil with good."

Submission to authorities

"I urge you," Paul says, "in view of God's mercy, to offer your bodies as living sacrifices, holy and pleasing to God— this is your spiritual act of worship" (12:1). A very important part of our spiritual service to God is the respect and obedience we pay to his representatives, the authorities whom he has placed over us, as prescribed in his Fourth Commandment. Paul, therefore, now directs our attention to this important phase of Christian living.

13 Everyone must submit himself to the governing authorities, for there is no authority except that which God has established. The authorities that exist have been established by God. ²Consequently, he who rebels against the authority is rebelling against what God has instituted, and those who do so will bring judgment on themselves.

Paul utters a profound truth when, by inspiration of the Holy Spirit, he makes the observation that there is no authority except that which God has established. In the final analysis, everyone and everything belongs to God. He is the Creator; we are his creatures. He holds all authority. It is he and he alone who divides out authority to his representatives on earth as he sees fit. Because God made the world and everything in it, he could rightly say to Adam and Eve, "Be fruitful and increase in number; fill the earth and *subdue* it. *Rule over* the fish of the sea and the birds of the air and over every living creature that moves on the ground" (Genesis 1:28). In reality, God was simply delegating his own authority to Adam and Eve when he put them in charge of his lower creatures.

In the same way, God has delegated certain aspects of his authority at various levels and in various areas to provide an ordered structure in human society. At its base, the Fourth Commandment deals with the authority God has given to those who represent him here on earth.

Obviously, not everyone has the same area of responsibility. For example, parents have a different area of responsibility regarding their children than do their children's teachers in school, but both are God's representatives and therefore deserve honor and respect as such in their areas of responsibility.

Paul, however, is not directing his remarks only, or even primarily, to children. Respect for authority is required of all. "*Everyone* must submit himself to the governing authorities," he says, "for there is no authority except that which God has established. The authorities that exist have been established by God."

In the context in which Paul is writing, his directives to the Romans especially include respect for secular government. That is perhaps the more remarkable when we realize that in Paul's day the civil government of Rome was undoubtedly totally pagan. In fact, if we were right in assuming, as we did in the introduction to this commentary, that this letter to the Romans was written from Corinth in the winter of A.D. 58, then Nero would have been the Roman emperor—hardly a model of kind and benevolent leadership! And yet Paul says, "He who rebels against the authority is rebelling against what God has instituted, and those who do so will bring judgment on themselves."

The "judgment" he is speaking of no doubt refers primarily to the punishment the courts would mete out to a criminal or lawbreaker. But the rebel against secular authority is, in a very real sense, on a collision course with God himself, the author and designator of all authority.

Paul pulls no punches. He bases his demand for obedience to government squarely on God's right to put authority figures over us. But the apostle employs yet another approach, and that is to invite willing and cheerful obedience by calling attention to God's good and gracious purpose for placing authorities over us.

³For rulers hold no terror for those who do right, but for those who do wrong. Do you want to be free from fear of the one in authority? Then do what is right and he will commend you. ⁴For he is God's servant to do you good.

We live in an age when there is considerable fear and distrust of government. Some of that, to be sure, is traceable to the fact that God's representatives are weak and sinful human beings who at times may not represent God properly. But by far the greater basis for fear and anxiety in the presence of authority figures is the guilt factor. People who know they are not in compliance with the law recognize that they properly should be punished for their disobedience. Hence they fear those to whom they are answerable, whether that be their workplace supervisor or a traffic officer or the Internal Revenue Service.

"Do you want to be free from fear of the one in authority?" Paul asks. "Then do what is right and he will commend you. For he is God's servant to do you good." Government and civil authority are gifts from a good and gracious God. Through them he wishes to bless us, and surely he has done so! In spite of flaws and defects in our leaders at the local, state, and national levels, we have been tremendously blessed. We are allowed to live our Christian lives without harassment and to proclaim our faith without hindrance. These are priceless blessings—ones for which we need to credit God's representatives and for which we daily ought to thank our gracious God.

God's overriding concern in providing government rule is to bless us with an orderly and peaceful existence. Hence it is the duty of God's representatives to encourage and commend those who do right. But when the peace is jeopardized by lawbreakers, God's representatives need to step in to restore order and punish evildoers. And when they do so, they do it not merely with God's permission but also in accordance with his command. Government is God's servant.

But if you do wrong, be afraid, for he does not bear the sword for nothing. He is God's servant, an agent of wrath to bring punishment on the wrongdoer. ⁵Therefore, it is necessary to submit to the authorities, not only because of possible punishment but also because of conscience.

Government has been set up to represent God. When the citizenry of a city or country disobeys its government, in the final analysis it is God himself who is being dishonored and whose righteous anger is aroused. Hence when Paul says that government is "an agent of wrath," he is not talking about personal anger on the part of the civil authorities. Rather, *God's* wrath against sin and disobedience is the basis for inflicting the punishment that is meted out.

Note the double negative: government "does *not* bear the sword for *nothing*." In other words, God has entrusted government with the task of punishing wrongdoers. He expects disciplinary action against them, even to the point of using the "sword." A sword is not used for simply reprimanding people or attempting to rehabilitate them. The sword kills. Paul clearly teaches that government has been vested with the right to inflict capital punishment. That does not mean the state must necessarily use capital punishment. But it does indicate that those who say that government may never inflict capital punishment are in the wrong.

Use of the "sword" is certainly calculated to instill fear of punishment in people. But fear is not to be the only check against disobedience, or even the main one. Rather, Paul says, it is necessary to submit "not only because of possible punishment but also because of conscience."

Christians regard civil government as God's representatives, carrying out God's will for him. Hence Christians will honor these representatives as they honor God, to maintain a good conscience.*

⁶This is also why you pay taxes, for the authorities are God's servants, who give their full time to governing. ⁷Give everyone what you owe him: If you owe taxes, pay taxes; if revenue, then revenue; if respect, then respect; if honor, then honor.

It is often said that nothing is sure except death and taxes. These two certainties were known also in Paul's day. He uses the latter, payment of taxes, to illustrate compliance to government. Paying taxes is generally viewed as an irksome civic duty. But even that becomes tolerable when viewed as being done out of respect for God's servants who are giving "their full time to governing." Their sole purpose, the apostle says, is the God-given task of serving and benefiting society.

Obedience to government, however, isn't restricted just to paying taxes. Paul generalizes, "Give everyone what you owe him." Paying our various kinds of taxes (income tax, property tax, sales tax, gas tax) is a tangible and measurable activity. But there's an even more important activity—an intangible one—that involves not just our hands (and pocketbooks) but also, and especially, our hearts. Paul calls for not just outward

---

* Paul's assumption, of course, is that the government properly represents the God from whom its assignment has come. If the civil authorities should require things that are in opposition to God's will, then Christians will have to follow their consciences and "obey God rather than men" (Acts 5:29).

and formal obedience but for the even greater tribute of a grateful and willing heart. Such a heart genuinely honors and respects the leaders and authorities who represent God in the many positions of service through which they daily serve us.

Love, the Christian's response

⁸**Let no debt remain outstanding, except the continuing debt to love one another, for he who loves his fellowman has fulfilled the law.** ⁹**The commandments, "Do not commit adultery," "Do not murder," "Do not steal," "Do not covet," and whatever other commandment there may be, are summed up in this one rule: "Love your neighbor as yourself."** ¹⁰**Love does no harm to its neighbor. Therefore love is the fulfillment of the law.**

There is a play on words in the opening verse here that reflects Paul's progression from the previous section to the current subject of love. What the NIV nicely translates as "Let no debt remain outstanding, except . . . to love" in the original literally says, "Do not *owe* anybody anything, except . . . to love."

Recall that in the previous section Paul urged his readers, "Give everyone what you owe him: . . . taxes . . . revenue . . . respect . . . honor." Those are obligations that can and must be fulfilled. But now he adds one obligation that should never be considered as completed, one bill that dare never be marked "Paid in Full." And that is the "continuing debt to love one another." Paul indicates the basis for that when he says, "He who loves his fellowman has fulfilled the law." One could paraphrase his logic by saying, "Love, because that's what God wants you to do."

As he goes on to point out, all of God's Commandments urge love. Paul cites four of them and summarizes the rest with a quotation from Leviticus: "Love your neighbor as yourself" (19:18). Every Commandment requires love for God or for our neighbor. Hence Paul can say, "Therefore love is the fulfillment of the law."

When we hear Paul speaking of fulfilling the law, let's not forget that we are in the section of his letter where he is speaking of the Christian's response to what God has done for us. Back in chapters 3 to 5, Paul clearly explained how the sinner obtains the righteousness that avails before God. It is not by keeping the law, but rather by accepting in faith the perfect obedience that Christ has rendered. Christ's merit alone makes a person acceptable to God.

In appreciation for having been accepted by God, the Christian now wants to show appreciation by living a new life that conforms to God's Commandments. Such a life reflects the life of love toward God and our neighbor that Paul urges here.

Love for God and our neighbor is a powerful motivation toward a life of holiness. There is, however, another consideration that also shapes the Christian's life. That consideration is a concern for our own spiritual welfare.

[11]And do this, understanding the present time. The hour has come for you to wake up from your slumber, because our salvation is nearer now than when we first believed. [12]The night is nearly over; the day is almost here. So let us put aside the deeds of darkness and put on the armor of light. [13]Let us behave decently, as in the daytime, not in orgies and drunkenness, not in sexual immorality and debauchery, not in dissension and jealousy. [14]Rather, clothe yourselves with the Lord Jesus Christ, and do not think about how to gratify the desires of the sinful nature.

For Christians of every generation, "the present time" is no time for spiritual slumber. In fact, the window of opportunity to lead a life of love and service to God and our neighbor becomes smaller with each passing day. The hymnwriter James Montgomery has it right when he says that the passing of each day brings us "a day's march nearer home" (CW 213:2).

Along the same lines, the apostle observes that "our salvation is nearer now than when we first believed." The full realization of our salvation, either at our death or at the second coming of Christ, is always imminent. It could be today! Hence in view of the rapid passage of time, the message is clear: seize the opportunity to live a life of righteousness. The apostle states that in a negative/positive combination: let us "put aside the deeds of darkness" and "put on the armor of light."

Putting aside the deeds of darkness means avoiding the disgusting things that sinful nature is inclined to do when it thinks it is operating under the cover of darkness and no one will see. Paul's list of such things is representative rather than exhaustive. He urges his readers (and us) to avoid orgies and drunkenness, sexual immorality and debauchery, dissension and jealousy. As indicated, Paul is not listing every possible sin. The apostle would have us tailor the list to include our own special temptations and pet sins.

The counterpart to *putting off* such "deeds of darkness" is *putting on* the "armor of light." Or as the apostle also states it, "Clothe yourselves with the Lord Jesus Christ."

Again, the hymnwriter Nicolaus L. von Zinzendorf serves us well when with picturesque language he says, "Jesus, your blood and righteousness my beauty are, *my glorious dress*" (CW 376:1). Paul used a similar picture when he wrote to the Galatians, "You are all sons of God through faith in Christ Jesus, for all of you who were baptized into Christ have *clothed* yourselves with Christ" (3:26,27).

Being clothed with Christ means, first and foremost, accepting by faith the righteousness Christ has earned for

us. Adorned with that glorious robe, we have the righteousness that avails before God and thus are assured of our eternal salvation. But having Christ's righteousness by faith
involves more. It also enables and empowers us to live a new
life marked by true holiness in our daily lives and conduct.

While such life and activity is not what saves us, holiness
of living is not simply an optional feature of the Christian life.
It is the mark and sign that our faith truly is living and active.
That's important! James states it very clearly: "Faith by itself, if
it is not accompanied by action, is dead" (2:17).

We realize then why Paul devotes almost four chapters of
this letter (chapters 12–15) to sanctification, that is, holiness of
living on the part of the redeemed children of God. Sanctification is an inseparable part of the Christian's life. For it to be
lacking would be a most distressing sign, even to the point of
putting the vitality of our faith into question. Hence we do
well to strive earnestly, with the help of the Holy Spirit, to
heed the apostle's double encouragement to put off the
deeds of darkness and put on the armor of light. Let us do so
all the more as we see the Lord's Day approaching. After all,
"the night is nearly over; the day is almost here."

Consideration for the weaker Christian

Throughout this letter the apostle Paul has been speaking of righteousness. His main theme, to be sure, is the
righteousness earned by Christ's perfect redemption and
received by faith in the heart of the individual believer. But
Paul also speaks of another kind of righteousness, namely,
the new life of righteousness practiced by the regenerate
believer. Paul has made it very clear that a change to a new
life of holiness is the inevitable result of a believer's having
received Christ's righteousness by faith.

Paul has already given us two examples of such holiness
in the Christian's life. Recall that chapter 12 dealt with an

encouragement to Christians to make faithful use of the special gifts given each of them for the benefit of others. Chapter 13 urged righteousness in the form of cheerful obedience rendered to government and to all those in authority. In chapters 14 and 15, Paul now adds a third example of righteousness. Here he illustrates Christian righteousness in the always delicate matter of strong Christians living together peaceably and harmoniously with their weaker brothers and sisters.

Instructions to both weak and strong

14 Accept him whose faith is weak, without passing judgment on disputable matters. [2]One man's faith allows him to eat everything, but another man, whose faith is weak, eats only vegetables. [3]The man who eats everything must not look down on him who does not, and the man who does not eat everything must not condemn the man who does, for God has accepted him. [4]Who are you to judge someone else's servant? To his own master he stands or falls. And he will stand, for the Lord is able to make him stand.

[5]One man considers one day more sacred than another; another man considers every day alike. Each one should be fully convinced in his own mind. [6]He who regards one day as special, does so to the Lord. He who eats meat, eats to the Lord, for he gives thanks to God; and he who abstains, does so to the Lord and gives thanks to God. [7]For none of us lives to himself alone and none of us dies to himself alone. [8]If we live, we live to the Lord; and if we die, we die to the Lord. So, whether we live or die, we belong to the Lord.

[9]For this very reason, Christ died and returned to life so that he might be the Lord of both the dead and the living. [10]You, then, why do you judge your brother? Or why do you look down on your brother? For we will all stand before God's judgment seat. [11]It is written:

> " 'As surely as I live,' says the Lord,
> 'every knee will bow before me;
>   every tongue will confess to God.' "

[12]So then, each of us will give an account of himself to God.

A notable feature of Paul's letter to the Romans is the attention he gives to Jews and Gentiles as individually identifiable groups within the Christian community of Rome. Blending these two together into one harmonious group was a significant undertaking. The great common feature, of course, was their joint faith in Christ. Both Christian Jews and Christian Gentiles looked to him as their sole hope of salvation, without adding any merit or contribution of their own. Hence in reality, they were perfectly united before God.

But outside of this all-important doctrinal base that served as the core of their unity, there continued to exist a host of cultural and ethnic differences. True, these differences were no barrier to the true spiritual unity among them, but in the matter of ordinary, day-to-day congregational life, these differences had to be addressed and dealt with. Paul does that when he gives to the strong Christian the following encouragement: "Accept him whose faith is weak, without passing judgment on disputable matters."

Note that Paul is specifically limiting the area under discussion to what the NIV translates as "disputable matters." The term in question refers to matters where two parties may legitimately hold a difference of opinion. Paul immediately identifies such an area by giving a practical example: choice of foods.

For centuries the Jews had been living under God's Old Testament ceremonial regulations, which clearly distinguished between clean and unclean foods. Eating pork, for example, was forbidden. These Old Testament ceremonies, however, were a teaching device imposed by God on the Jewish nation only until the promised Messiah came (Colossians 2:16,17). With the coming of the New Testament, these regulations were no longer binding. But even though Christian Jews knew and understood the full spiritual implications of the new covenant, changing their eating habits wasn't so easy, and making the change took some time.

The Gentiles had never been under the ceremonial laws. They had been eating pork all along, but for them now to do that in the presence of Jewish Christians or to put pressure on Jews to join them in a meal including "unclean" foods would have strained their congregational ties. In cases such as these, the Gentile, comfortably making full use of Christian liberty by eating anything and everything, was in a manner of speaking more mature than the Jewish Christians who still had reservations. Hence the Gentile was the strong brother who needed to be considerate of his weaker brother. The difference was one of degree of maturity, not presence or absence of saving faith. Paul summarizes such a situation when he says, "One man's faith allows him to eat everything, but another man, whose faith is weak, eats only vegetables."

The situation as described held the potential for either of two problems. The strong Gentile, cheerfully eating anything, could easily look down on the hesitant Jew as being something of a spiritual wimp. Paul cautions against that: "The man who eats everything must not look down on him who does not."

The Jew, on the other hand, could look disapprovingly at the Gentile who heedlessly helps himself to everything on the menu, and complain, "He shouldn't be doing that! Eating ceremonially approved foods is more God-pleasing than partaking of those other things." Hence the Jew could easily become critical and improperly judge the Gentile's actions.

To such a weak brother Paul says, "The man who does not eat everything must not condemn the man who does, for God has accepted him."

With his closing observation "for God has accepted him," Paul comes to the heart of the matter: God doesn't care what you eat. You may have reservations about oysters on the half shell, or snake steak, or chocolate-covered caterpillars, but God hasn't forbidden such fare. Each believer is God's "servant," and if God as "master" is satisfied, "Who are you to judge someone else's servant? To his own master he stands or falls. And he will stand, for the Lord is able to make him stand."

From the example of foods, Paul now moves on to another area: special sanctity of one day over another. It seems logical in the Jewish-gentile setting Paul is dealing with to think of the change in worship days from the Sabbath Day to Sunday. Here too Jews had lived for centuries under the strict regimen of the ceremonial laws, which prescribed six days of labor and the seventh, the Sabbath, as the day of rest, on which no work was to be done. All of that changed when God sent his sabbath rest in the person of Jesus Christ. Believers in Christ were now free to choose a new day of rest and worship, as they did in moving their weekly worship service from Saturday to Sunday in recognition of the Lord's resurrection. But again, making that change took some time, and it required the adjustment of some people's thinking.

Without using the terms *weak* and *strong,* Paul alludes to differences of opinion that prevailed in the two groups when he says, "One man considers one day more sacred than another." Either choice is acceptable. The only requirement is that the advocate of that day be fully committed in his mind to doing this to the glory of God. "Each one should be fully convinced in his own mind. He who regards one day as special, does so to the Lord."

Just as in verse 4 where Paul indicated that the basis for the commonality between all believers is that all are God's "servants," so here he calls attention to our common status of "belong[ing] to the Lord," whether in life or in death. "For none of us lives to himself alone and none of us dies to himself alone. If we live, we live to the Lord; and if we die, we die to the Lord. So, whether we live or die, we belong to the Lord."

The universality of death particularly suggests to the apostle yet another commonality between us and our fellow Christians. We will all individually have to give an account of ourselves to our just and holy God. In view of the great day of our own reckoning, how foolish it is to get all worked up about judging our brother! Reinforcing that sobering thought with words from Isaiah, Paul writes, "For this very reason, Christ died and returned to life so that he might be the Lord of both the dead and the living. You, then, why do you judge your brother? Or why do you look down on your brother? For we will all stand before God's judgment seat. It is written: "'As surely as I live," says the Lord, "every knee will bow before me; every tongue will confess to God."' So then, each of us will give an account of himself to God."

Instructions for the strong

Twice in the previous section, which was addressed to both strong and weak Christians, the apostle appealed to a commonality that bound these two groups together: We're all servants of the same Master; we'll all have to face our individual judgments before God.

Paul now narrows his focus and speaks more directly and pointedly to the strong Christians. Particularly in view of the coming final judgment, Paul urges the strong to be helpful to their weaker fellow Christians. The opening verse of chapter 15 summarizes the whole section nicely with its encouragement, "We who are strong ought to bear with the failings of the weak."

Note that Paul is speaking of "failings" on the part of the weak. These failings are not sins or doctrinal aberrations that the strong are to gloss over and minimize. No, he's still talking about the "disputable matters" of 14:1, matters where two Christians may legitimately hold different opinions, such as what foods to eat or what day of worship to observe. In such matters it falls to the strong, mature Christians to be considerate of the weak.

In the portion of the letter before us, addressed to the strong Christians at Rome, Paul divides his remarks into two sections. The first part (verses 13-23) is predominantly negative, strongly urging them not to put any roadblocks, or obstacles, into the weak believer's path. The second part (15:1-6) is decidedly positive, providing the motivation and strength for considerate, God-pleasing conduct toward their weaker fellow believers.

Let us first look at the entire negative section, noting the many prohibitions it contains. Then, grouping these negatives together, we will see that they all warn against one great disservice, namely, a strong brother leading a weak brother to go against his conscience and thus commit a sin by doing what in itself would be neutral and permissible. Leading a fellow Christian into sin is a grievous offense that merits all the negatives Paul relates.

¹³Therefore let us stop passing judgment on one another. Instead, make up your mind not to put any stumbling block or obstacle in your brother's way. ¹⁴As one who is in the Lord Jesus, I am fully convinced that no food is unclean in itself. But if anyone regards something as unclean, then for him it is unclean. ¹⁵If your brother is distressed because of what you eat, you are no longer acting in love. Do not by your eating destroy

your brother for whom Christ died. ¹⁶Do not allow what you consider good to be spoken of as evil. ¹⁷For the kingdom of God is not a matter of eating and drinking, but of righteousness, peace and joy in the Holy Spirit, ¹⁸because anyone who serves Christ in this way is pleasing to God and approved by men.

¹⁹Let us therefore make every effort to do what leads to peace and to mutual edification. ²⁰Do not destroy the work of God for the sake of food. All food is clean, but it is wrong for a man to eat anything that causes someone else to stumble. ²¹It is better not to eat meat or drink wine or to do anything else that will cause your brother to fall.

²²So whatever you believe about these things keep between yourself and God. Blessed is the man who does not condemn himself by what he approves. ²³But the man who has doubts is condemned if he eats, because his eating is not from faith; and everything that does not come from faith is sin.

Let us outline Paul's line of thought by pulling together the verses that support the main concepts he is advancing here. First of all, again using the example of food, Paul establishes that he is talking about matters that are really neutral and indifferent in themselves. "I am fully convinced that no food is unclean in itself," he says in verse 14. Two verses later he includes such eating in what he calls "good," and in verse 20 he makes the generalization "All food is clean." Hence there is nothing wrong in itself with the strong Christian eating the food in question.

The problem, however, comes when the strong Christian, by using his Christian liberty to eat anything, thereby puts pressure on the weak Christian to eat what in his heart he feels God has forbidden. "All food is clean," the apostle says, "but it is wrong for a man to eat anything that causes someone else to stumble."

Such "stumbling" by the weak brother occurs when he acts contrary to his conscience. Recall that Paul says, "As one who is in the Lord Jesus, I am fully convinced that no food is unclean it itself." He continues, however, "But *if anyone regards something as unclean,* then for him it is unclean." Paul enlarges on that idea when he says in verse 23, "The man who has doubts is condemned if he eats, because his eating is not from faith; and everything that does not come from faith is sin."

The weak brother thinks he should not be eating this or that kind of food, but he goes ahead and does it anyway, following the lead of the strong brother. Even though the eating really is permissible, even for the weak brother, by doing what he thinks is forbidden, the weak brother rebels against God and thereby involves himself in a deliberate, soul-destroying sin. To prevent the tragedy of a blood-bought soul losing the salvation Christ bought for it, Paul urges the strong brother to employ the greatest care. "Do not destroy the work of God for the sake of food," he pleads. Then he adds, "All food is clean, but it is wrong for a man to eat anything that causes someone else to stumble. It is better not to eat meat or drink wine or to do anything else that will cause your brother to fall."

The strong Christian knows that he has every right before God to partake of any kind of food, but for love's sake he won't use that right if it is going to confuse or mislead a weak brother. Hence Paul's advice, "So whatever you believe about these things keep between yourself and God. Blessed is the man who does not condemn himself by what he approves."

After completing the rather lengthy section consisting mainly of negative commands, Paul now turns to positive encouragement. In this section he provides the incentive and motivation necessary for proper treatment of the weak Christian. That motivation consists basically of urging his readers to look at what Christ has been willing to do for them.

15
We who are strong ought to bear with the failings of the weak and not to please ourselves. ²Each of us should please his neighbor for his good, to build him up. ³For even Christ did not please himself but, as it is written: "The insults of those who insult you have fallen on me." ⁴For everything that was written in the past was written to teach us, so that through endurance and the encouragement of the Scriptures we might have hope.

⁵May the God who gives endurance and encouragement give you a spirit of unity among yourselves as you follow Christ Jesus, ⁶so that with one heart and mouth you may glorify the God and Father of our Lord Jesus Christ.

The NIV's translation "We who are strong ought . . . not to please ourselves" is a literal rendering of the original, but perhaps it falls a bit short of our English idiom. Paul's point is that we shouldn't be guided simply by self-interest and do as we please. Rather, our concern should be for our neighbor. We should act "for his good, to build him up." That kind of looking out for others doesn't come naturally. We are all inclined to be very protective of ourselves—to look out for number one.

Then where are we to find the strength to rise above such natural, selfish inclinations? Paul's answer: Christ, who didn't do just as he pleased but rather looked wholly to the interests of others. His situation was like that which the psalmist describes: "The insults of those who insult you fall on me" (Psalm 69:9). What happened to the psalmist as a result of following God's will was but a dim foreshadowing of the ultimate "insult" that fell on Christ for doing his Father's will. In describing his mission on earth, Jesus says of himself, "Even the Son of Man did not come to be served, but to serve, and *to give his life as a ransom for many*" (Mark 10:45). In Christ's sacrifice lies the power source. Christ's love for us enables us in turn to love our weaker brother and do what's in *his* best interest.

Still thinking of the psalm quotation, the apostle continues, "Everything that was written in the past was written to teach us, so that through endurance and the encouragement of the Scriptures we might have hope." It is therefore as true for us as it was for the Twelve to whom the Son of Man first said, "Whoever wants to become great among you must be your servant, and whoever wants to be first must be slave of all" (Mark 10:43,44).

It bears repeating that such a spirit of humble service to weak Christians is not self-generated. It is rather a gift of God given through the Holy Spirit that enables us to imitate Christ more and more. In his prayer asking God to give this gift to his readers, Paul also includes us when he writes, "May the God who gives endurance and encouragement give you a spirit of unity among yourselves as you follow Christ Jesus, so that with one heart and mouth you may glorify the God and Father of our Lord Jesus Christ."

What we do for a weak brother is in reality being done for Christ himself as well. Regarding such deeds done by his believers, our Savior testifies that on the Last Day he will declare, "I tell you the truth, whatever you did for one of the least of these brothers of mine, you did for me" (Matthew 25:40). Hence in living a life of loving service for others, we are actually "glorify[ing] the God and Father of our Lord Jesus Christ."

Instruction for both weak and strong

⁷**Accept one another, then, just as Christ accepted you, in order to bring praise to God. ⁸For I tell you that Christ has become a servant of the Jews on behalf of God's truth, to confirm the promises made to the patriarchs ⁹so that the Gentiles may glorify God for his mercy, as it is written:**

> "Therefore I will praise you among the Gentiles;
> I will sing hymns to your name."

¹⁰Again, it says,

> "Rejoice, O Gentiles, with his people."

¹¹And again,

> "Praise the Lord, all you Gentiles,
> and sing praises to him, all you peoples."

¹²And again, Isaiah says,

> "The Root of Jesse will spring up,
> one who will arise to rule over the nations;
> the Gentiles will hope in him."

¹³May the God of hope fill you with all joy and peace as you trust in him, so that you may overflow with hope by the power of the Holy Spirit.

When Paul says "Accept one another, then, just as Christ accepted you," he is clearly turning his attention once more to both groups, the weak and the strong. Both are to bring praise to God by accepting each other. Such acceptance is not an unrealistic expectation on Paul's part, for he states emphatically that Christ has served both groups equally on behalf of God's truth.

We have previously noted that, in a general way, many of the issues that divided the weak and the strong were culturally conditioned, such as eating habits and worship styles. To the extent that the issues are cultural, they reflect some of the inevitable tensions between Jews and Gentiles that needed to be resolved in the early Christian church. It is in the hope of relieving this tension that Paul, in bringing this section of his letter to a close, calls attention once more to the common salvation they both share.

Solemnly, Paul testifies, "I tell you that Christ has become a servant of the Jews on behalf of God's truth, to confirm the promises made to the patriarchs." Going as far back as God's calling of the patriarch Abraham (Genesis 12:1-3), the Jewish nation had been God's chosen people to whom he had promised the Savior. In sending Jesus of Nazareth as that promised Messiah, God "confirm[ed] the promises made to the patriarchs." For Paul and his readers, there could be no doubt that God was the God of the Jews. That was clearly proven by Christ's "becom[ing] a servant of the Jews on behalf of God's truth."

But Paul's solemn assertion doesn't stop with his testimony of God's faithfulness *to the Jews*. Paul's sentence continues, "I tell you that Christ has become a servant of the Jews on behalf of God's truth, to confirm the promises made to the patriarchs *so that the Gentiles may glorify God for his mercy.*"

Recall the major section in the middle part of this letter (chapters 9–11) that Paul devoted to the relationship between Jews and Gentiles. As the apostle there pointed out, when the Jews, for the most part, turned their backs on God's salvation in Christ, God took that salvation to the Gentiles. Even though the pagan Gentiles were no better than the Jews, and though they were in no way looking for salvation, yet in his great mercy God sent Paul and his missionary peers to bring the gospel to them. Thus, pagan nations "who once were far away" were now "brought near" (Ephesians 2:13), so that the Gentiles might "glorify God for his mercy."

In observing this progression, the Gentiles might seem to be latecomers to the church, but their inclusion was not an afterthought on God's part or the alternative to a failed first plan. No, the Gentiles were a part of God's gracious plan all along. That Gentiles were indeed the object of God's mercy from the beginning is evident from four Old Testament quotations Paul now presents:

"Therefore I will praise you among
    the Gentiles;
  I will sing hymns to your name."
        [Psalm 18:49; see also 2 Samuel 22:50]
"Rejoice, O Gentiles, with his people."
        [Deuteronomy 32:43]
"Praise the Lord, all you Gentiles;
  and sing praises to him, all you peoples."
        [Psalm 117:1]
"The Root of Jesse will spring up,
      one who will arise to rule over the
      nations;
  the Gentiles will hope in him." [Isaiah 11:10]

These verses lead Paul into a prayer asking for the blessing of hope on the part of both weak and strong, be they Jew or Gentile. He prays, "May the God of hope fill you with all joy and peace as you trust in him, so that you may overflow with hope by the power of the Holy Spirit."

The NIV's double use of "hope" in this verse is a faithful translation of the term used in the original. A possible confusion, however, lies in the fact that our English understanding of the term *hope* allows for considerably less than what the original intended. We might say, "I hope to finish this job today," or "I hope the rain won't spoil our picnic." That use of *hope* leaves considerable room for doubt and uncertainty as to whether these desires will come to be.

There is none of that uncertainty in what Paul is saying here. Joy and peace from God come "as you *trust in* him." Hence Paul intends *hope* to mean "sure and certain confidence." We might paraphrase the verse as follows: "May the God who gives certainty fill you with joy and peace as you trust in him, so that you may overflow with sure confidence worked by the power of the Holy Spirit."

The joy and peace brought by being absolutely sure of God's loving care both for the present and for all eternity is something that the Holy Spirit works through the Word, the means of grace, as Paul will be pointing out in the next section.

PART EIGHT

Righteousness Shared with Others
(15:14-33)

This relatively short section of 19 verses is a highly personal portion of the letter, in which Paul leaves the doctrinal and practical matters that have engaged his attention so far and now turns to his own situation and his personal relationship to the Romans. Although the section is short, it is very interesting, because it gives us a glimpse into the heart and mind of the greatest apostle ever. It lets us see what makes Paul tick.

Actually, this section is a follow-up to what Paul briefly introduced already in the opening chapter of the letter (it might be useful at this point to review the commentary on 1:8-15, pages 15-18). For our purposes here, a brief summary of the main thoughts of that section will have to suffice:

- Paul has not yet visited Rome.
- For years Paul has been wanting to come to Rome but has been prevented until now.
- When he now finally can come, he looks forward to edifying them with the Word—or rather, he trusts that there will be *mutual* edification between Paul and the Romans.

In chapter 15 Paul explains more fully why he has been prevented from visiting Rome until now. In addition, he also alerts the Romans to one very important new subject: their role in the outreach plans he has for sharing the gospel—the righteousness of God that comes by faith in Christ—with those beyond Rome to the west, including the inhabitants of Spain.

> [14]**I myself am convinced, my brothers, that you yourselves are
> full of goodness, complete in knowledge and competent to
> instruct one another.** [15]**I have written you quite boldly on some
> points, as if to remind you of them again, because of the grace
> God gave me** [16]**to be a minister of Christ Jesus to the Gentiles with
> the priestly duty of proclaiming the gospel of God, so that the
> Gentiles might become an offering acceptable to God, sanctified
> by the Holy Spirit.**

One of the striking features of Paul's epistles is his gen-
erous estimate of the faith and spiritual maturity of his readers. Almost every letter begins with a long, glowing sentence in which Paul thanks God for the progress in faith that
his readers have made.

Paul did not put people down! He doesn't here either.
Note the commendation he gives the Romans: "I myself am
convinced, my brothers, that you yourselves are full of
goodness, complete in knowledge and competent to
instruct one another." The Romans are assumed to be competent to instruct not only one another but even great Paul
himself. That's why he could expect *mutual* edification
when he comes to them (1:12).

Although the apostle obviously knew many of the
Romans (witness the number of people he greets in chapter
16), Paul had not necessarily been the one who taught
them. Yet he credits them with knowing scriptural truth. His
letter dealing "quite boldly on some points" was not written
to bring them new teachings but simply to remind them
again of known truths.

Why did Paul remind them of truths they already knew?
He continues with his reasoning: "because of the grace [gift]
God gave me to be a minister of Christ Jesus to the Gentiles
with the priestly duty of proclaiming the gospel of God."

And what did Paul hope to accomplish by such a ministry? He himself supplies the answer: "so that the Gentiles

might become an offering acceptable to God, sanctified by the Holy Spirit."

The apostle is using Old Testament imagery to describe his privileged New Testament task of ministering with the gospel. In Old Testament times, a priest would present the worshiper's offering to the Lord. So too Paul, in a manner of speaking, is bringing believing Gentiles to God as an acceptable offering. But Paul immediately points out that their being an acceptable offering is no credit to him. Rather, these gentile converts are God's handiwork. They have been "sanctified by the Holy Sprit."

¹⁷Therefore I glory in Christ Jesus in my service to God. ¹⁸I will not venture to speak of anything except what Christ has accomplished through me in leading the Gentiles to obey God by what I have said and done—¹⁹by the power of signs and miracles, through the power of the Spirit.

Paul was certainly aware that the Lord had permitted him to achieve extraordinary things in the church. In a sense, Paul "gloried" in the success of the gospel, but that success was never a personal victory for him or a feather in his cap. Before this letter, Paul had written to the Corinthians, "Not that we are competent in ourselves to claim anything for ourselves, but our competence comes from God. He has made us competent as ministers of a new covenant" (2 Corinthians 3:5,6). Now he says to the Romans, "I will not venture to speak of anything except what Christ has accomplished through me in leading the Gentiles to obey God by what I have said and done—by the power of signs and miracles, through the power of the Spirit."

Unquestionably, Paul was empowered by God to do great things. Luke tells us in Acts that signs and miracles were not unusual phenomenon in Paul's ministry, as evidenced by numerous miraculous healings and even raising Eutychus from the dead (Acts 20:9-12; see also Acts 14:8-10; 16:16-18; 16:25-28; 28:8,9).

So from Jerusalem all the way around to Illyricum, I have fully proclaimed the gospel of Christ. [20]It has always been my ambition to preach the gospel where Christ was not known, so that I would not be building on someone else's foundation. [21]Rather, as it is written:

> **"Those who were not told about him will see,**
> **and those who have not heard will understand."**

[22]This is why I have often been hindered from coming to you.

We need to be careful not to miss the importance of the little introductory word *so.* The original term could also be translated "consequently" or "as a result." The apostle is saying, *As a result of what Christ has done through me,* I have fully proclaimed the gospel of Christ. Paul is not bragging; he is simply giving credit where credit is due, namely, to God. Under God, Paul has been able to accomplish remarkable things. He has "fully proclaimed the gospel of Christ" from Jerusalem to Illyricum. Paul is here including the whole northeastern seaboard of the Mediterranean. From Jerusalem, where the New Testament church started on Pentecost, Paul has carried the message in a northwesterly direction as far as Illyricum, which is the modern area of Albania and Yugoslavia.

Acts gives us no record of Paul's having worked in Illyricum, so perhaps his words here are best understood as saying that he took the gospel from Jerusalem up to the borders of Illyricum. Note how the geographical progress of the gospel corresponds to the marching orders Christ gave his disciples before his ascension: "You will be my witnesses in

Jerusalem, and in all Judea and Samaria, and to the ends of the earth" (Acts 1:8).

When Paul says, "I have fully proclaimed the gospel of Christ [from Jerusalem to Illyricum]," that doesn't mean he did all the preaching himself, or that he personally shared the message with each convert. Paul's pattern was to go to the major urban centers and plant the gospel there. Like spokes coming from the hub of a wheel, Paul's coworkers would then fan out from the city into the neighboring countryside. Ephesus serves as a good example of the Pauline missionary methodology. After Paul and his Christian group were expelled from the synagogue in Ephesus, he held daily discussions in the lecture hall of Tyrannus. Although this activity took place solely within the city, Luke still can say, "This went on for two years, so that all the Jews and Greeks *who lived in the province of Asia* heard the word of the Lord" (Acts 19:10).*

When the NIV translates Paul as saying, "It has always been my ambition . . . ," it could seem as though Paul is following his own inclination and setting up his own game plan. Such is not the case.

Recall that on his second missionary journey, when he wanted to go to Ephesus, Paul was "kept by the Holy Spirit from preaching the word in the province of Asia" (Acts 16:6). And "when they came to the border of Mysia, they tried to enter Bithynia, but the Spirit of Jesus would not allow them to" (verse 7). Instead, Paul and his partners were led by the "Macedonian call" to go into Europe.

---

* Colosse was one of the cities in the province of Asia most likely evangelized from Ephesus. Paul apparently didn't know the Colossian congregation personally, because in his letter to them he speaks of his having "heard of" their faith in Christ (1:4). Epaphras was the founder of their congregation, not Paul, for Paul writes, "You learned it [the gospel] from Epaphras, our dear fellow servant, who is a faithful minister of Christ on our behalf, and who also told us of your love in the Spirit" (1:7,8).

Recall also that Paul thought of himself as an "ambassador" for Christ (2 Corinthians 5:20). An ambassador does not speak for himself. He does not choose his own time or place. Rather, he is totally committed to representing the interests of his superior. Hence instead of assuming personal ambition as Paul's motivation, we do better to see Paul's approach as reflecting a directive from God that caused him to *strive earnestly* "to preach the gospel where Christ was not known." The apostle then immediately adds the reason for using this mode of operation in his work: "so that I would not be building on someone else's foundation. Rather, as it is written: 'Those who were not told about him will see, and those who have not heard will understand.'"

In telling us of the limitation God has placed on his ministry, the apostle is not complaining or being defensive. This approach, after all, has resulted in the fulfillment of what Isaiah already foretold regarding the successful outcome of the Suffering Servant's work: "What they were not told, they will see, and what they have not heard, they will understand" (Isaiah 52:15).

Paul's remark, however, does provide an explanation as to why he has been so long in coming to Rome. First of all, the Roman church rested largely on the work of others: to use Paul's picture, it had been built "on someone else's foundation." Thus, it technically could be viewed as falling outside of Paul's assignment.

But a more compelling reason for Paul's delay was that, until now, there had been major areas not yet served with the gospel that required Paul's attention first. "This is why I have often been hindered from coming to you," he explains. That situation has now changed.

²³But now that there is no more place for me to work in these regions, and since I have been longing for many years to see

you, ²⁴I plan to do so when I go to Spain. I hope to visit you while passing through and to have you assist me on my journey there, after I have enjoyed your company for a while.

After having planted the gospel in the major urban areas between Jerusalem and Illyricum, Paul can say, "There is no more place for me to work in these regions." This does not by any stretch of the imagination mean that Paul's work is finished, however. He is quick to point out that he had his eye on another area where Christ was not known. That area is Spain—beyond Rome, to the west. Hence on his way to Spain, Paul intends to stop off at Rome and thus fulfill his long-felt wish of visiting the Roman Christians.

A personal visit with brothers and sisters in the faith—important as that was—was by no means the only reason for coming to Rome, however. Paul also intends to involve the Roman Christians in his projected mission expedition to Spain.

We should not think of Paul's missionary procedure as being entirely comparable to our current methods of conducting overseas mission work. When a church body (through its world mission board) sends out a team of missionaries to distant lands, it assumes responsibility for outfitting and financing the endeavor.

In early New Testament times, Christian missionaries were much more on their own. Think, for example, of Paul's tentmaking in Corinth to support himself (Acts 18:1-5; see also Acts 20:33,34). Also, traveling missionaries often depended on Christians along the way to help them and outfit them for the next field of labor they were going to. John's third epistle gives us a clear indication of such mission support from local congregations (verses 5-8).

Similarly, Paul seems to be expecting such aid when he comes to Rome, for he tells the Romans, "I hope to visit you while passing through and to have you assist me on my journey there, after I have enjoyed your company for a while." Those plans, however, are for the future. For the moment they will have to wait.

25Now, however, I am on my way to Jerusalem in the service of the saints there. 26For Macedonia and Achaia were pleased to make a contribution for the poor among the saints in Jerusalem. 27They were pleased to do it, and indeed they owe it to them. For if the Gentiles have shared in the Jews' spiritual blessings, they owe it to the Jews to share with them their material blessings.

A recurring theme in the New Testament record of early church life is a concern for the poor and needy "saints" (believers) in Palestine. Accepting Christ and his gospel apparently deprived these Jewish Christians in the homeland of the support system they previously had in the synagogue and the local structures for emergency help and relief.

Recall the appointment of the seven deacons in Jerusalem to handle the relief work when that task became too burdensome for the Twelve to administer effectively (Acts 6:1-6). In Acts 11:27-30 Luke speaks of a collection taken by the predominantly gentile congregation in Antioch to alleviate the hardships of Jewish Christians caused by a famine. Paul's account of a meeting in Jerusalem at which the Christian "pillars" James, Peter, and John recognized Paul as their lead missionary to the Gentiles concludes with this intriguing encouragement: "They agreed that we [Paul and Barnabas] should go to the Gentiles, and they to the Jews. All they asked was that we should continue to remember the poor, the very thing I was eager to do" (Galatians 2:9,10). Both of Paul's letters to the Corinthians also have key sections dealing with the collection that they and other congregations were gathering for the saints in Jerusalem (1 Corinthians 16:1-4; 2 Corinthians 8,9).

The collection Paul is referring to in the Corinthian correspondence apparently was finished just prior to Paul's arrival at Corinth in the fall of A.D. 57, where it seems he spent the winter (1 Corinthians 16:5,6; Acts 20:2,3). Now at the time of the writing of his letter to the Romans, Paul is about to leave for Jerusalem to deliver the collection.

Wisely Paul had invited representatives from the participating congregations to serve as a committee to carry the money. In writing to Rome, Paul mentions only the European participants in the collection, Macedonia and Achaia (Greece). From Luke's listing of the seven-man committee in Acts 20:4, we know that the Asia Minor congregations also participated. The Asia Minor congregations were represented on the committee by Gaius from Derbe, Timothy from Lystra, and Tychicus and Trophimus from the province of Asia, presumably from Ephesus.

This collection was a major event in the life of the early church, for its intent was not merely to provide physical relief for the Jewish component of the church. It was also to show the spiritual unity that existed in Christ between Jewish and gentile Christians (2 Corinthians 9:12-14).

Recall that Paul spent a great deal of space in this letter to Rome stressing the need for Jewish-gentile solidarity. It will not surprise us, then, to see Paul take the opportunity here once more to make that point with his readers. Speaking of the mostly gentile participants in the collection, he writes, "They were pleased to do it, and indeed they owe it to them. For if the Gentiles have shared in the Jews' spiritual blessings, they owe it to the Jews to share with them their material blessings."

²⁸**So after I have completed this task and have made sure that they have received this fruit, I will go to Spain and visit**

you on the way. ²⁹I know that when I come to you, I will come in the full measure of the blessing of Christ.

The task Paul intends to complete is not merely that of handing over the collection; he especially wants to make it clearly understood that this gift is a "fruit" of faith on the part of the gentile Christians. Paul has gone through great pains to emphasize in this letter, and throughout his ministry, that gentile Christians are perfectly united with their Jewish brothers and sisters.

After the important business of the collection has been taken care of, Paul can set out for Spain, stopping off at Rome en route. Incidentally, this is the last direct reference we have of Paul's going to Spain. The apostle may have accomplished that goal in the period between the release from his first Roman imprisonment (about A.D. 63) and his death (mid to late years of that decade). The time frame would seem to allow it, but we have no specific information from Scripture to confirm such a mission journey to the west.

³⁰I urge you, brothers, by our Lord Jesus Christ and by the love of the Spirit, to join me in my struggle by praying to God for me. ³¹Pray that I may be rescued from the unbelievers in Judea and that my service in Jerusalem may be acceptable to the saints there, ³²so that by God's will I may come to you with joy and together with you be refreshed.

We have previously noted the high esteem Paul places on his fellowship with brothers and sisters in the faith. We see it again here in the value he attaches to their prayer for him. Two things especially are weighing heavily on his heart and mind. First of all, he wants the matter of the collection to go well, both in its delivery and its distribution. Hence the Romans are asked to pray that Paul's service in Jerusalem "may be acceptable to the saints there."

But there also is another matter of grave concern, namely that of Paul's personal safety. Recall that Christ had predicted a time when those who violently opposed Christianity would think they were doing God a service (John 16:2). Paul was encountering that very thing from his Jewish compatriots, particularly from "the unbelievers in Judea." That Paul was not being paranoid but rather was concerned about real dangers is shown by events on the ensuing journey to Jerusalem. Along the way, in one place after another, people warned Paul that trouble and imprisonment awaited him in Jerusalem (Acts 20:22,23; 21:4,10-14). What was foretold actually happened, of course, when Paul had to be rescued from a Jewish lynch mob in Jerusalem and then fell under Roman custody for the next four or five years.

At the time of Paul's writing to the Romans, all of this still lay in the future, so Paul very properly requested his readers' prayers so that "by God's will" he would arrive "with joy" and "be refreshed" together with them. As indicated above, it is entirely possible that Paul might have gotten the opportunity to go to Rome and Spain after his release from Roman imprisonment. If so, it simply came later than he was hoping for when he asked the Romans to pray for his speedy arrival to them.

[33]The God of peace be with you all. Amen.

Paul closes the section with a benediction. The sentence has a note of finality, bringing the letter proper to a close. All that remains for Paul to do is attach a commendation for Phoebe (who may have been the carrier of the letter), send greetings to some two dozen acquaintances in Rome, and transmit the instruction of 16:17,18.

PART NINE

Conclusion

(16:1-27)

Commendation

16 I commend to you our sister Phoebe, a servant of the church in Cenchrea. [2] I ask you to receive her in the Lord in a way worthy of the saints and to give her any help she may need from you, for she has been a great help to many people, including me.

When Paul refers to Phoebe as "our sister," he is likely not thinking of her as a blood relative but as a fellow believer. Phoebe came from Cenchrea, one of the seaports serving Corinth. Corinth is located on an isthmus and has two harbors, one serving westbound shipping (for example, Italy) and the other serving the east. Cenchrea was on the eastern (Aegean) side of the isthmus.

The term used to describe Phoebe is *diakonos*. It could very properly be translated "deaconess." What her exact capacity was as a "servant of the church in Cenchrea" is not known, nor are we told what her role in Rome was to be. One thing is very clear: she had been most helpful to the Christian cause. Paul gives her high praise and an unqualified recommendation to the Christians in Rome.

We need to remind ourselves that in ancient times there was no international postal service such as we take for granted. A standard method of sending correspondence was for a letter to be carried by a traveler who happened to be going to the place you wanted to send it to. A likely scenario would be that during his three-month stay in Corinth, Paul, who wanted to send a letter to the Romans, learned that

Phoebe was going there. Hence he prevailed on her to carry the letter and deliver it to the Roman Christians. It might also have served as a letter of introduction for her.

Greetings

[3] Greet Priscilla and Aquila, my fellow workers in Christ Jesus. [4] They risked their lives for me. Not only I but all the churches of the Gentiles are grateful to them.

[5] Greet also the church that meets at their house.

Greet my dear friend Epenetus, who was the first convert to Christ in the province of Asia.

[6] Greet Mary, who worked very hard for you.

[7] Greet Andronicus and Junias, my relatives who have been in prison with me. They are outstanding among the apostles, and they were in Christ before I was.

[8] Greet Ampliatus, whom I love in the Lord.

[9] Greet Urbanus, our fellow worker in Christ, and my dear friend Stachys.

[10] Greet Apelles, tested and approved in Christ.

Greet those who belong to the household of Aristobulus.

[11] Greet Herodion, my relative.

Greet those in the household of Narcissus who are in the Lord.

[12] Greet Tryphena and Tryphosa, those women who work hard in the Lord.

Greet my dear friend Persis, another woman who has worked very hard in the Lord.

[13] Greet Rufus, chosen in the Lord, and his mother, who has been a mother to me, too.

[14] Greet Asyncritus, Phlegon, Hermes, Patrobas, Hermas and the brothers with them.

[15] Greet Philologus, Julia, Nereus and his sister, and Olympas and all the saints with them.

**¹⁶ Greet one another with a holy kiss.
All the churches of Christ send greetings.**

An unusual feature of the letter to the Romans is the large number of personal greetings Paul attaches—over two dozen! No other letter comes close to having that many. Such a quantity of greetings is the more remarkable when we recall that Paul had never visited the Christian community in Rome. The likely explanation is that many of the "Romans" may have been people whom Paul got to know earlier during his days of working "from Jerusalem . . . to Illyricum" (15:19) who subsequently moved to Rome, either permanently or temporarily. Note, for example, that Epenetus was "the first convert to Christ *in the province of Asia.*" There was, after all, a good deal of truth in the ancient generalization that all roads lead to Rome.

As for the people Paul simply mentions by name, the Roman readers would obviously know exactly who was being greeted. It's a pity that we know so little about them. Once we're past Aquila and Priscilla,* they tend to be mere names for us.

Paul, however, adds some intriguing tidbits of information that allow us to do some grouping. One feature that leaps out from the list is the number of women who are commended. Paul's inspired teaching on the role of women has occasionally (and incorrectly) gained him the reputation of being a woman-hater. How far that is from the truth is indicated by the fact that approximately a third of the people greeted here are women—and all are given unreserved praise. The list includes the following women and tributes:

---

* Known from Acts 18:18-26; 1 Corinthians 16:19; 2 Timothy 4:19.

> *Priscilla:* "my fellow [worker] in Christ Jesus . . . risked [her life] for me. Not only I but all the churches of the Gentiles are grateful to [her]."
>
> *Mary:* "worked very hard for you"
>
> *Tryphena* and *Tryphosa:* "women who work hard in the Lord"
>
> *Persis:* "my dear friend . . . another woman who has worked very hard in the Lord"
>
> Rufus' *mother:* "who has been a mother to me, too"
>
> *Julia*
>
> Nereus' *sister*

Incidentally, the gender of Junias (verse 7) could be debated. The ancient Greek manuscripts didn't have accent marks, so adding them was a later editorial addition. *Junias* could be accented as either a man's name or a woman's name. Note that in crediting Andronicus and Junias with being "outstanding among the apostles," Paul is using a wider definition of *apostle* than only those who were called directly by Christ himself.*

Another interesting feature is Paul's mention of "relatives." Three of them—Lucius, Jason, and Sosipater (16:21)—are with Paul in Corinth and are sending greetings. They would no doubt have a special interest in the three relatives in Rome: Herodion (verse 11) and Andronicus and Junias (verse 7). The latter two are commended as having "been in prison with [Paul]" and are further described as people who "were in Christ before [Paul] was." This second piece of information suggests a highly interesting situation where Paul's family

---

* Paul uses this wider sense when he calls James, the Lord's brother, an "apostle" (Galatians 1:18,19), as also does Luke in calling Barnabas an apostle (Acts 14:4,14). In 1 Thessalonians 2:6, Silas and Timothy seem to be included among the apostles.

members became Christians while Paul was still a vicious persecutor of Christians.*

A final observation drawn from incidental pieces of information incorporated into Paul's list is that there does not appear to have been one formally organized congregation in Rome at this time. Rather, the Roman Christian community seems to have consisted of a series of house churches convening in private homes. We are clearly told of that arrangement in the case of Aquila and Priscilla, where Paul speaks of "the church that meets at their house." "The household of Aristobulus" sounds like a similar grouping. Also, the apostle sends greetings to Christian leaders and "the brothers with them" and "all the saints with them." The impression left is that these are loosely organized house churches.

When Paul says, "Greet one another with a holy kiss," he is urging a common practice that was in use in the early church** and is still practiced in some churches. Then, as now, it was a sign of Christian fellowship and did not bear any romantic implications.

Warning

¹⁷**I urge you, brothers, to watch out for those who cause divisions and put obstacles in your way that are contrary to the teaching you have learned. Keep away from them. ¹⁸For such people are not serving our Lord Christ, but their own appetites. By smooth talk and flattery they deceive the minds of naive people. ¹⁹Everyone has heard about your obedience, so I am full of joy over you; but I want you to be wise about what is good, and innocent about what is evil.**

---

* For additional support to the Christian cause by Paul's relatives, see Acts 23:12-22, particularly verse 16, where Paul's nephew ("the son of Paul's sister") tips off the authorities to a Jewish plot against Paul.

** 1 Corinthians 16:20; 2 Corinthians 13:12; 1 Thessalonians 5:26; 1 Peter 5:14

²⁰The God of peace will soon crush Satan under your feet. The grace of our Lord Jesus be with you.

Because this section of the letter sounds different from the surrounding sections, some have questioned whether this section belongs here. The solution to that supposed problem lies in observing how Paul has structured the material under discussion.

It is essential to realize that Paul starts verse 17 with the connecting word *but*. Unfortunately, many translations drop that conjunction, including the NIV. When we take that conjunction into account, the progression of thought between verses 1 to 16 and 17 to 20 becomes clear. After listing numerous people whom the Roman readers were to greet, the apostle then continues, *"[but] watch out for* those who cause divisions and put obstacles in your way."

Note whom Paul is warning against. These are not people of different political persuasions or different cultural practices. They are religious people—but religious people who teach false doctrine, doctrine "contrary to the teaching you have learned."

Also, the original makes it clear that these are not people who have simply become a little confused in their thinking and would be willing to correct their teaching if their errors were pointed out to them. No, they are people who may fairly be described as regularly and intentionally causing divisions and questioning beliefs. They have an agenda; they are teachers seeking to win others to their point of view.

Paul is very definite in his advice concerning false teachers: Watch out for them and keep away from them! Or to cast it in the terminology of the first 16 verses of this chapter, Don't greet them as if they were brothers in the faith.

Avoiding fellowship with false teachers ourselves and warning others against them is not a popular message, particularly in our age of false ecumenism. But as Paul points out, such avoidance of false teachers and false teaching is very necessary, for two reasons.

First of all, "Such people are not serving our Lord Christ, but their own appetites." A standard assumption on the part of the ecumenicists is that unity of doctrine is neither possible nor necessary. Thus they follow their own inclinations ("their own appetites") rather than our Lord, who sent his heralds out with the commission to teach all nations "to obey *everything* I have commanded you" (Matthew 28:20). Ignoring some doctrines or incorrectly teaching what Christ has entrusted to us is simply unacceptable to our Lord.

But there is another very practical reason to steer clear of false teachers and false teaching. False doctrine is a grave danger to saving faith! Or as Paul says, "By smooth talk and flattery they deceive the minds of naive people." This "naive people" is not just other people; it includes us as well. False doctrine is nothing to trifle with. "Don't you know that a little yeast works through the whole batch of dough?" Paul warns (1 Corinthians 5:6). "If you think you are standing firm, be careful that you don't fall!" (1 Corinthians 10:12).

Although Paul feels the need to warn very earnestly, he is not being critical of the Romans or implying that they have not been avoiding false teachers. Quite the contrary! He commends their faith and their faithfulness. With his usual generosity toward others and enthusiasm over any growth and maturity in the faith of his readers, Paul says, "Everyone has heard about your obedience, so I am full of joy over you; but I want you to be wise about what is good, and innocent about what is evil."

With a promise and a benediction, the apostle now concludes his letter. "The God of peace will soon crush Satan under your feet. The grace of our Lord Jesus be with you."

Just as there was a note of finality at the end of chapter 15, so there also is here. Paul has finished his part of the letter, but there still remains a bit of unfinished business. His colleagues in Corinth, who, like Paul, also knew many of the same people in Rome, would like to take advantage of the rare opportunity to send their greetings. Therefore, Paul lets them piggyback on his letter.

²¹Timothy, my fellow worker, sends his greetings to you, as do Lucius, Jason and Sosipater, my relatives.

Timothy, of course, is well known from Scripture. Since joining Paul's missionary team on the second missionary journey (Acts 16:1-5), he has been Paul's constant companion and coworker. By contrast, we know nothing about Lucius, Jason, and Sosipater, except that they are Paul's relatives.

²²I, Tertius, who wrote down this letter, greet you in the Lord.

Fortunately, Tertius identifies himself. He was the professional scribe, undoubtedly Christian, who wrote what Paul dictated. Paul always used secretarial help. The secretary would write the body of the letter, and Paul personally added merely a closing section as his signature (2 Thessalonians 3:17). That practice is evident at the close of Galatians where Paul says, "See what large letters I use as I write to you with my own hand" (6:11). Here in Romans, verses 25 to 27 of this last chapter are very likely the sign-off in Paul's own handwriting.

²³Gaius, whose hospitality I and the whole church here enjoy, sends you his greetings.

This Gaius is often assumed to be the same person referred to in Acts 18:7. There we are told that after Paul and his Christian group were driven out of the synagogue in Corinth, they "went next door to the house of Titius Justus, a worshiper of God." The assumption is that this benefactor's full name was Gaius Titius Justus.

Regardless of whether or not that association of names is correct, this verse does substantiate the assumption that early Christians regularly operated as house churches that met in homes rather than church buildings. Gaius must have had a large home to accommodate the "whole church" in Corinth, which seems to have been more formally structured into one congregation than was the Christian community of Rome.

Erastus, who is the city's director of public works, and our brother Quartus send you their greetings.

The observation is occasionally made that the majority of those who were attracted to the Christian message were from the lower classes of society, also including many slaves. For example, attention is called to the fact that names such as Ampliatus, Urbanus, Stachys, and Apelles (16:8-10) turn up in the listing of slaves in the imperial household. Not all Christians were from the lower classes, however. As "director of public works," Erastus obviously held an important civil position. Archeology has unearthed a fascinating bit of information possibly related to this verse. While working on an ancient paved square in Corinth, archeologists discovered a reused stone block bearing this Latin inscription: "Erastus, commissioner of public works, bore the expense of this pavement." That *may* be the same man who sent greetings to the Romans, but we cannot be certain. "Brother Quartus" remains totally unknown to us.

To close out this section of greetings, many Greek manuscripts have another doxology such as we saw at 15:33 and 16:20. Some translations include this doxology as verse 24; the NIV has entered it as a footnote: "May the grace of our Lord Jesus Christ be with all of you. Amen."

Paul's signature closing

[25]Now to him who is able to establish you by my gospel and the proclamation of Jesus Christ, according to the revelation of the mystery hidden for long ages past, [26]but now revealed and made known through the prophetic writings by the command of the eternal God, so that all nations might believe and obey him—[27]to the only wise God be glory forever through Jesus Christ! Amen.

As indicated earlier, these verses were very likely written in Paul's own handwriting. They are his signature, if you will. This signature certified the genuineness of the letter. Although he doesn't say so here, one is reminded of the apostle's closing comment to the Thessalonians: "I, Paul, write this greeting in my own hand, which is the distinguishing mark in all my letters. This is how I write" (2 Thessalonians 3:17).

Not only is the handwriting Paul's, but the theology as well. Actually, this doxology reflects virtually everything Paul said in the letter. Recall how the body of the letter began with Paul's bold assertion, "I am not ashamed of the gospel, because it is the power of God for the salvation of everyone who believes" (1:16). Paul closes the letter by focusing once more on that same gospel and power of God.

Paul tells the Romans, "[God] is able to establish you by my gospel and the proclamation of Jesus Christ." When Paul says "my gospel," he is not contrasting it to the gospel his coworkers are preaching. Rather, Paul's gospel is the message that was uniquely given him when Christ personally confronted him on the road to Damascus and totally changed his life—from persecutor of Christ to witness for Christ.

The meaning of "my gospel" is further defined by the expression Paul sets next to it: "and the proclamation of Jesus Christ." Considering two grammatical points may help us better understand the relationship between these two expressions. First of all, the word translated as "and" does not work as a connective here, joining "gospel" and "proclamation" as if they were two different things. Rather, the word introduces an appositive, a second expression that restates or explains what is previous to it. Hence instead of translating the word as and, one might more correctly use *namely* or *that is.*

The second point to be noted concerns the phrase "the proclamation of Jesus Christ." The word *of* would have been better translated as *about.* The proclamation is not something that Christ possesses or does; it is the proclamation *about* Christ. Hence Paul is confidently asserting that God is able to establish the Romans by the gospel given to Paul, namely, the proclamation about Jesus Christ.

Jesus Christ is the heart of Paul's message. Christ is the key, the revelation that unlocks "the mystery hidden for long ages past." God's gracious plan of salvation has been in effect ever since Adam and Eve—yes, even from eternity. But for a long time it looked like the personal possession of the Jewish nation.

All of that changed, however, when Christ came to earth, completed his saving work, and commissioned his followers to proclaim that salvation to all the world. Thus the "mystery" of God's grace—disclosed to Paul and proclaimed in his gospel—is that by faith in Christ, God's salvation is for all people, Jews and Gentiles alike. Or as Paul says, God's grace has been "revealed and made known through the prophetic writings by the command of the eternal God, *so that all nations might believe and obey him.*"

Paul had experienced the power of God in the gospel not only in the spiritual rebirth it brought into his own life but also in seeing that miracle repeated in hundreds and thousands of lives in connection to the work the Lord had privileged him to do. His gospel had brought the power of God into the hearts of both Jews and Gentiles, setting up centers of Christian worship all the way from Jerusalem to Illyricum.

Hence Paul is confident that this Word will now also "establish" the Romans, both through the written message he is sending them and through the spoken Word when he comes to visit them. So confident is Paul that he could say, "I know that when I come to you, I will come in the full measure of the blessing of Christ" (15:29).

But this gospel also gives Paul confidence for the establishment of future congregations. He has invited the Romans to be partners with him in the proposed outreach work to Spain, so that he may have "a harvest . . . among the other Gentiles" there also (1:13). Paul can be confident of that because the gospel *is* "the power of God for the salvation of everyone who believes" (1:16).

Paul's confidence, of course, was not misplaced. For almost two thousand years now, that Word has advanced, particularly to the west—to Spain and beyond—to the point of also having reached us and won our hearts. Moved by that gospel in general, and in particular by Paul's exposition of it in his magnificent epistle to the Romans, we too join with the apostle in saying, "To him who is able to establish [us] by [the] gospel . . . to the only wise God be glory forever through Jesus Christ! Amen."